COMPARATIVE PHYSIOGNOMY

OR

RESEMBLANCES

BETWEEN MEN AND ANIMALS

BY

JAMES W. REDFIELD, M.D.

> With his hand thus o'er his brow,
> He falls to such perusal of my face,
> As he would draw it. SHAKSPERE.

ILLUSTRATED BY 330 ENGRAVINGS.

NEW YORK:
W. J. WIDDLETON, PUBLISHER.
1866.

PREFACE.

The word *preface* is an indication that a book, like its author, must have a *face;* and unless it be a misnomer, there is no reason why it should not be illustrated with faces. That it comes first and foremost it would be useless to observe, had not certain persons been inclined to put it in the background. We will state frankly, at the outset, that this particular preface is intended to "face down"—not by "barefaced assertions," but by a presentation of faces and arguments—the unjust treatment to which the face has been subjected.

Why should a periodical, that professes to be a "Journal" of Phrenology and of kindred sciences, look out at the back of its head whenever it takes a peep at Physiognomy? We know not, but humanity claims that the eyes in such a case should be set right. We address ourselves, therefore, to answering the objections contained in two articles on this subject in the "Phrenological Journal," both of them new-year's presents, for which we have reason to be thankful.

The first formidable obstacle we meet with is this: "The naked skull of poor Yorick, notwithstanding its yawning eye-sockets and ghastly grin, presents the evidences of his former warmth of affection and his racy wit, although the signs of these emotions in the face are obliterated for ever." Is there, then, nothing left of the skull but the cranial portion? and does not Physiognomy claim that the character is indicated in the *features* of the face, as well as in the expressions?

The idea conveyed by the objection is, that the "naked skull" is the all of Phrenology, and only a part of Physiognomy. The naked skull, says the writer, "is the only organic memento of the character of the dead;" but Physiognomy claims the advantage of the *naked face, while living*, and of being able to say, "Blessed be the art that can immortalize!" In portraits, the skull remains in the background, where nature placed it; and the power of art is expended upon the face, in making it live, and breathe, and grow warm with life, and almost speak. Would the "naked skull of poor Yorick" have been treated contemptuously in the third person, or gibingly in the second, if it had been as good an index of character as the face? "How abhorred in my imagination it is! My gorge rises at it. Here hung those lips that I have kissed I know not how oft. Where be your gibes now? your gambols? your songs? your flashes of merriment that were wont to keep the table on a roar?" Contrast this with Cowper's address to his mother's picture:—

> "That face is thine, thy own sweet smile I see,
> The same that oft in childhood solaced me!"

What if somebody should become so phrenology-mad as to hang up "the only organic memento of the character of the dead" on the parlor-wall! Pity it is that Nature should have made "the only reliable index of character" so inaccessible; and that Art, when Nature fails in her attempt, should substitute a wig, and add such a fashion of head-dress as to be a burlesque upon the reliability, pretensions, and significance, of the cranium!

The second formidable objection is this: "The temporary effects of an emotion may be set forth in the face, obscuring for the time being the natural traits of character, while the form of the head remains the same, offering to the phrenologist equal facility to read the *real elements* of the mind, whether it be lashed into fury, and the face distorted with rage, or lulled to a calmness of spirit and placidity of countenance by all the soothing appliances of peace and love." We would like particularly to see the author of this thrilling passage examining a head when the mind was "lashed into fury, and the face distorted with rage;" and we would inquire if, under the "soothing appliances" of his fingers, the bones of the cranium ever discovered themselves to be more osseous than those of the face?

Not far from this stage of the criticism several faces are introduced from the "favorite delineator of eccentric character," Dr. Valentine, showing how a man may "frame his face to all occasions." Let us compare "Monsieur Grenoble," or the representation of "a sympathetic, good-natured, confiding, simple-hearted Frenchman," with a genuine exhibition of the same traits, and see if there is not a difference. Here is a

Frenchwoman whose habitual character is that described above, and where is the hesitation in deciding which is the genuine and which is the false? In the first, the feeling which appears upon the face is superficial; but in the other the feeling is the character itself, and the expression is not put on, but is the very face.

By the side of a countenance that is said to exhibit "every

line, angle, and expression, of moping melancholy," and is called "the embodiment of sadness—a visage fit to freeze the soul"—let us place the expression of sullen gloominess and frigidity in a woman who resembles but is seen to be in a very different mood of mind from the other. In this com-

parison, the pretended "hypochondriac" is easily distinguished from the portrait, which has the expression of genuine sentiment and stern reality.

The second criticism is now in turn. First, it says of the brain, that "it is the trunk of the mental tree, and that all outward signs of character and emotion spring from and depend upon it, as do the branches and leaves of the natural tree upon its trunk." According to this, "all the outward signs of character and emotion" are in the arms and hands, and the features and expressions of the countenance, which are compared to branches and leaves. This is more than we are willing to accept, for we acknowledge that there are *some* outward signs of character in the skull.

The next objection is the more formidable on account of being an assertion, which is this: "We often find a person, whose father and mother are very unlike in character, who resembles in head one parent and in face the other. Such a person's character is always found to follow the phrenological development. . . . . The face will everywhere be recognised as being very much like that of the father, for example, while the character is precisely that of the mother .... and as unlike that of the father .... as can well be imagined." The premises in this case will not sustain the conclusions. That from a father and a mother, whose opposite characters are indicated by opposite faces, can be produced an offspring whose face and character are opposite to each other, is a contradiction in terms. If the face and the character "belie" each other, the one may as well be convicted of falsehood as the other: but the truth is, whatever belies one belies them both; and the assertion, that one is true and not the other, belies itself.

The next assertion which strikes us as being very singular is this: A person "looks at the face, but the scenery above it gives him, after all, his idea of the man. We say an eye is beautiful, but it is as much the scenery around the eye that gives it beauty and expression as the eye itself, and even more." The first sentence teaches us that we can have no idea of a man till he doffs his hat; but the second descends from that high empyrean, and acknowledges that there is scenery *around* the eye, which, as the eye is very expressive, must be an important index of character. But the most ridiculous thing is, that a "a glass eye keeps pace exactly with the natural one, in all apparent changes of that speaking organ." Of course, then, when a high-spirited horse "darts the fire of passion" from his eyeballs, it is "the change of scenery around the eye, and not the eye itself;" and, of course, Art may do as well as Nature in manufacturing eyes! Accordingly, our critic has caused a pair of eyes to be executed for the picture of the bust of Vitellius—with what intention we shall presently see. It is quite probable, too, that Art can manufacture a face out of the odds and ends of different characters that shall be quite equal to one of Nature's own productions. On this principle, faces are manufactured that are intended to be, and that are, perfect contradictions to Physiognomy.

"To illustrate how the appearance of the head changes the expression of the face," the inventor introduces "four engravings."—"These," says he, "are *made up* from two portraits, each of which is engraved on two pieces of wood, divided just above the eyes, so that the head of each may be united to the other. These parts are *mismatched.* Two of the four are *as Nature made them;* the other two are composed of the head of each on the face of the other." In this quotation the man-

ufacturing process is well described. It would seem as if the writer intended that his own two charming productions should be taken as illustrations of the principle that the head may be derived from one parent and the face from the other. As "the character is always found to follow the phrenological development," Vitellius and Wilson, having changed heads, must be described thus. First, Vitellius: "A man remarkable for talent, purity, and elevation of character; a pattern of benevolence, of enlarged and liberal views, a zealous friend of the poor; who lived, like Oberlin, for the human race." In his physiognomical judgment of Vitellius, the writer exclaims: "What a beastly face! how sensual and gluttonous! what tyranny and severity! How much of the base robber and murderer are seen in that countenance! how savage and how repulsive!" But, as the head of this beastly Roman emperor is turned over to the Rev. Dr. Wilson, this description of character must go with it. We have presented above the portraits of these two individuals, and surely the thought of a mutual exchange of heads and faces between characters so perfectly opposite is horrible.

One other objection remains to be answered. It is the idea that in certain cases "the changes of expression are so great, and so mingled in their effects upon the facial muscles, as to make the reading of character by that means a complete puzzle." The writer of the following description of Kossuth did not think so:—

"A word of the orator's personal appearance. He is a little under size, perhaps five feet eight; erect, of fine form and figure, quick and elastic in movement, and of admirable and commanding gesture. The flexibility of his physical frame is the type of his flexibility of nature, and accurately obedient to its command. When he is roused, the soul speaks through the entire person. Hence comes the electric shock, the magnetic effusion, that captivates and controls his hearers. His face is suffused with emotional indications, and is eminently susceptible of every expression. It melts in sadness, it lights up with enthusiasm, it grows fierce in passion, it flashes with mirth. Upon no man's face is the sunshine glow of delight more effectively expressed, yet is the prevailing expression sad and subdued. The eye tells of the treasures within. It is full, liquid, and in him the very window of the soul; it is the ready outlet of a heart filled with emotion, and feminine in a gushing sympathy of expression, that needs not the poor interpreter of language. It mirrors a depth and reveals an inspiration of nature, cognizable to the dullest sense, as rare as it is captivating."

In refutation of the above objection, we offer also the following:—

"The artists," said Mr. Clay "have not generally succeeded well in taking my features but that has been in a great measure my own fault; for my face never retains long the same expression, and, especially when I am under any excitement, it changes every moment. John Randolph once paid me a high compliment, not intentionally—for he seldom complimented any man—but, without intending it, he paid me what I esteem one of the highest compliments I ever received. He said, 'Whenever a debate is coming on, if I can get a sight of Mr. Clay's face, I can always tell which side he is going to take.'"

The practice of affectation, or dissembling, so far from adding lineaments and expressions to the countenance, absolutely obliterates them. It makes the face, on which was originally "the royal stamp of man," like a smooth shilling, which, though very attractive and pleasant to the feel, is liable to be called in question; to be more closely scrutinized than a coin with an honest face upon it; to be set down for something less than its original value; to be branded as claiming to be of more value than it really is; to receive the curse of Cain, to bear his mark, and thereafter be suffered to wander unmolested.

Finally, we would observe that generally the brain and face are harmonious, but that always the former is subservient to the latter. The divining of character by the skull is subordinate to the practical, every-day reading to which the face is appropriated. Physiognomy is available on all occasions, and it is even a breach of etiquette not to look a man in the countenance: but Phrenology can be employed only professionally, and discovers character "by fumbling up the hair and rubbing the organs," which in most cases would be regarded as a gross impertinence.

NEW YORK, *August*, 1852.

CONTENTS.

LIST OF PORTRAITS

COMPARATIVE PHYSIOGNOMY.

CHAPTER I.

ARISTOTLE, or some other equally sage philosopher, has said, "Man is an animal." If man was not well aware of this fact long before the saying was uttered, he has certainly confirmed it in innumerable instances since, not only in words, but in actions. It is a humiliating truth, of which many people seem proud; but, as humility is a rare and inestimable virtue, it is well that we should be reminded of our frailty by a just comparison of ourselves with the brute creation. What does hinder man from speaking like an angel on the topic that most interests him, and upon which he most wishes to interest others? It is the animal nature that oppresses and clouds his mind, alas! alas! But there is a divine fire within him that struggles

against the superincumbent mass, and ever and anon casts it high in air, mingled and confounded with substances of a lighter and more ethereal nature; and there is a sun of truth and love that clears away the dark mists that obscure his vision.

If, now, we were going to write a poem, we would commence with an invocation, like that with which Milton introduces his "Paradise Lost;" but, "gentle reader," we claim for our subject a scientific character, and we intend to treat it accordingly. An invocation, uttered within the chamber of the soul, is none the less appropriate on that account.

We commence, then, with the admission that "man is an animal." A comparison of himself with the inferior animals has led him, in all ages of the world, to apply the names of animals to men, and the names of men to animals, on the ground of a resemblance between them. There is often great significance in the words *calf*, *goose*, *dog*, *monkey*, and so on, when applied contemptuously. They betray fragments of a true science, perverted to the degradation of human beings. There is equal evidence of the rudiments of this science in the popular mind in the use of the words *kitty*, *lamb*, *duck*, *dove*, and the names of other gentle and favorite pets, applied to those who have corresponding traits. In a rude and simple state of society, the designation of an individual by some ruling trait of character, embodied in the form of some animal, shows what foundation this department of Physiognomy has in nature and in the human mind, and how easily and naturally it is learned. It is not probable that the American Indians are indebted to our modern civilization for an observation of those correspondences which have led them to apply the terms *wild-cat*, *black-hawk*, *alligator*, *snapping-turtle*, and the like, to their chiefs and warriors.

But, lest the reader should suppose that his estimation of

man is much higher than our own, we will here state that, in our opinion, the essential attributes of a human being elevate him to a point beyond comparison with the animal creation. The term *man*, in its highest sense, is synonymous with *angel*. Men are not born, and peradventure we are not men when we "come to man's estate." It may be that we are but "children of an older growth." Man is the result of education, of improvement. He is "self-made," if he be made at all, and the character which he forms for himself is indicated in his countenance. But if truly a man, he considers himself the workmanship of a higher power, for in his own creation he works from a sense of duty, and in opposition to himself, or to the animal which Nature has made him. We say emphatically—

"MAN is a name of honor for a king"—

though, according to the definition, most men who are promoted to royalty are worthy of the title of "king of beasts."

"Man is an animal," but he is more. He has the privilege of naming all the fowls of the air, the beasts of the field, and the fishes of the sea. The lion is to eat straw like the ox, but he is no less a lion on that account; and so it is with every other savage beast, or passion in the human beast. If the beast be made human, the comparison is favorable to the man; but if the man be made animal, the comparison is favorable to the beast. Dear reader, we do not wish to puzzle you, but do you not see the difference between comparing a beast with a man, and comparing a man with a beast? Yes, you see there is some difference between calling an ass a faithful servant and calling a faithful servant an ass! If, therefore, in the following pages, we fail to observe this distinction, you will, for humanity's sake, pardon us, knowing that it was not intentional.

The inferior races are like infants, who, as is well known, go on all-fours. The Ethiopian who opened this chapter is like a brat just learning to stand. Observe the posture — the arms, body, legs, and feet — and you will be struck with the similarity. What a reminiscence of infancy is awakened by that physiognomy! Let it teach thee not to despise one who is as Nature made him, until thou canst deny that thou wast ever a child. Thou wert misshapen, and some time in coming to the condition even of a quadruped, from which thou mightst have grown a satyr —

> ——— "Thy face itself
> Half mated with the royal stamp of man,
> And half o'ercome with beast!"

Plato's definition of man was, "A bird without feathers." This is carrying the comparison rather too far, but it may be said that in many respects man has a striking resemblance to the bird. The bird aspires to a similar standing, though wisely he never takes advantage of his position. The feathered gentry are, we believe, biped animals without an exception, and it is upon his position upon two legs that man prides himself. Birds show something of the same vanity, without therefore laying any claim to superiority. They do, indeed, make use of all-fours in travelling, but it is never with more than two at a time. Birds, however, have a greater likeness to some people than to others. There are certain persons for ever flying about, making a greater flourish with their arms than with their feet: they preserve their hands in gloves, as carefully as a bird does his in feathers; and when they are not swinging their arms, in imitation of rapid travelling, they carry their hands tucked under their coat-tails, behind their backs. They are bound at all events not to show their hands, lest people should know that they have any, and should insist upon their making use of them. The man who very much resembles a bird invariably attempts to live by his wits, however little his noddle may contain. But he is not, by any means, the only person who adopts this method of gaining a livelihood. Those who resemble foxes and pussy-cats do the same.

But as every person has an individuality of his own, which is not to be confounded with that of any other, it is necessary that we should be more particular. Here is a person (see next page) with a sharp, bird-like countenance, who is trying to assure himself that he has a genuine bill, or that it is not a jaw with teeth in it, by which he is in danger of being bitten. The result of the examination will probably be, that he has a long bill, and that he feels like a bird. He is evidently of the kind that was forbidden to the Jews, for the reason probably that he is too much like them to be "taken in;" and his partiality for bills is entirely on account of the havoc they make among the frogs, and young lizards, and other small-fry, that are found in shallow places. His ear is a mighty small one, just fitted to be the lodging-place of a quill; and you might know, without asking his attention for a few moments, that he is a "deaf adder." Think you he makes any great use of the quill upon which he prides himself so amazingly? It is an apology for not grasping with his hands something more substantial than a feather, and it is a token that he plumes himself upon his ability.

Here is a bird on a roost, sharpening his wit with a penknife, a mighty labor of his hands, considering the disposition of his feet to take upon themselves the office of handling. Examine him from top to toe, and you will expect that when anything comes in his way, he will remove it with his foot; and that when he wishes to draw anything nearer to him, his feet will be found more accommodating than his hands. The hand, in his opinion, has a higher of-

fice to perform. It is a quill-holder, and there is no knowing what high flights this gray goose may take into the regions of *space*, to bring down fancies and imaginations—

> "Such as take lodgings in a head
> That's to be let unfurnishéd"—

into the regions of tangible reality.

What have we here? A bird, saving the feathers, which might be supplied with a few tatters, or else with a coat more smooth and glossy. This also is one of the creations of Darley, who seems ambitious to have his creations classed with those of Nature. Those legs!—there is something in their position that beggars description. What need we to speak of the body, the arms, the head, the features, the expression? they speak for themselves, and it is fortunate for a good example that it teaches its own lesson.

By dwelling too long on the subject of birds, we are in danger of becoming flighty. We will simply say that the specimens of the *rara avis* are, if the popular opinion be true, very frequently met with. The individual above, no more than those preceding him, can be accused of soiling his hands by very hard labor, and will certainly get his living in some easy way, without any greater tax upon his wit than is natural to him.

On the following page is a real "fly-away"—and she is but one of a multitude of the same variety. Whether it be a robin, a tomtit, or a lady-bird, it is not important to decide But let us, if our subject does not keep us up in spite of ourselves, descend from birds in general to birds in particular. We can not make minute observations upon the wing—and are not so skilled in marksmanship as not to require our bird to be at rest in order to hit him. When the artist has made a capital hit, and fixed his quarry to the spot on which it stood, which is generally some old limb of a tree, we are prepared to aim at the mark, and may stand some chance of hitting it too.

CHAPTER II.

In likening human beings to animals, people sometimes blunder. Somebody took it into his head to call Jenny Lind the "Swedish nightingale;" and, in endeavoring to conform her face to the theory, the most untruthful and insipid representations have been palmed upon the world as likenesses. The truth is, Jenny Lind, in the expression and contour of the face, and in gait and mien, resembles a lioness. There is something in the unimposing dignity and active strength of the lioness that contents us, while it awakens an almost *unconscious* admiration; we feel that she is fully deserving of her kingly mate. And these same qualities strike us in the character, personal appearance, and manners, of Jenny Lind. It is no objection to this resemblance that her voice is powerful, resonant, and of great compass — for it is the counterpart of the most splendid base that was ever heard.

A prominent characteristic of those who resemble the lion is boldness of project, and a bringing of distant places and objects into a state of equilibrium, by a law like that which governs commerce and the sea. "De Witt Clinton and the Grand Canal" is a very natural association of ideas, and the face of that individual shows a strong resemblance to the lion. That very face, if it approached more literally to the lion, to which it bears a resemblance, would be that of a "regular bruiser;" for the theatre in which his lion-quality exercises itself is one requiring pickaxe, and crowbar, and "horse-power," literally to the end of time. Where this is the case, horse-power may be considered as synonymous with reason caught in the process of a demonstration and unable to extricate itself. It is there bound like Ixion to a wheel, to suffer torture, till the power that resides in a complication of wheels comes to its relief. The horse, it should be observed, is horribly afraid of the lion.

The person represented on the preceding page (De Witt Clinton) has a German face, and the Germans as a nation resemble lions. Of the next two figures, the countenance of

the female is almost literally that of a lion fast asleep, while the face of the man is deprived of this dignified resemblance

by a paltry pipe. In whatever the German descends from his proper characteristics, he approaches the hog. Canals, where Nature has failed to establish intercommunication by rivers, are such works of art as bold minds alone are capable of projecting—and Germany abounds in these. In literature, science, theology, and in everything, the Germans are distinguished for the vastness of their projects, and for execution equal to their designs. Everything, from the crown of the head to the sole of the foot, and

from the treasury to the chest in which the laborer deposites his earnings, is upon an extensive scale. What people in the world make cakes of such vast circumference and diameter as they? Whether Reason has enough concern in their national affairs to substitute intellectual and moral power for physical, and labor-saving machinery for animal force, is a problem in the course of solution.

A noble lion is that of which we are reminded by a face like the following. Some large project of usefulness, in his own proper field, is as necessary to this person as the breath he draws. His animal nature is suited to his moral and intel-

lectual, and is subservient to the higher. Of the lion, it may be said—

> ———————"He has, I know not what,
> Of greatness in his looks, and of high fate.
> That almost awes me."

He is a symbol of the mighty passions that slumber in the human breast, waiting to be taken into the service of Benevolence, which is "mightiest in the mighty," and of Truth, which is "mighty and will prevail." The face of the lion, therefore, has a wonderful resemblance to the human, but to some persons much more than to others.

The next example which we present of a resemblance to the lion is John Jacob Astor. The history of this individual, in

connection with his face, is a confirmation of the principle stated at the outset. A sordid look, we see, is compatible with the lion, otherwise there would be no pertinence in the allusion to "the lion's share." But there is no littleness in anything that he thinks or does. It is not emulation that makes the lion-like individual do things on a larger scale than others. He has the desire of doing great things, but they are little in his estimation when he has done them. He therefore takes no pride in what he does; and to show that what others stare at, is nothing in his eyes, he may give it away. The "Astor House" was given by the father to the son, for a dollar, it is said, directly after it was completed.

There is a strong infusion of the noble qualities of the lion into the mastiff, and the dogs of St. Bernard; but the dog that bays the moon is like those who magnify a sixpence to the size of that deceitful luminary, and are slightly lunatic.

The individual before us bears a perverted resemblance to the lion, but resembles more nearly the variety of dogs just referred to, and may be supposed to hold on to a shilling so tightly as to press a hole through it!

The resemblance between Andrew Jackson and the lion, in character and physiognomy, may be easily traced in the representations given on the following page. Magnanimity, in one of its phases, is synonymous with heroism, with greatness of soul, and greatness in noble deeds. It is fitting, therefore, that the "old hero" should resemble a lion. The sign of the choleric temperament is characteristic of both, and of those previously mentioned. How could Jackson brush that hair of his in any other way than Nature disposes it? His disposition is to resemble the lion, as well in the external as the internal, or he would resemble him in neither. How obvious it is, therefore, that the character must impress itself upon the countenance, and that they must correspond with each other perfectly! What an interesting face is that of Jackson, when we read his character indelibly impressed upon it, and trace the resemblance which we here discover!

Let it be borne in mind that the animal passions, when governed by the moral and intellectual faculties, are very different from what they are in animals. This is necessary, if we would form a correct idea of the person who has any of the marks of the lion in his countenance. Such a person is either generous or cruel, peaceable or savage, noble or treacherous, magnanimous or mean. The most truly magnanimous person is not above performing menial offices for the sake of the happiness of others, and this is from a faculty that in animals and in bad people is the very opposite of magnanimity — it is from a faculty that may be called meanness. This faculty has a large sign in the lion; but as it aspires to be the servant, and to do the bidding of Magnanimity and of all the higher faculties, the lion stands for nobility in the human race, as his physiognomy shows.

The love of overcoming and the love of triumph are elements of tremendous power in the lion, and are prodigious in those who are to be classed under the head of "lions." The traits which distinguish this animal are suitable to royalty. Of the British sovereigns, William the Conqueror, William II., Henry I., Richard I., King John, Edward I., Richard II., Richard III., James I., William III., and George I., have the lion strongly marked in their countenances; while nearly all the rest have a wonderful resemblance to oxen. We have examples also of likenesses to the lion in the persons and characters of Mary Queen of Scots, Oliver Cromwell, and Prince George. Robert Boyle is another of the same class.

CHAPTER III.

Puss, with her nose in a pan of milk, is called *Trollop;* but it is impossible to say that it is on account of her likeness to Madame T———, whose portrait is here presented. There is no doubt but that the "milk of human kindness" is as grateful to the one as *milk* is to the other, and the two appetites generally go together. The cat is remarkably fond of both, though a little at a time satisfies. She relishes petting and fondling very highly, but is soon satisfied, and then "no more play."—"Too much of a good thing" she studiously avoids; and, if you observe, you will see that she acts upon the principle of "not casting her pearls before swine." She is very nice and very particular, and when things do not go to suit her she is a perfect virago—of which we have a fine sample o' nights, when she may be supposed to be engaged in giving curtain-lectures to her spouse, or having a dispute with her neighbors. You would not think, to see her so quietly sleeping the next morning, that she had been playing the termagant so fiercely. The wonder is, that after such serious difficulties she could get to bed and sleep so sweetly, and look the next day such a perfect picture of amiability and contentment. Should any one call her a "spit-fire," you would declare it to be slander; but wait, and presently you shall see for yourself.

But it is very wonderful how the cat can have such a sweet, amiable, loving countenance, when her disposition is the very opposite of that. No—you must not exaggerate her faults: she has affection and forbearance as well as cruelty and slander. Besides, it may be said in extenuation, that her quarrelsome disposition is connected with great love of neatness, for the simple reason that she is "*put out*" when things are in disorder, especially when her choler is ruffled, or any part of her dress is disarranged. The effort to set things to rights disturbs them all the more; and this is an excuse for still more scolding, pulling hair, scratching, screaming, spitting, chasing, and all that. Very amiable this! but we shall come at the amiability by-and-by.

It should be known that those who spend several hours a day in dressing, preparatory to placing themselves on a cushion, or some elevation where they may be seen, are generally pleasant in society, but in private life ill-tempered and ill-tongued. The cat and those who resemble her are no exceptions to this general rule.

But allowing that the cat has a great deal of softness, quiet, love of repose, contentment, love of children, love of kind treatment, and love of milk, how is it that these are so much more observable in her face than the opposite traits? The reason is this: the cat has a wonderful degree of affectation. She can assume a character that does not belong to her; or, rather, she can wear the *semblance* of it, and that is often mistaken for the thing itself. Who would doubt, on looking at this individual, of his ability to dissemble? He looks like a cat, and may be placed in the order of lynxes. The same faculty which induces dissembling gives the power of "acting" or of "play-acting" (whichever term we may choose to employ). The cat is

remarkably fond of play; and as play is the opposite of "sober earnest," it takes Affectation into its service, aud changes the deceiver into a comedian. A playful cat is an honest puss, while a demure one is deceitful, treacherous, cruel. Playfulness is associated with innocence, as it is in children; and it is not till "sober age comes hastening on," that human beings are tempted strongly to play the hypocrite. When children do so they are not playfnl, they are not happy; and examples of "juvenile depravity" are of those that are gloomy, morose, and inclined to disturb rather than to assist in the plays of other children. Here, then, are the *moral advantages* of play—the advantages of such theatricals as children engage in, and of public theatricals, if they are what Nature designed them to be. When *play itself* is an affectation, then the players are deceivers, and the acting is deception; their innocence is lost; and, being themselves corrupt, they do all they can to encourage corruption in others, and to corrupt the morals of the good and pure.

The reader hardly need be told that the cat is sly. It is her nature to take by surprise—she lives by it, and therefore she surprises you in everything. It makes her very soft and quiet in her manners, and this, if we would understand her character, must be distinguished from gentleness. If she had gentleness, she would enjoy her nights undisturbed by brickbats; and in that case, if all people were like her, "midnight outcries and alarms" would cease for ever. It is very hard for those who resemble cats to be gentle, and for the same reason it is next to impossible for them to be gentlemen. Between them and gentlemen there is as great an antagonism as between cats and dogs.

But we were speaking of slyness. The cat enters a room so slyly, that you are not aware of it until she is near you; and she withdraws without your knowledge, so that you are surprised at her absence. You feel something rubbing gently against your leg: it is "Miss Puss," come to soothe the whirlwind of passion that she has excited against herself the night previous, and to say: "There, don't be angry—you see how I can be quiet; let us now make up, and I will lie in your arms, and purr you to sleep!" Slyness, therefore, in the cat, is a good thing. It goes out entirely when she is angry, and after a while it comes to drive anger away. Without it, how would quarrelsome people get over their difficulties, and look more bright, smiling, and affectionate, than ever?

People who entertain a large number of cats, and therefore look like them, steal upon you unawares, whether they intend it or not, and they depart as slyly as they came. But they also meditate surprises—sometimes of an agreeable nature, and sometimes of a disagreeable—for the sake either of enhancing the pleasure of others, or of exciting alarm. As the cat catches a mouse by surprise when it fancies itself enjoying its full of liberty in the bounties and luxuries that surround it, and lets it go that it may be again deceived—so does the individual who resembles a cat delight to disabuse people of their halcyon enjoyments, and to catch them "just as they are," in the midst of their domestic disorder, or comfort, as the case may be. The people they like to come in upon are those "undisturbed"—at their ease—"not dressed to be seen." Slyness, therefore, plays into the hands of Cruelty, and is exercised along with dissembling; but in this case there is no anger; it is destructiveness in cold blood, and meditated hypocrisy.

On the following page is a portrait of Cortez, and it is seen to resemble a puma. A formidable cat this to pounce down upon the mice whose portraits are sculptured on the monu ments of Central America, and represented in the "Aztec children!" Now, gentle reader, do not deprive us of the pleasure of describing to you the resemblance between the Aztecs and mice, which animals we reserve for another chapter. Pray, take your mind from that subject, and trace the feline qualities a bit further. Of all animals, cats are the most savage: the faculties that make them so are love of triumph, contest, hurling, and resistance. Savage and bloody men have the signs of these faculties very large, in consequence of which they have a resemblance to pumas, tigers, leopards, panthers, and wild-cats. Warriors

make special use of the faculty of hurling; and their cheekbones are wide, like those of cats, indicating the strength of this faculty. Storms and tempests, with lightning and thunder, are imitated by warriors on the battle-field, and by cats in spitting fire at each other, and uttering all sorts of strange, unearthly, and portentous sounds. They exhibit gusts, whirl winds, and a tempest of passion; and the place for these exhibitions is the top of the house, as near the clouds as possible: and seeing them there, their looks and motions may remind you of streaks of lightning. The cat is excited by corresponding things in nature, for the worst performances of this kind we have observed to be when—

> "The speedy gleams the darkness swallowed;
> Loud, deep, and long, the thunder bellowed;
> When e'en a child might understand
> The de'il had business on his hand."

To do justice to our subject, we must mention that the cat and those like her have great parentiveness. Who has not witnessed the tender care of the cat for her kittens, in selecting a place, in providing food, in comforting them, and in carrying them in her mouth from a place of danger to one of safety? Who has not witnessed her love for children, her forbearance toward them—as well as learning her kittens to mouse, and, when they come to years of discretion, teaching them propriety and good behavior by an occasional box on the ear? She is, indeed, very affectionate; and when her tempests of passion are over, she is as warm, and sunny, and serene, as the atmosphere and sky after a thunder-shower. It is truly so with those who resemble cats: occasional outbursts purify their spirits from the unhealthiness that is engendered by quietude and stagnation, and their enjoyments are enhanced by contrasts all their lives long. Especially are they so tenderly attached to children, that even half the domestic feuds are controversies respecting the modes of bringing them up and giving them the advantages of education, polish, and refinement.

Fondness for children, an aptitude to teach, and the other dispositions of the cat, are the component parts of that variety of the *genus homo* called the "schoolmaster," and his resemblance to the cat in the external is susceptible of ocular demonstration. There is something feline in his appearance as a whole, and in everything he says and does. He requires the pupils to be "still as mice," and watches them slyly, while the pupils of his eyes wander about in every possible corner. He takes the cat for his model in everything. She says to her kittens: "You may be allowed to play with my tail, which is the pleasantest thing you can do; but, if you do thus and so, I shall punish you!" This is the perfect model of instruction, aimed at, at home and at school, but requiring a knowledge of human nature for its application. The Prussians resemble cats—some one kind and some another. They care more for children than other nations do, and have the best system of education in the world. Annexed is the portrait of Frederick the Great, and by his side that of the ounce, which he is seen very much to resemble. His prominent traits are the same that have been mentioned as constituting a likeness to the cat; but the ounce is the noblest of the cat-kind, and a worthy representative of so great a man. In our category of cats, the lion is not included.

CHAPTER IV.

The "king of beasts" and the "king of birds" are characters fitted to represent royalty in the human race. Who can look upon this portrait of Maximilian without admiration, connected with the impression of its kingly attributes, and of its

resemblance to the eagle in those qualities which constitute royalty? Although this is a kingly countenance, it is very different from that which resembles the lion; but the difference is merely that which exists between birds and beasts—or, if it will make our idea plainer, the one may be called a lion-bird and the other an eagle-beast. In our estimation the eagle-countenance is more noble—it is more intellectual—it has more of greatness—more of that something godlike which we discover in the "bird of Jove." He looks down, not in humility, nor yet in pride, but because his eyry is on high, and he was born to soar above the clouds, and to look on things below as little and insignificant. There is scorn of meanness in his look, but no arrogance; that noble countenance belies a sneer; he has no ambition to soar higher and to explore more lands than others, for his superiority stands confessed. Envy may rankle in others, but in him it is subordinate; and those whom he takes in his talons and "drops on Fortune's hill," may feel contempt for and sneer at those below them.

In this last remark we have hit upon a class of persons who resemble owls. In the formation of certain individuals, Nature seems to have had an eye to the preceding, but to have fallen just so far short as she falls short of creating an eagle when she makes an owl! They may be referred directly to "chaos and old night" for their origin. The nocturnal influences overshadow and rest down upon them, and their souls are filled with howlets, gloomy forests, deserted castles, haunted steeples, and graveyards! They see only by moonlight; and if love ever enters their hearts, and they essay to express it in sounds of affection, accompanied by a guitar, at that witching time of night to which their nature and sentiment incline them, all nature should be hushed, and there could be nothing more appropriate than the injunction—

"Silence, ye *cats*, while Ralph to Cynthia *yowls*,
And makes night hideous—answer him, ye owls!"

Envy and Jealousy are birds of night, and are associated with love, and with every other faculty, in owls and in those persons of whom this bird is the most suitable representative. Such people have also in their faces very large ostentation and love of eminence, the latter being converted by the former into a perpetual sneer. From envy and jealousy, with subterfuge and the love of contest, are begotten detraction, and robbery, and other things, for which the patroness Diana is to be held responsible. Subterfuges are delicate morsels to those who resemble owls, as moles and mice are to owls them-

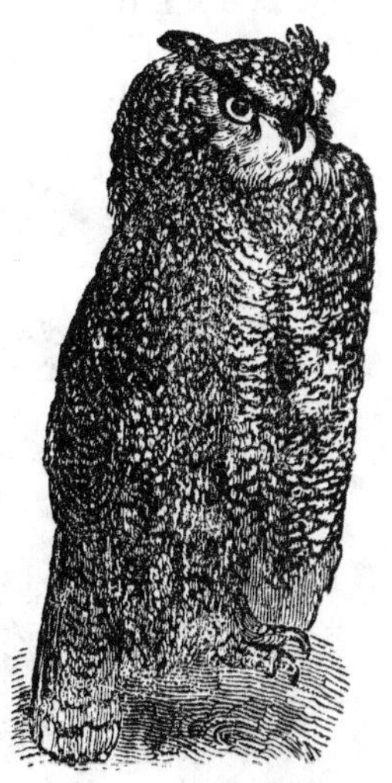

selves; and ofttimes these gnawing, undermining, burrowing, mischief-making little gnomes are elevated on the wings of paltry ambition in the endeavor to outsoar the eagle. As bats and vampires flit through the air in the darkness, and impart a spirit-fire to the owl, so these spirits of the shades flit through the minds of the owlish, and are the nectar and ambrosia that make them fancy they are gods.

Strange things happen sometimes, as when Subterfuge becomes ambitious. Then the cunning and artifice of the cat are owlish, and are exhibited in sublime humbuggery — in fortune-telling, sorcery, magic, and the like; in other words, the cat is turned into an owl. The ogling and staring which are so characteristic of the owl, are no less conspicuous in those who resemble him. The trait exhibits itself in a love of *raree-shows*, and inclines its possessors to the profession of showmen. They take it for granted that what they themselves are most fond of, there must be a demand for; and thus they "kill two birds with one stone" — stare all the time at wonderful sights, which they are exceedingly fond of doing, and make money by exhibiting to others. The men who provide these things they consider the greatest curiosities of all, and are confident of being so regarded by the community. They have no idea of people being so stupid as not to appreciate them. Their self-complacency, therefore, grows to something very decided in the expression of the face.

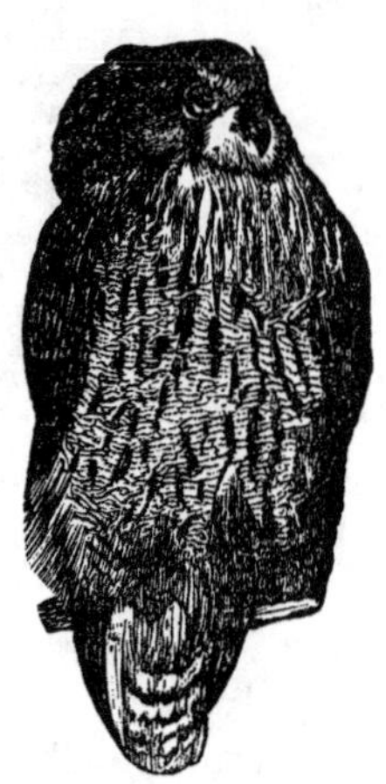

The owl has dignity—he has no notion of being put out of countenance. He fancies that all the birds of the forest have come to see him, when in reality they have come to pick at him: therefore he stands stock still, like a wax figure, as highly gratified at being looked at as in looking. He sets the example of "mute astonishment," as that which is most becoming to the spectators, interrupted now and then by a hoot or a screech, according as the subject is merely wonderful or of the nature of something terrific. He exhibits an indifference to the honors that are paid him, for the simple reason that Nature compels him to affect the eagle, and has given him a vast deal of ostentation. He sits in judgment on others—is the severest, and in his own estimation the wisest, of critics. "As wise as an owl" is a proverb that places him on a level with Solomon, whose fondness for collecting all the strange and wonderful sights in nature and art furnished him with knowledge, and made him all the wiser.

The noble use which is performed by those we are now de

scribing is the imparting of instruction, by means of illustration and example, in whatever is most interesting and important in the arts and sciences. It is the storing up in cabinets and museums, and thereby in the mind, of historical reminiscences, and the wonders of the world, and the exercising of a powerful moral influence by the interest and sympathy awakened for the inhabitants of other climes, and by the memorials of generations that are past and gone. But what need has anybody to be told of this? This mode of instruction, it is perceived, is especially juvenile. In those who resemble owls there is very great love of children, as there is also in those who resemble cats; and this love is connected with the desire and the ability to teach.

The most easy and impressive manner comes, as a matter of course, from that juvenile love of exhibition and wonderment that has been already described. The love of surprise in this case is not gratified by falsehood, but by knowledge — not by the hallucinations of the mind, but by the evidence of the senses; and thus the love of *truth* is cultivated, and with it the love of nature and the love of man, and every good and noble sentiment in the human breast. In our view, there is no picture of tender, earnest, devoted parental affection equal to that of an owl caring for her young, if the representations we have seen be true, as we doubt not that they are. Yet the notion which most people have of the owl would cause them to pass these pictures by without appreciation or sympathy. They suffer the worse features of the bird to eclipse this shining quality (maternal love), and they conceive that the appearance of it is either a burlesque on something touching or sentimental (all the more ridiculous for its attempting to elicit a feeling in the beholder which has no existence in the object), or else that there is no truth in physiognomy. But however the cat and the owl may deceive in other things, they do not deceive in this—and just that beautiful love of children which is by them expressed is exhibited by those who resemble them, more especially if their peculiarities are turned into the highest channel, and subserve the noble ends which Nature designed.

CHAPTER V.

Insensibility is Sensibility in the lowest degree. Knock him on the head, pinch his tail, beat him about the body, and he will show no signs of being hurt. But take care that you do not serve Sensibility in this way, which is the way to reduce it to the condition of its negative and to make the shell of Insensibility thicker than at first. There is such a thing as treating a rhinoceros tenderly: but truth demands that we should show what stuff he is made of. If it seems to thee, gentle reader, that we treat some of our subjects too plainly, remember that *sensation* is pleasant to all animals; and that the degree that is awakened by a touch in some, is only awakened by a blow in those that are protected by a shell.

In the rhinoceros, feeling is kept under. As hardness is the *summum bonum* of a mere animal existence, he has a happy life of it. He may be considered to have attained, very nearly, to the full stature of a perfect beast! But before we can come to a conclusion in regard to him, we must comprehend his two essential qualities, insensibility and appetite.

Insensibility, it should be observed, has a partiality for the tail. In fact, Nature has provided this posterior appendage expressly for its accommodation. This is fully illustrated in the alligator, not to mention the similar animals that are now extinct. Insensibility is nearly synonymous with stupidity, and oblivion is the bliss which it longs for, and to which it finally attains. People who believe in annihilation resemble animals with very long tails, with the exception of this latter appurtenance. Tails are peculiar to animals—are worn as badges of honor in the order of beasthood. They are in many instances more or less scaly when the body is not at all so, as we see in the mouse, the opossum, and the beaver; and the habit of the lemur, of gnawing off the end of his tail, shows that very little sensibility resides there. It shows also that there is an antagonism between Appetite and Insensibility. But the latter in beasts is superior to the former. Insensibility lords it over a wide domain. When he would show his power, he makes an extensive sweep, as may be observed in the use which animals make of their tails when they are enraged. He holds the supremacy over every passion, and "blind rage" is no more blind than he.

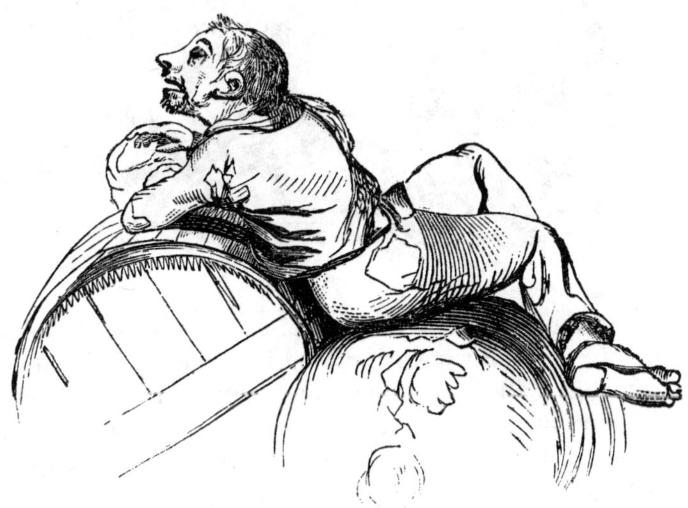

But, like all other sovereigns, he is dependent on his vassals. Appetite is his principal servant. He is supplied with the grossness that is essential to his existence through the demands of Appetite, which himself is obliged to supply. Thus the alligator sweeps his prey into his mouth with his tail; and the brandishing of the tails of lions, tigers, &c., is from the same cause. It is the mighty lord Insensibility that sways this sceptre of power—turning living bodies into dead carcasses, flourishing it about the body to keep his vassals in fear, and extending it over the head to keep his principal servant in subjection.

Thus much of Insensibility. We come now to speak of Appetite. It resides as far as possible from its lord and master, for it is the very opposite. Of course, then, it occupies the head, and has the same relation to the anterior extremities

that the other has to the posterior. Appetite is essential attractiveness, drawing everything into relation and conjunction with Sensibility. It refines and softens the skin as much as Insensibility hardens it, and does always the very reverse of what its master does. It begets Sensibility, which feels intensely, suffers pain, and is carried to the degree of torment. Who, if he has not felt it, has not heard, of the *feeling* of hunger and of *tormenting* thirst? Appetite, therefore, is the very opposite of Insensibility, and, to indicate this, is assigned to an opposite position in the body.

When Appetite grows strong, it dispenses with Insensibility altogether. It makes use of teeth, tongue, claws, &c., to surprise its food, and tosses up its head in perfect contempt of the pretensions of its former lord. It grows bold, saucy, and independent, and says of the tail, that it is "no great shakes, after all!" The consequence of this is, that it turns out as Appetite says: Insensibility is obliged to withdraw from the tail into the body, that he may receive a portion of the nourishment that Appetite would otherwise appropriate entirely to its own use. He reasons, with regard to the state of the case, by the method called *à posteriori*. He considers himself the rightful sovereign; and though he does what he can to conciliate Appetite, he has no notion of consenting to a rebellion.

He makes a virtue of necessity, and becomes on familiar terms with the servants that he was formerly in the habit of chastising. He lets down his dignity wonderfully—deserts the tail, which, "like a pile without inhabitant, to ruin runs," and takes up his residence in the back.

But the less of a gentleman he becomes, the more selfish is

he. He converts the body into a fortification; he builds on a larger scale, and in a style of greater magnificence, than before—a sure index of his waning fortunes. He is swayed by fear, and what he does is an indication of it; he substitutes grasping cupidity for the title of sovereign in just the degree that his sceptre is in danger of being wrested from him; he parts with his courage and magnanimity as a prince with his sceptre and his crown. Fear draws him into close communion with Appetite, and enlarges headquarters for his reception. Finally, he becomes the very slave of Appetite, and takes up his residence in the head, which is gradually enlarged for his accommodation. When this is the case, we may ascertain it by the fact that there is no tail left. He may be called, first and last, *Endurance*, because, as he suffers nothing, he suffers anything you please. He is the common ground for all sorts of impressions: he is at first the pavement, then the stepping-stone, then the marble hall to the palace of the soul; and finally he is the luxurious carpet, upon which, though there is less danger, men tread more softly than on stones. What we have described is Endurance, indicated by the brain and nerves of sensation, upon some of which impressions are made more lightly than on others.

We are now prepared to speak more particularly of the rhinoceros. Insensibility has lost all dignity in him. You see by his looks that he is supremely selfish, and that Insensibility in him would sacrifice pride rather than the services of Appetite. By remaining in the tail when the servant was likely to become independent of his master, the latter would vacate entirely, and the whole animal economy would be destroyed. Here master and servant dwell peaceably together, in the back and head, surrounded by the tokens of unbounded prosperity; while the tail hangs idly, having been resigned for things more substantial and enduring.

The condition of the rhinoceros, for a beast, is truly a happy one. The means of subsistence are before him, but never a great way off. Not so with those animals that have a predominance of insensibility in the tail, as the alligator, or that have a predominance of laziness, like the bear. "Proud and lazy" is an epithet that can not be applied to the rhinoceros. Insensibility keeps such good pace with Appetite, that his food is always under his nose. He is ever reaching forth for the supreme good—the gratification of Appetite, and the closing up of the avenues of Sensation. His belly is therefore of the largest dimensions, and is fortified around with shields and bucklers, so that the vulnerable part is long in being discovered. He keeps his servant busily at work in closing the avenues outside and in. As he has so much selfishness, it is appropriate that he should be formed specially for *self-defence*. The sign of this is the most prominent feature in his countenance. As Self-Defence follows Attack, he must invariably, in every controversy, have the last word. It is impossible to find anything new about him, for he is fortified against encroachment, and is encased in the old. He has but one logic for all who dare to assault him, and his last word is always the same. He assures you that "facts are stubborn things," and the toughness of his hide inclines him to deal in these, and makes it impossible that any other should have an impression upon him. He puts effects for causes, and in going forward supposes that he is going backward; and this he dignifies with the name of reasoning! But this is more the case with those who resemble alligators—where Insensibility attaches greater dignity to the tail—than in him. What you attack in the rhinoceros is "cut and dried." It has stood the test of time and of innumerable assaults, and why should he change it? He knows how to give you mathematical demonstrations, for it is his business to *fortify* himself. This is his *fort*, and he applies it to the erection of defences against all who war with him, whether the weapons be spiritual or carnal. It is against the *possibility* of an attack that he fortifies himself, and he is therefore impregnable. He is prejudiced: what can you do with him? His motto is, "In peace prepare for war, that no enemy may be tempted by your weakness to pounce upon you!" This is the dictate of fear, and also of Insensibility, when there is no danger to be apprehended. But when it shows no fear of reason, and takes reason for its counsellor, it serves a noble use.

The man who resembles the rhinoceros is either one of the wisest or the most senseless of individuals. Look at that countenance, and say if it is not destitute of Sensibility. Was there ever anything so stupid? You may anticipate the time when, like the hog, he will testify his content-

ment with a grunt. But let us turn from this example of the brute creation to another that is very like him, and yet in a certain sense the very opposite.

CHAPTER VI.

WHAT executioner is this, come to wield his monstrous lash, more effective than the club of Hercules? He is inclined to try the stability of those mathematical certainties which the rhinoceros puts his trust in — to feel the ground upon which he treads, and to make impressions on defences that bid defiance to attack. Everything about him is formed to be the counterpart of that which is discovered in the rhinoceros. That trunk of his, which is the only thing of the kind in existence, is curiously and wonderfully made. It is a maul unparalleled, and has at its end an instrument for pinching, so that it is suitable to the execution of every sentence. He punishes both great and minor offences, with an exactness of justice that is truly admirable. As he is physically suited to carry it into execution, so his belief is —

"That when a man is past his sense,
The method to reduce him thence
Is twinging by the ears and nose,
Or laying on of heavy blows."

He has the feeling that he is formed to be an executioner. When the sentence has gone forth, it is never revoked. The punishment must come if ever the opportunity offers; his duty must be discharged. In the East, he is chosen to execute the laws. There is no variety of execution short of infernal that he is not prepared to inflict. The man who is so wanting in Sensibility as to play a hoax upon the elephant, will have it dinged into him by the elephant's trunk if ever he comes within the reach of that flexible instrument. By "the elephant," be it understood, we mean the man who resembles the elephant, and by "the rhinoceros" the man who resembles the rhinoceros.

The animal we are now speaking of may be styled the "Executive." He is the very embodiment of "physical force." As the rhinoceros represents Endurance, so does the elephant represent Effectiveness. Like an immense water-wheel, he rolls, and tumbles, and pours the water over him; and the *animus* which he applies, or the motive-power, is like water tumbling over a precipice, to which his forehead and descending trunk bear a close resemblance. His countenance

is all dripping, and seems to invite a torrent of water to be poured over it. His whole body is like a sea, with its ebb and flow, and moving forward with a slow current to its outlet, where the mighty force of descent invites to the demonstration of the principle that "knowledge is power." He is the wisest of the brute creation, for physical force should be governed by intellectual, to which it corresponds. He represents all things mighty—the water-power, the ponderous wheel, and the whole machinery through which power overcomes a resistance equal to itself in the production of the most wonderful results.

As there is in the rhinoceros that which involves the principles of mathematics, so there is in the elephant that which involves the principles of mechanics; and as Nature illustrates these principles in the animal economy of both, so Art, in those who resemble the rhinoceros and the elephant, applies them to the demonstration of the laws which govern the material creation, and to the production of machinery. Astronomy is the result of the one, and wheels and their complicated revolutions are the result of the other. The Effectiveness that resides in the human frame is still greater in the instrument that man produces. There is a resemblance to the elephant, not only in those who make an extensive application of machinery, but in those who invent it.

The *inferior* class who bear this resemblance, are suited physically to perform the function of executioners, and to be the instruments of power. The stoutest laborers—in size, form, motions, and expressions of the countenance—resemble the elephant. This is so with herculean negroes particularly, and they have been re-

garded as the executors and as the labor-saving machinery of the world from time immemorial. This is doubtless in some degree a perversion of the grand principle which they illustrate, but it shows an instinctive recognition of this resemblance, not only in those who make a slave of the negro, but in the negro himself. There is something peculiarly noble, dutiful, and trustworthy, in the features of the "black fellow" who bears this resemblance—rude when caught, and yet beautiful from his adaptation to his various uses.

The elephant exhibits this beauty of adaptation the very day that he is captured; he takes to service almost immediately, which can be said of no other animal. His susceptibility of improvement is uncommonly great. This is true of the African, and hence he is capable of attaining to the highest condition morally and intellectually, the correspondent of which is the lowest physical condition when the former and the latter are not united. But his development is exceedingly slow, as is also that of the elephant.

The negro presented in the first of these chapters is a mere babe. Precocity in the human family, although highly flattered, is less to be desired than the tardy development of the negro. Every one may judge what the difference will be in the final ıesult. Mrs. Harriet Beecher Stowe has some fine remarks on this subject, in her popular work entitled "Uncle Tom's Cabin, or Life among the Lowly," which it would be superfluous to quote, since it must be taken for granted that everybody has read them. The features which resemble the elephant are characteristic of childhood, as in this and the preceding examples.

There is also characteristic childhood in a child like this, who is exceedingly fond of a ride on the elephant's back, and whose features are seen to bear a striking resemblance to the profile of that animal. It must be confessed, too, that he has reason to be grateful for affection on the part of his bearer, for they are congenial spirits. In the negro-looking female who stands above, we can hardly fail to see that the features are elephantine, and to ascribe to her all the docility, faithfulness, caution, substitution, and love of children, that are characteristic of the elephant.

The African may be called deformed and monstrous, like the elephant· but there is an old proverb which says, "Homely in the cradle, handsome in the saddle." Besides this, the highest beauty is the result of the highest use, and is founded on the lowest. In his adaptation to the lowest, which is that of a dutiful child, the African is still handsome:—

> ——— "his mother's eye,
> That looks upon him from his parent sky,
> Sees in his flexile limbs untutored grace,
> Power in his forehead, beauty in his face."

This beauty is latent in him, and will be developed. It should be observed, however, that certain negro races do not resemble elephants, and these in market value are good for nothing except to play the banjo, and exhibit white collars and pocket handkerchiefs: but we shall speak of these in another chapter.

CHAPTER VII.

What a man loves, he generally is: hence he is generally himself, for it is himself that he loves. Self-love is the most natural solution of the fact that the animal a man most likes he most resembles. The man who resembles the ostrich has more of the spirit which says, "I'm myself," than the generality of mankind. It is the staring, wondering owl that says, "Who? who?" and provokes the response just alluded to. In children, who are more spontaneous than grown people, question and answer of this sort are expressed literally. The one that says, "I'm myself," is a young ostrich, and promises to resemble that bird more and more. There is progressively developed in him a spirit of independence that is truly noble. He throws off infantile weakness rapidly, and relieves his parents of the responsibility of taking care of him. This is one of the characteristic things in which he resembles the ostrich. His appetite for knowledge, his power of mastering stubborn truths and of appropriating the results to the development of his own mind, and the possession thereby of an uncommon degree of strength and maturity, correspond to the appetite, powerful digestion, and wonderful hardiness and strength of the desert-bird. He has an abundance of self-love; but his love of liberty, in raising him above dependence, elevates him above the lower gratifications of selfishness, and he exhibits a high-mindedness that is truly admirable.

Be it observed, however, that the resemblance to the ostrich may be too literal. In that case the individual is weak-minded, foolish, self-conceited, light-headed, and likes to be odd, at the same time that he "asks no odds" of any one, prides himself upon his originality (which is mere oddity), and reasons in a circle from one end of a single idea to the other, as the ostrich runs when pursued by a horse. He is a sort of mathematical reasoner, considering that if by any means he can return "to the place of beginning," the thing is "proved." In other words, he is a sort of transcendental rhinoceros, for whoever resembles

the one animal has a certain resemblance to the other. It may be mentioned at the same time that the relationship between the lion and the eagle, and the cat and the owl, causes that the person who resembles the beast should resemble also the bird, and *vice versa.*

But the ostrich, and the man who resembles him too literally?—A horse, unaided by the cunning and prudence of the rider, can no more overtake the one, than reason can overtake the other. The sandy desert which you will have to traverse, if you follow in his footsteps, will not furnish you with a single oasis to gladden the eye or to refresh the exhausted spirits. Water there is none, but only a vast sea of sand; and instead of genial warmth, there is burning heat, that withers every verdant thing, and destroys the life. If this strange bird can live there, others can not, and it is because he is adapted to a situation that to others would be a "place of torment."

Most persons can tell you without much hesitation what animal they are most fond of, but this is not so with the person who resembles the ostrich. He never saw the animal that

he had any particular liking for and the truth is, he has no particular liking for any. The reason is, he has never had the opportunity of making a pet of the animal he most resembles. He is minus also the love of children to the degree that he has no disposition to pet and fondle them. As he has no idea of leaning upon parents and being a burden to them, so he expects that children will take care of themselves, and relieves himself of responsibility concerning his own. As he has no opportunity to love the animal he is like, he loves it in himself, and the definition of this is—

> ——"he loves himself so much,
> He owes all others else a grutch!"

On the contrary, the person who is like a horse, a cow, a cat, or a dog, or any familiar animal, is fond of creatures of all sorts. The gratification of a predominant affection opens a channel for the exercise of other affections of the same nature. Thus it is necessary that conjugal love should be awakened, in order that the domestic and social affections should be fully developed; and that a man should love the animal he most resembles, in order that he may exercise love and compassion toward animals in general. The fondness for animals, like that for human beings, is founded upon a partiality for *one*. As the love of God is the love of ONE, the love of mankind is founded upon that.

The animal nature of which the ostrich is an embodiment forms the groundwork of a character as exalted as the foundation is low, and as chaste and beautiful as the basis is coarse and strong. In nature and art the barren rudeness and ugliness of the foundation are in proportion to the perfection of the design. The most beautiful temple is reared upon the unsightliest and most rugged rock. The hardest material is formed for the most exquisite finish. Its roughness and deformity give place to symmetry and proportion; its rigidity is changed to the appearance of softness. The most solid substance becomes spiritual, and thereby yielding; the shapeless mass acquires the highest degree of individuality; it becomes ethereal by the flow of life and beauty that surrounds it; it is an embodiment of the sublimest conception — an image of the DIVINE.

The stubborn hardness of the substances which the ostrich takes into his stomach, and the more obstinate stomach that resists and overcomes them, correspond to facts the most difficult of solution, and to a mind capable of grasping and resolving them. The barren sand traversed by the ostrich, and the vain effort at progress (the running around and returning to the same place, which makes it impossible ever to escape, either from the desert or the enemy that pursues him), correspond to universal truths which in the process of reason are never to be lost sight of, and to the true order of reasoning, which, as it follows Nature, is in a circle — but in a circle that is progressive, being that of "end, cause, and effect." We see, therefore, what connection there is between folly and wisdom, silliness and simplicity, and consequently what connection there is between pride and selfishness on the one hand and respectability and usefulness on the other. The independence of care and protection, and the consequent deficiency of these in the ostrich, correspond to the independence which seeks to increase itself by establishing a commerce of freedom, and to the consequent kindness and protection which relieve the dependence of others, and enable them to confer independence in their

turn. The self-sufficiency or proud independence of the bird corresponds to the humble Sufficiency which acknowledges Mutual Dependence for its father. From this action of Independence proceed the most admirable relations of parents and children, and of society at large. The most perfect order and harmony are the result of the rudimentary traits which constitute a resemblance to the ostrich, or of the highest degree of improvement which these qualities are capable of. The Swedes, as a nation, bear a resemblance to the ostrich, as a comparison of faces and of the characteristics mentioned above will show.

CHAPTER VIII.

THE distinction between matter and space will explain the difference between beasts and birds. It would seem at first glance as if the elephant and the stork were altogether dissimilar, but the difference between them is as the difference between *size* and *distance.* In everything relating to measurement, the stork is a model of perfection. There is no part of his body in which length is disregarded; consequently his proportions are faultless. His appearance may remind us of something awkward and ungainly, but it is not in him. His gait is easy and graceful, and it is association of ideas that reminds us of the opposite. In our disposition to find in him something to laugh at, is illustrated the saying that "there is but one step from the sublime to the ridiculous." His height is contrasted with the low, and instantly we think of littleness and insignificance being elevated upon stilts, for contrast is the very essence of the absurd. If we observe the length of his bill, the contemptible idea of a noddle which is suggested by the height to which his extremities elevate him will pass over to the flamingo, the crane, the ostrich, and birds of that ilk, whose heads are little in proportion to their height. A head whose lightness elevates it among the clouds is ridiculous in the extreme.

The class of persons who, on account of the length of their limbs, are compared to cranes, are many of them exceedingly graceful, and these resemble storks; while the remainder have greater length in particular portions of their limbs than they can well dispose of. Their not knowing what to do with their hands and feet is connected with a shortness of nose, chin, or other features of the countenance. Proportions being dependent upon length are looked for in connection with it, and by length want of proportion is rendered conspicuous. The man who resembles the stork is suspected of being awkward and

ungainly when he is not so; and if the suspicion prove true. even in the least degree, he is poked fun at. For the reason that there is but one step from the sublime to the ridiculous, it is a dangerous step for a man to grow tall, particularly if it be a hasty one, as is frequently the case between the ages of fifteen and twenty. For the same reason it is dangerous to aspire to an elevation in rank. A high position is one which commands criticism quite as much as respect; and perfect consistency, or *truth*, is looked for in this case as perfect proportion is looked for in the other. The man whom *Nature* makes tall, and at the same time harmonious, has nothing to fear. Like the stork, he will outlive ridicule. He is not born to be idle—he must vindicate himself—and should be reckoned among those things that are "comely in going." His talent is discovery, not invention—observation, not theory. In this consists the principal difference between him and the person who resembles the ostrich: the one is prone to be odd and ridiculous, the other the reverse:—

> "That lifts a mortal to the skies,
> This calls an angel down."

Invention proceeds in its development from the earth to the heavens; Discovery from the heavens to the earth. The former, with its head among the clouds, is silly and self-conceited, or is liable to become so, like the ostrich; the latter, with its high thoughts directed to the earth, is distrustful of appearances, like the stork:—

> "Who bade the stork, Columbus-like, explore,
> Realms not his own, and seas unknown before?"

If he traversed in a circle the little spot where he was born, he would find out nothing. As he is a discoverer, it is suitable that he should be high, where he can look down upon those whom he enlightens, and enlighten every object that he sees. It is suitable that he should be high, for his matchless proportions defy criticism; and however much we may be disposed to ridicule him in his standing position, he inspires a sense of sublimity when we see him stretched out in his aerial voyage.

As length is a predominant thing in the stork, he walks with measured tread. So does the person who resembles him. His life is portioned out to various pursuits, each in its season, and he keeps pace and time with others, and sets them an example of regularity. The *adjutant* is well named, so far as marching, or measuring time and distance by paces, can make a

soldier of him. But it should be remarked that tall persons, who resemble storks, adjutants, herons, and the like, are deficient in *courage*. This essential of a soldier generally falls to the lot of short people, and to short, thick-set animals, like the bull-dog. The combination of caution, which is characteristic of the long, with courage, which is characteristic of the short, is exhibited in the *military character*. The courage of the lion, as the lion should be, is mated with the military instinct and genius of the stork, and the animal which embodies these two in perfect proportion is the horse.

Want of courage, in man or animal, induces consumption; and caution, being changed to fear, increases it. The adjutant is a giant-bird, with a formidable jaw, but he is a shameful coward. If the increase of flesh and fat is not in proportion to the food taken into the stomach, the food is *consumed:*

it is wasted, and this waste indicates one degree of cowardice, and the wasting of the body another. It is the destiny of the stork, the flamingo, and the like, and of those who resemble them, to grow long and spindling, and consumption is a means to that end, whether it be a perversion or not. Stout-hearted people are stout built, and hearty appetite and hearty food promote their stoutness. But the person who depends upon his food and drink to give him courage, or upon any kind of narcotic or stimulant to supply his mental deficiencies, becomes intemperate, and wastes in body and mind as he does in money and provisions. As there is something natural in this (the herons and cranes setting them the example), they spin out quite a life of it, after all!

CHAPTER IX.

Whoever has seen the "Aztec children," whatever may have been his speculations respecting them, will jump at the idea of their resemblance to mice. The feeling they awaken is a compound of repugnance, playfulness, curiosity, and fondness. But however much, gentle reader, you may feel a disinclination to touch them, you will be ready to spring upon them as the embodiments of a truth, and clasp them to your hearts. Besides, if you are capable of seeing beauty in a mouse, with his peculiar habits, his confidence, his distrust, his audacity, his silken hair, his delicate structure, his active temperament, his tiny limbs, his round chest, his little big head, his sparkling black eyes, his disproportioned chops, in which mischief is concealed under gravity—if you are capable of sympathizing in his misfortunes, of desiring to protect him, or of a temptation to enlarge him when he has unluckily fallen into a trap—then you are capable of seeing beauty in the Aztec children, and of feeling an affection for them. You will have no disposition to call them fools: *they are noodles.*

Their resemblance to mice is in everything they do, and in every part from top to toe, but most in the countenance, and in those things which it is impossible for the artist to portray. The only correct impression that can be made upon them is upon the retina: a second-hand solar impression, like the daguerreotype, will never do. In the proportions of the jaws, in the peculiar form and expression of the mouth, in that nose, so full of fire, energy, and comicality, and in a certain something diffused over all so like what we discover in the mouse, we can not fail to see a wonderful relation between the two. From such lips as those you argue a pair of incisors similar to those of a mouse; and the truth is, the boy, who has his second set, has but one pair of cutting-teeth in each jaw. To the exercise of gnawing we should imagine that nothing could be better suited than the cracker which constitutes their principal food. They are wonderfully mischievous but not

wilfully or maliciously so. The boy is fond of teasing his sister, of intermeddling, of having "a finger in the pie," but it is all for the sake of fun and frolic, the gratification of curiosity, the largest liberty, and the indulgence of the senses.

You must not look in their countenances for the expression of delight so much as in their feet: their nether extremities are curiosities equal to those of the mouse, and the appearance and feeling of their hands confirm the resemblance. There is no warmth in them — they are like dead things; and though there is a certain glow in the countenance of the girl, it is too literally ruby to answer the expectation arising from the association of "ruby lips." If you would understand the strange sensation that is produced by contact, you can experience it by kissing the lips of a marble statue. Of this we are assured on good authority, for it is no unusual thing for matronly ladies to manifest the common fondness for children toward the girl Bartola. But the countenance of Maximo is absolutely dead, except a faint attempt at roguishness which may be occasionally discovered in the corners of his mouth. The greater amount of love which falls naturally to the female, gives a lifelike appearance to the face of his sister, and thus an interest, which his has not

There is no accounting for tastes except on principles of Physiognomy. People who resemble owls are attracted to the Aztecs, and find in them a gratification of their tastes and an ample field for the exercise of affection and fondness. The same is true of those who resemble cats. In the cat the qualities of the mouse are assimilated, and she can but love that which gratifies her, and which corresponds to the playfulness, the refinement, the cunning, and so many other things, in her own nature. The part of her nature that is not mouse is made up of bird and fish, both of which she is exceedingly fond of. That a cat is fond of mice in a higher sense than is usually understood is manifest from the delighted expression of her eyes when she sees one, and from her playing with it before she appropriates its little flesh and bones to the gratification of appetite. You can see that the mouse "fills her eye," as something both good for food and fair to look upon. Thus it is that the eye expresses taste and appetite in relation to beauty and quality, which are in most cases inseparable. The little mouse appeals to the cat through her love of infants, which is wonderful; and it is affection, not hatred, in connection with her appetite, that makes her devour it. Females who resemble cats threaten to devour their little ones, play with them as a cat with a mouse, bite harder than they intend, and really feel as if it would be a pleasure to swallow them alive if there were not a higher law of nature, the "sovereignty of the individual," to oppose it. We saw one man in whom the Aztec children excited extraordinary affection and delight. He kissed the girl, was enthusiastic in his admiration of their beauty, and went into an ecstasy at the grace and liveliness of their manners. He had a very parental expression of countenance, and resembled a cat almost as much as the children resembled mice.

These children never walk; they always run. Explaining the constant flexure of their legs by the idea that they may have had the rheumatism some time or other, is ridiculous. Except when they jump, they run with a gliding motion, which requires a peculiar step, like that of the mouse. There is no elevation upon the toes, or from straightening of the limb, so that (as in the absence of locomotion, or of steps and paces) the attention is directed principally to the head, that glides mysteriously along, like a mouse, or like a ball that is kicked from one end of a room to the other: the force seems to be not in itself, but behind it, or out and around. The whole expression of the countenance is external, as if in the gratification of the senses it would spend its existence. In this, too, the Aztec children resemble mice. The first time we saw the boy Maximo, there was so little expression of internal consciousness, that we questioned whether he was alive. In our imagination he was a first man, made of red clay, with life breathed into his nostrils, where it seemed to reside, but that he had not yet become a living soul. As for Bartola, she should be called "Undine," but how she crept into the soul of the author of that delightful story it is impossible to conceive. We should not be more surprised to see her in a little chariot drawn by mice, than we were at the first sight of her. Poets may cease dreaming of fairies, for their dreams are realized. If spirits should claim that these were the first fruits of their endeavor to clothe themselves with material forms, we should be inclined to believe them.

But, seriously, these children do not seem like beings of flesh and blood. They may be taken for souls without bodies, or bodies without souls, whichever we please:—

"All eye, all ear, the disembodied soul"—

and that is what these Aztec children are, though it is pretty evident that their spirits are upon the outside, and that their senses are external. Their spirits may be said to have "stepped out," and this gives the impression that they are dead. This, and the instant association of their features with the Aztec images, and with the sculptured heads on the Central-American ruins, to which they bear so striking a resemblance, impressed our minds with the idea that they were the work of some modern Prometheus who had discovered the art of creating human beings artificially. That grave countenance, like that of a graven image; those lively extremities, which might owe their activity to galvanism rather than to a head so motionless as theirs; those animated dead eyes; that stifled voice, extorted as it were by screws and pinching; that unearthly attempt to speak; those threads and hinges on which the motive power, whatever it is, is intended to operate — these, and other things too numerous to mention, constitute a resemblance to the mouse. On the whole, they are pretty little contrivances for the diversion of ladies and gentlemen, old and young.

CHAPTER X.

For all that ethnologists can discover to the contrary, the origin of the "Aztec children" is hidden in impenetrable obscurity. They are mysterious little beings certainly. If they are not the productions of witchcraft, they have at least a something about them that will cure "the blues." No ghost can haunt a castle that is not deserted of mice. One sprite, or fairy, or eldrich thing, will drive out another, and so it is with the little elves we are speaking of. From hall or cottage they will keep away annoyances of a more serious nature. Like mice, they are weak and helpless. They are born to frisk and frolic, and to live on preserves and confectionery, in a lordly mansion, where they are permitted to make free use of whatever they can find. They are wholly incapable of providing for themselves; and should the mansion be deserted, they would starve to death. Yet they are useful in their way, and pay for the immunities that are afforded them. Think not, gentle reader, that they are the only persons who resemble mice!

But the spirit personated in the rat—oh, horrible! Sordid, sensual, its energies bent on plunder; carnivorous, insatiable; hiding his plunder in subterranean holes, where he expects to find it; torturing the earth to uncover and conceal his cherished gold; extorting confessions and disclosures from the miserable victims of his cupidity and lust; incarcerating men and women in excavations of his own, where his ratty soul takes refuge in times of danger—these are the characteristics of the worst of tyrants, or of those who resemble rats. On the following page is presented a full-length portrait of the Hindu nabob, Suraj-a-Dowlah, the incorrigible wretch who thrust a hundred and forty-six Englishmen into a dungeon not twenty feet square, known to fame as the "Black Hole of Calcutta." It was about eight o'clock in the evening when they were forced in, and "at eight o'clock in the morning the narrow space

was so completely blocked up with the dead lying one upon another, and those who yet lived were so weak and faint, that it was with the greatest difficulty that the door was opened. At length twenty-three ghastly figures were brought out—figures that would not have been recognised by the mothers that bore them." What better could be expected from a man who resembled a horrible black rat? If there be such a thing as transmigration of souls, it might be some gratification to the English to imagine that he was among the number of infernal rats that the city of Paris made war upon, killing thousands in "black holes"—and that among the skins they purchased of the victors, to manufacture into gloves, his was one!

Those whose faces resemble hares or rabbits are much prettier. They are attractive, simple, lively, ready to act at a moment's warning, but somewhat selfish and quarrelsome withal. As with the mouse, there is very little fraternal affection in them, though filial love is strong. They are remarked for wonderful aptitude and desire to learn, and for extraordinary susceptibility of improvement. The portrait of Sir Henry Clinton, which follows, may be taken for a model of a schoolboy countenance. It is that also of a "hewer of wood and a drawer of water." It is the representative of a useful class, but of one that learns to do mischief and good with equal facility. You can see impudence in that countenance, requiring only to be let go in order to exhibit itself in words, and to act hand-in-hand with mischief, to which it is near akin. If that were the case, filial love would be selfish, like the fondness of a cat for a mouse—requiring to be fed and clothed, and making insolent demands, and thereby retaining the character of weakness and infancy. The person who resembles a rabbit is either saucy, impudent, idle, disobedient, or the very reverse; for the animal faculties acting in subserviency to those that are peculiarly human are reversed, and manifest themselves in the very opposite direction. Thus there is no harm in resembling a savage beast, for the traits of character in such an animal tend to innocence, peace, comfort, contentment, and felicity, as is manifested in the faces, expressions, postures, motions, and air, of the feline animals, when their passions are withdrawn from the external, which is the region of disturbance, to the internal, which is the region of tranquillity. It is as the difference between the surface of the ocean and the depths beneath.

The person who resembles the mouse has tendencies toward refinement and elevation, while the one who resembles the rat has none. The one aspires, ransacks drawers and closets, buries himself in books and papers in garrets, gleans knowledge from every source, finds profit in being alone, and "all the bread and cheese he has he lays upon a *shelf*." The other sinks in the mire of corruption, delves for filthy lucre, and has no disposition to rise except upon the heaps that he can accumulate.

The person who resembles the squirrel has nobler tendencies than the one who resembles the mouse. The squirrel-countenance which we see here is interesting, charming, good, and improves on acquaintance. It indicates interest, simplicity, truthfulness, cheerful and lively emotions, domestic virtues, providence, industry, aspiration, liking for children, tenderness, and the love of being well housed and made comfortable. It resembles the squirrel in everything, as a higher may correspond to a lower; and who is there that, from the countenance alone, would not confirm our judgment of the character? It is the face of Anne of Cleves, the fourth wife of Henry VIII.

Of the traits mentioned in the last character, maternal love is the centre, around which the others cluster. This is still more remarkably the case with the individual who resembles the opossum. But the latter is as homely as the former is beautiful; and this word "homely" is the very one to express the

looks and dispositions of the person referred to: the parental feeling is so strong, that even in the male it seems maternal, and in the female it seems more than that. This is a rude sketch of a South African, an old Bossouto warrior, a convert to Christianity. For a resemblance to the opossum, that carries its young ones in a pouch, and loves to do so, we may well look to the African mothers, who carry their children continually about them, so that the office of child-bearing never ceases. The Ethiops are children, as before described, and parental love in children exhibits itself chiefly in carrying babies in their arms, which is the more servile employment, but easy, because it is a child's affection, the exercise of which is play. Whatever animal the Africans resemble is fond of carrying young things; and this is the principal secret of the elephant's wonderful docility, for men are playthings to him, and he serves his master as a negro does a child, or as a heathen does his idol. He rides him on his tusks, tosses him on his back, takes him down again, teters him up and down, as if he would say, "This is my doll-baby."

CHAPTER XI.

It would be a strange thing indeed if, in tracing the resemblance between men and animals, we should overlook the monkey. The class of animals called *simia* similate man so perfectly as often to create the suspicion that there is something human in them. The orang-outang is justly entitled to the appellation of "wild man of the woods," though some consider it too high an honor to bestow upon him for his mockery of the human species. But man was born to be created, to labor as an artist in the production of an image and likeness of the Divine; and, until he has made himself a man, he is a mere child, a mere production of Nature, a wild man of the woods. The orang-outang has not one particle of the artist about him, and therefore he is not and never can be a man.

The ape, as a representative of the class to which he belongs, is a parody on the human race. He represents the perversions of human nature in the extreme, and operates as a check, without which man would set no bounds to his folly and madness, his vanity and pride, and would degenerate into the ape he now despises.

Of the perversions to which man is liable, and which constitute his resemblance to the monkey, let us speak in order. First, his assumption of appearances and manners not belonging to him; his affectation of qualities superior to his own; his ambition to pass for a being of superior mould — to palm himself off for a god. It is Dr. Adam Clarke (is it not?) who supposes that the temptation of our first parents (that by eating the forbidden fruit they should be as gods, knowing good and evil) was suggested by an orang-outang; but now-a-days the creature operates as a preventive to such a vain ambition.

The rock on which they split is a warning to their posterity; and those who disregard it must appear very much to the angels as monkeys do to us:—

——— "Man, proud man,
Dressed in a little brief authority,
Plays such fantastic tricks before high Heaven,
As make the angels weep—who with our spleens
Would all themselves laugh mortal."

Human beings are pleased with a reflection of themselves in a glass, in the minds of others (particularly when they can have their characters described to them), in every object that they resemble, even in a monkey. Hence they are more amused with these animals than any other, laugh heartily at their grimaces and mannerly ways, and in doing so resemble them still more.

Be it observed that apes are not ambitious to be men, but *as* men, and the ambition of men is not to be angels, but *as* such. It is a great mistake to suppose that men should not aspire to be angels. The error is in wishing to appear such when they are not. They rob heaven of its sacred things, that they may appear divine, and receive the homage that is due to the Supreme Being, not considering that these things are forbidden fruit. They rob humanity, which is robbery of Him who created man in his own image, and with the things they steal from their fellow-beings they invest themselves, and thereby claim for themselves divinity, and command that those whom they have robbed should fall down and worship them—worship the garments, the equipage, the gold, the power, which they have filched from the hands of the poor and needy. There is not a thing they wear but that is a token of something heavenly, and is therefore too good for them. It is the proper clothing of beings that are good and pure, humble, and moved by charity in everything they do. It is not one man, but the majority, that "steal the livery of heaven to serve the devil in." Hence the ape is a representative of mankind in general, and combines in his physiognomy and character all sorts of animals—some men resembling one species of monkey, and some another!

The disposition to take what does not belong to him is conspicuous in man's social relations, especially in the commercial department, and this also is strikingly exhibited in the monkey. In a community of apes it is the practice to look, every man, on the things of his neighbor, with an eye to their appropriation to his own use; and we can well imagine what sort of order and harmony must prevail in a community that is regulated by such a principle as this. Monkeys are actuated by the feeling that what another has is theirs; that "stolen waters are sweet;" that what is stolen is better than what is given to them—are always reaching their arms into their neighbors' provinces, grabbing at each other's food, pulling tails, kicking up a row, causing hubbub and confusion, abusing and insulting each other to the face, and "robbing Peter to pay Paul" in every possible way they can think of. This is all in the disposition to similate man; and if they will rob man of his distinctive attributes (for this is humanity perverted), of course they will rob each other.

The second liability to perversion which constitutes a resemblance to the monkey is that of the *domestic affections.* The ambition to *seem*, rather than to *be*, withdraws everything from within and expends it upon the surface in a deceptive appearance, which is worse than nothing at all.

> "How little do they know what *is*, who frame
> Their hasty judgment upon that which *seems!*"

The mere shell-of-an-individual is hollow-hearted. Like a balloon he exalts himself on account of his greatness, and proves rather how vapid is his intellect, and how little there is in him. Of sensibility and shame he has so small an amount, that they are hardly appreciable. To make room for pride and vanity, he deprives the domestic affections of their home, where alone they are capable of existing; he turns them out upon the surface, where they grow cold, die, and are petrified into an appearance of reality. It is worse than naught, for love without tenderness is inhuman. Its feeling, its consciousness, its susceptibility to pleasure and pain, which is internal, is lost in brutality, or mere instinctiveness, which is upon the outside.

The instinctiveness of a faculty exhibits itself in gesture. Parental love in a child is chiefly this, and expends itself on dolls. In parents it is developed interiorly, and relates to conscious infants that can laugh and cry. The first and lowest action is instinctive; the last and highest is a conscious one. In the monkey there is the same action of parental love that there is in a child. The creature handles its young one as if it were a rag-baby, and this appears like an imitation of a human mother, though it is far more like the actions of a little girl. Anything that can be made a baby of, like a marmozet, attracts the attention of an orang-outang instantly; and his actions when he sees it—his desire to have it, his manner of holding it, and every sign and movement that he makes under the excitement of this superficial impulse—is strikingly similar to that of a little girl under the excitement of the passion for dolls. The simplicity, gravity, earnestness, and eagerness, of this mockery of a mother's love, is exceedingly ludicrous, when we reflect that it is merely instinctive; that there is no emotion of tenderness in it, no feeling of responsibility, no exercise of consciousness, prompted by susceptibility to pleasure or pain, in the object of attention. In assuming the dress and manner of superiors, in taking what does not belong to them, in the affectation that accompanies parental love, and in parental love itself, mankind are "children of an older growth;" and in so far as they are children they are natural, and in so far as they are natural they resemble monkeys.

That monkeys act as men naturally do, is too plainly attested by the senses to admit of a contradiction. In superficial people, especially, parental love is upon the outside; their children are dolls, and they dress them accordingly, as if they were insensible to pain and invulnerable to disease. That comfort and health are not the first considerations is quite certain, and hence the conscious action of parental love is less than the instinctive. The latter is a blind idolatry, that defends its young with one hand, while with the other it presses it to death. Where mankind are most like monkeys, children are most like dolls — the objects of idle ceremony and parade, of passionate attention alternating with cruel neglect. At one time they are addressed as if they were fools, and of no account; at another they have powers imputed to them equal to those of Shakspere: and, in keeping with this idea, they are at times considered helpless, and at other times have tasks imposed upon them that are suited to giants.

This blind, instinctive action of parental love is the origin of idolatry. It is like the devotion of an ant to the egg that he is going to place in his temple. Idols are the dolls of foolish, wicked people, who retain the characters of children when they ought to be men. As dolls are exalted into objects of importance, so are these; though, as they are "children of an idle brain," they are at times treated with contempt by those who made them. They are the objects of a thousand childish conceits, of ridiculous ceremonies, of pantomimic show, of unmeaning jibber and nonsense. The places in which they are kept are such as children choose for baby-houses. The attention that is shown them passes for filial reverence, though, as they are objects of parental affection, the appearance of respect is mere mockery. Of a mother who shows this blindness of parental love, it is often said, "She worships that child," and the reverence of an idolator is this, and nothing more.

The first of the domestic affections in a proper and orderly state is the conjugal, but in

a state of perversion the first is the parental; and the character of the primary affection is the character of all the rest. But we forbear to speak further of the resemblance between mankind and the monkey. It may be observed, however, that the more angles there are in the countenance, and the greater angularity in the corners of the mouth and eyes, and in the dimples, the greater is the resemblance to the monkey, in both character and physiognomy. In those who resemble the mouse, there is the opposite, viz., roundness. The most perfect contour is a medium between the two, and this is the symmetrical.

CHAPTER XII.

FROM time immemorial human beings have exhibited a fondness for clothing themselves in scales and armor, and have chosen circumstances which would afford occasion for doing so. This is very appropriate in one who is like a fish in physiognomy, as in the individual before us, or in one who resembles a serpent. The strongest element in military ambition is the love of contest, the object of which is the palm of victory, or a prize; and this it is which governs the actions of a fish, and fills up the measure of existence in the life of a snake. In the pursuit of food there is a contest for the greatest mouthfuls, and for the greatest number of prizes; and hence the serpent lays in a month's provisions at a single swallow, and the fish rushes forward in the pursuit of food, eager to get it first, and dashes it down without stopping to enjoy his meals. It is always a race with others for the prize, which he who is the swiftest wins.

By the union of contest with the love of food, Appetite is rendered rapacious; and, never satisfied, it rushes onward for more. The laurel won in battle is lost by the ambition for another still. It is neither tasted nor enjoyed, and is therefore nothing gained. The love of contest is not limited by appetite: it wants the whole, so long as one atom of it is in danger of being seized by another. It gives the poor fish no rest—it urges him on continually, as it does those who are actuated by a like ambition, of whom it is said, "There is no peace to the wicked." The finny tribes not only race, but do battle with each other; they have swords and bayonets, as well as shields and bucklers, and engines-of-war for beating down barriers, as well as barriers for resisting assault. They belabor each other with their tails, as if they had boasted to "beat each other all hollow," and the trial had commenced.

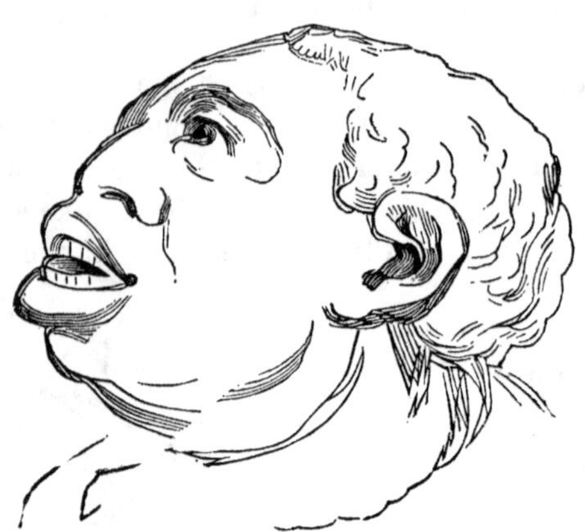

The African tribes whose contentions furnish victims for the slave-trade are of the variety of negroes that are like fishes rather than elephants. The negro fisheries along the coast of Africa depend on the same exigencies, the fishermen cruise about with the same uncertainties and hopes of success, are prompted by the same tastes and associations, are stimulated by the same desire of gain (only far more intensely), as the fisheries on the coast of Newfoundland and elsewhere. But there is a piratical bloodthirstiness in the one case which there is not in the other. Catching negroes is akin to fishing, and the caught are stowed away on board vessels like codfish and whale-oil; and were it not that they resemble fishes, and that there is a feeling of this, and a dim perception of it, the business would be perfectly infernal. There is always something to relieve men from the charge of being devils incarnate, and to place them in a position in which their reformation is not to be despaired of.

Allowing that the class of negroes we are speaking of resemble fishes, as we see by the foregoing figure and the one following, what could we expect from them in slavery, and in any other country than their own, but that they should act like "fishes out of water"? They are not in their element, but the talents natural to them are put forth in a new direction. The last time we had the pleasure of hearing a negro play the banjo, we were delighted to see how strikingly the music corresponded to the twitches and vibrations of a fish that is trying to live on air, and to make it a substitute for water. Whoever will pay attention to it, will be equally struck with the similarity. Then, again, the dancing that accompanies the banjo, and in which fifty negroes may be engaged, is like the flopping of so many fishes up and down, and from side to side, on their fins and tails. You might fancy that you had fallen down into some charmed region beneath the ocean, into a company of mermaids.

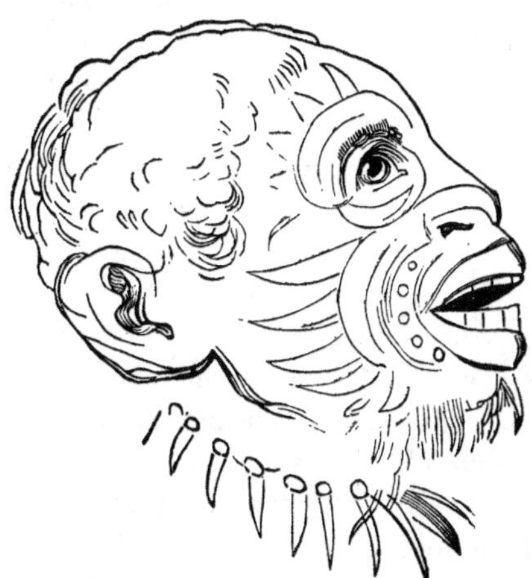

We have heard it said that the West India negroes are extravagantly fond of fish, all the more if it has swum in brine since it was alive. Negroes of the kind that may be compared to weeds on a plantation are excessively prolific, as they should be to resemble fishes. In slavery the[illegible] no field for the exercise of the love of contest, which in a state of cultivation would make them pant to excel and to outstrip others in the pursuit of noble objects. The ambition which is the principal ingredient in their natures is turned into a strife for superiority in laziness, in eating and drinking, in lying and stealing, and in various kinds of profligacy. But they are in the first stages of training. There are many degrees between the lowest action of the love of contest and the highest; let them be elevated to the latter, and they will aspire to "glory, honor, and immortality," as individuals of them have done already. There are no people who are naturally more ambitious than they. In dancing, music, and religious exercises, so far as *exertion* is concerned, they excel all others; and exertion, other things being equal, is the measure of ambition.

Of the class of negroes who resemble fishes, some are similar to whales, and these are akin to those who resemble elephants. Both are fond of *spouting*, as are the animals themselves, and this opens a channel for their ambition to flow in. It is in proportion to their feeling of greatness; and it may be the same feeling in the elephant and the whale that causes them to engage in the corresponding exercise. The negro distinguishes himself for his *laugh* as well as for his speechifying, and the stress which he lays upon the former shows that he attaches importance to it. There is very great character in the sudden explosion of sounds called "laughter," for it proceeds from the bottom of the heart, and shows the depths of a man's soundings (which are in some cases exceedingly shallow), together with the quality of the ground—whether it be rock, sand, clay, or gravel. The negro's "Y-e-w-a-h!—yah! yah! yah!" is wonderfully like the sound which we have often heard in a menagerie, proceeding from the elephant—especially the first, "Y-e-w-a-h!"—of which "yah! yah! yah!" is the echo. It seems as if the negro struck upon the resemblance in his nature to the elephant, and sent it forth in a sound expressive of his consciousness of it; and then, to show his pleasure, and at the same time a little of shame at the foolishness of what he has discovered, laughed at the sound, or *echoed* it—for echo is laughter.

This is our opinion of echo, and of the philosophy of laughing. and we think that others will be inclined to agree with us. The reason why animals do not laugh is, that there is no echo in them; they have nothing but themselves — they are the original sound, and the echo is in man. Laughter is a reflection of nature; it shows man to be an artist. Echo is in exact proportion to the perfection of art. A landscape or a temple, to be beautiful, must be full of echoes; this will prove that it is in harmony with nature, or that it is a reflection of beauty of which nature is the original. Artists resemble horses, and the horse utters a sound that is exceedingly like laughter: this is so faithfully imitated by a large number of people, that the "horse-laugh" has become proverbial.

A volume might be written on the varieties of laughter, showing that those who laugh like horses resemble horses; that those whose laughter is an echo of the voice of the lion resemble lions; that those whose laughter the parrot is fond of imitating, resemble parrots; that those who echo the voice of the crow resemble crows; and so on.

CHAPTER XIII.

MAN is reared upon the animal, as a temple is reared upon its base. The mineral kingdom is the substratum of the vegetable, the vegetable of the animal, and the animal of man. The human temple, as a whole, is based upon the entire animal kingdom; and one stone of that temple is raised upon the back of a turtle, another on an eagle, another on a horse, another on a lion, and so on to the end of the catalogue. The basis and the superstructure, of course, resemble each other; but the former is created for the latter, the lower for the higher, the animal for the human: and hence it should be said that animals resemble men, and not the reverse, except by implication. In a city where no two houses were of the same appearance and dimensions, each foundation would correspond to its own house better than to any other; and as persons differ from each other, it is evident that one animal will resemble one, and another another.

————" There are
More things in heaven and earth, Horatio,
Than are dreamed of in your philosophy."

There is a science of poetry as well as of physics. All general truths are made up of particulars; and no one will deny that the kingdoms of Nature rise one above another, and that each kingdom is composed of parts, and that the parts above must have an orderly relation to those beneath. For each vegetable there is a mineral, for each animal there is a vegetable, and for each man there is an animal; and the vegetable that is the animal's, and the mineral that is the vegetable's, are man's also. Why not, if the second kingdom of Nature rests upon the first, the third upon the second, and if man is supported by them all?

This relation does not imply that a particular man subsists upon a particular animal; for the truth is, each man is a representative of his race, and comprehends in himself all sorts of animals, so that he somewhat resembles them all. He is an individual, and not to be confounded with things in general. It is true that he "eats everything," selecting at will from the three kingdoms of Nature, and balancing himself into a likeness of all things; but his resemblance to some one particular specimen of natural history is still retained. If his foundation be a lion, self-love will cause him to love and admire that animal, and he will cherish in himself the attributes that he admires and loves. But the superstructure which he rears may be so beautiful, so perfect, that the basis will not be observed. He may, indeed, love the foundation so greatly as to care for nothing higher; but when he has reared a beautiful temple upon it, which is himself, he values it all the more for the sake of the use. His first affection is self-love, and looks to nothing beyond the animal; his second is benevolence, and looks to humanity, and to elevating himself into a representative of his race, and this is his true and noble self, in the love of which the love of the neighbor is included. It is a beautiful conception which places a hero upon the back of a lion, another of a different character upon a leopard, another upon a horse; but what would we think of the artist who should place his hero upon a cow, a hog, or a deer? The impropriety of such a thing arises from the fact that man is reared upon the animal kingdom *once*, and not twice; upon the horse in one way, and upon the cow in another.

The animals which men in general have the greatest resemblance to are those that they are most inclined to rear themselves upon, by either eating their flesh or riding upon their backs. Thus the resemblance is increased. This is desirable, for in this world at least man must have a foundation to stand upon. He derives a stamina from the animal kingdom which the vegetable does not afford, and from the vegetable a substance which is supplied in a very scanty degree by the mineral. But for a foundation to his feet the mineral kingdom is the best. Man has a feeling that, whatever animal it is proper for him to bestride, it is not proper for him to eat, and *vice versa.* Hence the ass, the horse, the elephant, the camel, and the llama, are not associated in the mind with the ideas of slaughter, nor with the desire for flesh : and Nature, to suit this law, has made the flesh of the animals that are most suitable for burden distasteful. But the ox, the deer, the sheep, the goat, suggest the propriety of sacrificing their lives for our own; and in proportion as they do so, the idea of sitting upon them, or of using them as beasts of burden, strikes us as absurd.

CHAPTER XIV.

PEOPLE who feel and think alike, and love the same things, are drawn together by their sympathies and by their attraction to the same objects. Associating with each other, their points of difference are reconciled, and they learn to agree more and more. This principle is applicable to the associations between men and animals, which are in many cases exceedingly intimate, and also to the intercourse of animals with each other. "Birds of a feather flock together;" and the bringing together of animals that are antagonistic may harmonize them in such a degree, that the cage in which they are confined may be compared to "Noah's ark."

We will take a special instance for the illustration of our principle. It must have been an agreement in the first place between the Laplander and the reindeer that brought them together. The former must have seen the adaptation of the latter to his own necessities and pursuits; and the latter, when brought into the service of his superior, acknowledged, by his submission and acceptance of favors in return, that no violence was done to his nature, but that there was afforded a wider field for the exercise of his predominant faculties. The Laplander, on the other hand, seeing what the reindeer could do, expanded his thoughts, inspired the spirit of the animal, and adapted himself to the instincts and habits which were to be called into his own service, and which required to be ministered to in order that they might be a benefit to himself; and it is very likely that powers that would have remained dormant in the deer, for want of exercise, were awakened by the duties imposed upon him.

This is the relation in which the Laplander and reindeer stand to each other at present, for they are as primitive as

ever, and the deer is ready at any time to go wild, and his master is in a state of exertion to reclaim him. And that they have a strong resemblance to each other is certain. Whatever produces similarity in character, produces similarity in countenance, in body, manners, and appearance. The reindeer is like the Laplander as a whole; and in the manner of standing, and in the features of the face, there is a striking similarity. The causes of this similarity are numerous and powerful. The reindeer is the animal that belongs to the Laplander especially; and the country to which the former is adapted the latter will inhabit, though he be threatened never so hard with being "imprisoned in chilling regions of thick-ribbed ice."—"That dreary region," says a writer, "owes to this animal whatever it possesses of civilization, and whatever comforts tend to make it supportable to the inhabitants." The Laplander's foundation-stone, the lap of earth on which he is reared, is the reindeer; and add to the causes mentioned above, the fact that he is principally reared upon the flesh and milk of this animal, and converts every part of the carcass into something of his own, and it is no wonder that the resemblance between them is so great.

It was remarked in the former chapter that for every animal there is a plant. Sometimes the animal lives upon its plant and sometimes it does not, but there is a resemblance between the one and the other, as there is between man and animals. The plant proper to the reindeer is his food, the reindeer-moss, and this he resembles, particularly in the horns, which are the more vegetable portion of his organization. Whoever admires deer's-horns admires trees, and branching shrubs, and flowers, of which lichens appear to be the types and originals. This portrait of an eminent painter of flowers

resembles a deer, and looks as if flowers and snow-flakes should be showered about his head in honor of his talent, as well as for the gratification of his taste.

The person on the following page is one who has more of the literal deer in him than is becoming, or rather he has too little of the higher attributes that are proper to man. His resemblance to the deer is more striking from the deficiency of that which conceals the animal by converting it into the higher use which it is intended to subserve. We should ascribe to him insensibility, wildness, impetuosity, love of liberty, determination to have his own way, a measuring of obstacles at a single glance, but never removing them, an aversion to others on account of scruples of conscience, which he is pleased to call *trifles*, and finally a disposition to elope with some fair one who may be taken with his dashing ap pearance.

To resemble an animal that has horns upon his head for ornament rather than for use, is to be subject more than others to depression of spirits — to "the blues" — to feelings like those which follow intoxication — and to that complication of nervous sensations called "the horrors." Ornaments prove the heaviest burdens, but where Nature grants them she gives also the strength to support them. Persons who resemble deers have their "ups and downs;" and whatever it is in the mind that corresponds to the horns on the head of a deer, is like two trees, barren in winter, but covered with foliage and flowers in summer. In the mind, summer should be perpetual: the trees and shrubs should be evergreens, like moss, and the flowers perennial; snowflakes in one season, and blossoms in another. Thus the person who resembles the deer may be happy always. In his "up and down" he should be elastic and bounding. Cowper's is a head that resembles a

deer very strongly. That spontaneous effusion, "John Gilpin," is the deer that, in his feeling of abandonment, he rested back upon — the deer that ran away with him.

"Away went hat and wig" —

and away went the heavy deers'-horns — the barren, leafless, winter trees—from the mind, and juvenile ones budded and blossomed in their places.

It may be said of those who resemble deers, that they are inclined to

"Look from Nature up to Nature's God."

They reason from effects to causes, and it would be a perversion of their natures to reason otherwise. They are delighted with those things that are full of spirit and animation, in which the life and soul, the desire and thought, and the Power superior to either, are easily discerned in the effect. Hence they are fond of birds and flowers, and everything beautiful, which are so full of the spiritual, that the grossness is scarcely perceptible. For the same reason these people are shocked at deformity, which, as it is the absence of the spiritual, is the characteristic of grossness. Beauty, they perceive, is the cause, and not the effect: it moulds its opposite (the effect) into a likeness of itself, and changes grossness and deformity into refinement and beauty. Their course is forward and upward, from the lower to the higher, "leaving the things that are behind and pressing forward to the things that are before." They set their eyes on beauty, and, progressing toward perfection, they come nearer and nearer to it, and nearer to the Final Cause to which they tend.

CHAPTER XV.

"WHAT distance have you made?" is equivalent to "What progress?" Length is synonymous with advancement—as when we say that a goose's head is six inches in advance of his body. In the neck of the goose there is something absurd, for the simple reason that there is advancement without progression. The organs of locomotion are unequal to the headway indicated in the neck. The man who resembles a heron

comprehends distance; if it were not so, he could not make a successful *coup d'etat* upon the frog—a creature that in measuring distances demonstrates perfectly that measurement, while it is synonymous with distance, is synonymous also with progression. A "strip" of something, a "stripling," and "outstripping" a deer, are ideas naturally connected. When a person goes very swiftly, he is said to go "like a streak," and a streak is nothing but a straight line. In the form of the heron the faculty of distance is indicated by chains and links. You might fancy that you could take him to measure a piece of ground with, by both links and paces. His length is the physiognomical sign of progression. There is the same connection between travelling and distance that there is between a faculty of the mind and the feature which indicates it. The face is synonymous with the person himself, and it is as ridiculous to deny the truth of Physiognomy as it is to separate distance from travelling.

It is true that, if we suppose a man's face always to be animated, we shall be in danger of ascribing to him what he does not possess. There are certain persons, as well as certain beasts and birds, that are the embodiments of absurdity and contradiction. They oppose the plainest physiognomical truths, and deny the principle that the face is an index of the mind. But we must understand that they are contradictions; we must take them for what they are. Who is so wanting in a sense of the ludicrous as not to see that the goose, in respect to the neck, and in respect to the organ of intelligence, which is supposed to have rule over the body, and to control the motion of the feet, is decidedly droll, queer, singular—so much so, that people are inclined to laugh at the absurdity of the thing? We must not look for confirmations of Physiognomy in such an animal until we have observed that the body, legs, and feet, belie the swiftness that is indicated in the neck. He is a bundle of contradictions, and this makes it necessary that we should put him into our intellectual crucible, and subject him to analysis and combination, and the test of reason, until we have compelled him to speak the truth.

A neck of unusual length is ridiculous, for the simple reason that it makes no progress unless the body does. It must be confessed, therefore, that in a bird that is all length, and at the same time destitute of animation, there is something intrinsically absurd and supremely ridiculous. Supposing him to be *dead*, even, we can hardly resist saying, "Get *a-long* with you!" It is only a less degree of ridiculousness which we discover in him supposing him to be standing stock still, indulging in laziness, or walking very slowly. Long legs that do not travel are of a piece with the goose's neck, which looks as if it were formed to leave the body an incalculable distance behind it. As the person who resembles the stork is sensitive to ridicule, and would avoid it, it be omes him to engage in high and noble pursuits. The heron in the sky stretches himself to the utmost. He is like a wisp of something whirled

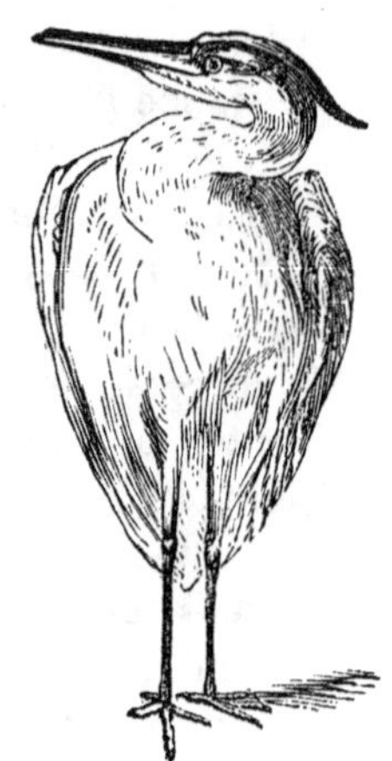

up from the ocean, and projected through the air like an arrow. He appears to outstrip the hurricane, and is an object of sublimity; but inertia makes him more ridiculous than the goose. In his proper character he is bold, daring, heroic, sublime, delighting in the terrific, sporting with the elements in their wildest mirth. Letting himself down from his true dignity, and becoming aristocratic, lazy, luxurious, intemperate, he is a perfect coward, and in this and every other respect perfectly ridiculous.

The heron has an instinct of what is proper to him, and an instinct of the absurd. Hence his long neck, which indicates progression, and has no locomotion of its own, he doubles up and winds around like an ear-trumpet, which he is ashamed of having exhibited; but when he flies, he holds it out like a spear which he is going to thrust into the heart of the wind. He flies through the midst of heaven, his long legs extended behind him; and there is nothing ridiculous in this—for he is a swift messenger, like those divinely commissioned to convey tidings, and to minister rebuke and happiness to man.

The ministration of those who resemble the heron, and are not perverted, is akin to the service of those who bear a noble resemblance to the deer. The one has an analogy to the magnetic telegraph, and the other to the railroad. The one is from causes to effects, and is hence a ministration of spiritual and heavenly things; the other is from effects to causes, and is hence a ministration of earthly and corporeal things, such as are essential to the body. If the former be subservient to the latter, it substitutes cordials, teas, and narcotics, for spiritual healing and comfort; it perverts appetite and taste, and is the cause of the intemperance in eating and drinking spoken of in the chapter concerning the stork. This is characteristic of those who resemble the heron literally. But if they (like Howard the philanthropist, whose portrait is annexed) minister to others instead of themselves, they relieve the distresses of the mind, remove the causes of its sickness, dissipate falsehood, and nourish the soul with truth; and so far as is necessary they minister to the body also. They can not do the one without doing the other. As body and soul are united and correspond, it is absurd to divide the office of physician into two.

We have observed that those who resemble the heron have a sense of what is proper to them, and consequently a sense of the improper or absurd. Short, duck-legged people, too, have a sense of the ludicrous when they are as Nature designed them to be. The wild goose and duck double up their necks while standing, and thrust them out when they are anxious to go ahead. The people who resemble them are fond of ridiculing those who resemble the heron, and then they forget that they are themselves ridiculous, and most so when they hiss at those who are above them, with the idea of "hissing them *down*." They "run out their necks" at people, but their short legs have never the office of running ascribed to them. It is as absurd for short things to travel, as for long ones to stand still. This renders the goose and the duck doubly ridiculous. It is the short and long together that makes a person awkward and ungainly; and the well-proportioned and graceful, like the heron and the stork, if they are employed in useful undertakings, can well afford to be laughed at, seeing they have nothing to do but to attend to their own proper business, and allow jokes and laughter to fall back upon the heads of geese and ganders!

CHAPTER XVI.

As between the camel and the Arab there is a likeness in habits and pursuits, in tastes and dispositions, so also there is in physognomy. They live in the desert because they are adapted to it, and they are adapted to it because they live there. Adaptation or accommodation is one of the essentials of hospitality. The camel accommodates himself to all sorts of inconveniences for the convenience of others, and the power of adaptation in the Arab is equally wonderful. His highest expectation is to render his own condition tolerable; and as this is the consequence and means of promoting the comfort of others, the Arab is an example of genuine hospitality. The conveniences of the camel depend entirely on accommodating himself to *in*conveniences. Look at his feet and legs: what accommodating members! Was there ever such a commodious hump, or such an accommodating stomach? Yet is his temperament choleric, or hot and dry, like the burning desert he inhabits, and to which he is so wonderfully adapted. The temperament of the Arab is the same. The kneeling of the camel, to receive his burden and to set it down again, is, figuratively speaking, for the sake of an oasis in the desert, and the hospitality of the Arab is for the sake of another and more beautiful one.

The camel and the Arab carry their heads erect and high. Their sight and hearing are wonderfully acute. Their faces are thin, and their bodies are always lean. Their eyes are sunken, and the brows projecting. They have high cheekbones, Roman noses, straight hair, and countenances of uncommon gravity. But there are shades of expression and feature that constitute the more particular resemblance between them, as is evident on comparing their likenesses.

Looking at the face of a camel, one would suppose that the person who resembled him would never smile; and the Arab, instead of smiling when he greets a friend, looks grave and solemn. There

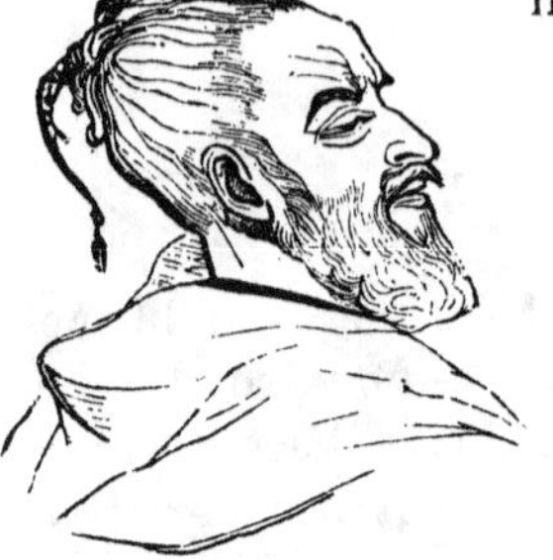

is something in the attitude and appearance of the camel that reminds us of the Arab salutation—placing the right hand on the breast and then on the forehead, and saying, "Peace be with you!" As the camel's foot is formed to press the sand, we should suppose that those who resembled him might find it more natural to press each other's palms (the right of one being adapted to the left of the other), than to clasp and shake hands in the ordinary way; and it is true that the Arabs do so. In the manner of the camel's eating, and chewing the cud, there is something exceedingly slovenly and disagreeable, and the Arab's cooking and eating are of the same character. The mutton which he serves up is sure to have a plenty of wool in it; and his butter, being churned in goat-skin bags, the hair of which is inside, contains a profusion of hairs. These extraneous substances the Arab does not object to, for if a person resembles the camel, and finds his subsistence in the desert, it will not do for him to be particular. Whatever provision is offered to him, the Desert says, "This or none!" He eats but two meals a day, though much at a time, and, like the camel, is capable of going several days without food or drink. He is dexterous though rather ungraceful in his movements, and trains his children to hardships as he does his camels.

It is adaptation to the worst of situations, or to Nature in her most hideous forms, that renders the camel ugly and uncomfortable. Who has not observed the ugliness in his disposition as well as in his looks? and in what animal is there such an air of discomfort as in him? Yet, as a compensation for this, there is in this ugliness something good; in human beings there is kindness and an obliging turn, willingness, self-denial, and whatever is included in that noble virtue, *hospitality*. Homely people have a home for all, and none for themselves; but it is well to remember that this goodness holds in check a vast amount of ugliness, which may at some time gain the advantage. Socrates acknowledged this fact with regard to himself, and the magnanimity of the confession was a part of that self-denial and accommodation to hardship which was a cause of his ugliness. The man to whom Nature is a harsh and capricious mother, grows up ugly and deformed; but if he have learned to love her, it is a sign that she has instilled good into him, and he resembles her more and more. There is grandeur and sublimity in the rugged virtues that he is compelled to practise, but vastly more in the rugged morality that is based on those, and that is as free and independent as those are compulsory. But the man to whom Nature is provident and tender, grows up handsome, and the more he sympathizes with charming objects the more beautiful he becomes

Yet beauty without sublimity has "a worm i' the bud;" it is fading and ephemeral; it relapses into effeminacy, and degenerates finally into ugliness, like that of swamps, in which the animals are not homely, but monstrous. The Arab who inhabits the delta of the Nile is the very opposite of hospitable, for he requires a certain amount of accommodation, and he imposes it upon Nature, since Nature does not impose it upon him.

The ugliness of the camel and the Arab in the deserts has a tendency to be of the very noblest kind. It contains the element of self-denial, or of virtue, as before observed, and this encloses an image of the most exquisite beauty—an object of reverence, of devotion, of self-sacrifice. Homely hospitality entertains a heavenly visitant, an embodied perfection, in every stranger, regarding him with the same deference, and administering to his comfort and happiness, as if it would make up for the heavenly felicities which he is supposed to have been accustomed to. Thus the homeliest people have the most intense admiration and devotion to the beautiful, as was the case with Socrates; and the beautiful in return have grateful love and exalted reverence for the homely. Thus, too, the homeliest animal and the most beautiful (the camel and the horse), the most perfect specimens in their way, live together in Arabia. The horse is the embodiment of the choleric temperament (which makes him high-spirited and noble), without the habit of accommodation to deform him. The camel and the Arab are accommodated *to him*, and the desert air is the most congenial to his temperament: hence in Arabia are produced the finest horses in the world. The barb is the Arab's guest, his especial favorite, and a better entertainment than is afforded by his honest keeper he could

not have. People who resemble horses find homely persons to be their most indulgent, faithful, enthusiastic, and devoted friends.

The countenance of a stranger is to the Arab what an oasis is to the desert. That countenance will smile if hospitality can make it, but the Arab's never, till the desert shall bud and blossom as the rose. The green spot owes the perfection of its beauty to the desolation that surrounds it, but from this the desert is to be clothed; and in like manner the beautiful have a mission to the ugly, and there is given to the latter the disposition to entertain them, and to emulate their graces by preserving and heightening their charms. The stranger is indebted to the Arab, not for hospitality merely, but for the blessings that are intended for all, and of which he is made the dispenser. This the Arab feels, and by feeling knows. When the Bedouins have committed a robbery, they say of the plunder, that they "have gained it;" and when reproved for the depredation, they reply that they "are Arabs." They do not take the life of the stranger when they rob him, but claim relationship, saying, "Undress thyself—thine aunt is without a garment." This is what the Desert would say to the Oasis, if it had a tongue, and it is the language of the ugly to the beautiful.

The plundering disposition of the Arab is compatible with the excess of their hospitality. When they have pitched their tents, the individual is fortunate who first discovers a stranger approaching the encampment, for he is allowed to claim him as his guest; and to tell an Arab that he does not treat his guests well, is deemed one of the greatest of insults.

If the Arab resembles the desert, he resembles the camel still more. He enters into the feelings of his companion, and enlivens him with a chant, that is said to make him travel more easily. There is something in the appearance of a camel that reminds one of an old astrologer: he looks as if he were eying the stars. The Arabs consult the stars on all occasions of importance, particularly in reference to their undertakings, and hold astrology in high honor. The camel looks as if he were born to do penance, and as if the sum of the penalties which he had to endure was to press the burning sands with his naked feet, which are thereby rendered insensible to the infliction. The penalty which the Arab suffers is that of blows upon the soles of his feet; he is bastinadoed to expiate his crimes. A traveller says of a case which he witnessed in Cairo, that the Arab, after receiving the punishment by the order of the governor, was unable to stand, and groaning with pain was borne out by his friends; and that "the governor, in the meantime, stood as though hardened to such transactions, munching his jaws like a sheep chewing the cud." We imagine that it was like a sheep, only excessively so—that is, like a camel.

CHAPTER XVII.

We have been thinking of the cowardice of a certain variety of the carnivorous appetite—that which waits till assured of the death of an animal, by the putridity of its carcass. Say, if you will, that the crow, the raven, the vulture, and the turkey-buzzard, live on carrion because they prefer it to fresh meat—still we maintain that the appetite for substances in a state of decomposition is promoted by cowardice; and it is equally true, we believe, that cowardice is increased by these substances. The proof of this is in the fact that all animals that live on carrion are cowardly, and that all cowardly animals have something to do with carrion. This statement will, of course, need considerable explanation. There is no coward who is not cruel. The benevolent individual, who would not harm a fly, does not prove himself a coward by refusing to accept a challenge; but the *ruffianly* fellow, who pleads that it is against his principles to fight, does not inspire us with such full confidence in his bravery. You can never say of the person who "would not hurt a hair of your head," that he is a coward. The harmless, inoffensive, vegetable-eating animals, are not cowards, for the simple reason that they are not cruel; but the carnivorous *are* so, in the degree that they *ought to be courageous and are not.* A timid hare will scare away a class of birds that have a scurrilous resemblance to hawks and owls; but as soon as he is poor, or sick, or lame, he will have the crows after him, with the whole posse of cowardly gluttons that spend their lives "waiting for dead men's shoes."

The caravans in the desert, it is said, are followed by vultures—signs in the heavens of the cruelty of human beings to the animals that serve them! The vulture resembles the camel, as may be seen by a comparison of their forms; and the Arab who is not merciful to his beast resembles the former more than the latter. He wishes his overburdened camel to fly like the wind (as certain persons do their horses when they drive them), and the consequence is, the poor animal is soon an object of expectation to the greedy vultures. The cowardly wretch who treats his horse or his camel thus can not bear to be looked at by the animal he abuses; the eye that he deprives of brightness he can

not meet; he never saw any beauty in it, that he should admire it; and when it appeals imploringly to heaven, with an eloquence that touches the hearts of the tender, and makes them almost curse the cruel master, he walks by it at a distance, or hastily pulls the blind over it, lest he should discover a feeling of pity and remorse in the heart of even so base a wretch as himself.

From a similar prompting, the dastardly vultures, when the eyes of the camel are turned upward (as they always are, to see what they are about), shrink away into the depths of air. They can not endure to be looked at by the innocent ones to whom they meditate injury. Like the ruffian, the vulture seeks to extinguish himself: he shrinks into nothingness, and is neither seen nor heard of till those eyes that he dreads have lost their fire—when suddenly he descends and plucks them out, and riots upon the carcass.

Constant apprehension of the motives of others—how cowardly! evil surmises against characters—how cruel! This is the action of Suspicion, and is nourished by *fermented food and drink.* The very *minds* of persons who have these tastes and dispositions are in a constant ferment. If they were not afraid of people, they would not whisper suspicions about them, and would not tear out the eyes of the dead. It is not one of these who can say—

——"I've not a vulture's bill,
To pick at all the faults I see,
And make them wider still!"

The person who confides in others trusts in God, and is not afraid. He can not be cruel to those he confides in, nor suspicious of those he loves; and that he chooses to trust mankind, is proof that he loves them.

All animals, be it observed, that are fond of carrion, are remarkable for suspicion: they are apprehensive of danger constantly. When a creature *is dead*, the crows pounce upon him; they tear him to pieces with savage ferocity, exulting in the triumph over an animal greater than themselves, as if the "King of Terrors" had nothing to do with it! But they are cowards: engrossed as they are in their riotous feast, you can not get within gun-shot of them; and there is not one of them that has courage enough to defend himself against the kingfisher, or the other small birds that give him chase. He is put to flight by a scarecrow: what could be more contemptibly cowardly than that?

People who ascribe wrath to the Almighty, and endeavor to escape it by denouncing it against others, are both cowardly and cruel. They are in constant terror of others, for they judge others by themselves; and as they suffer from fear, they try to make others *afraid of them.* It is well that they should be governed by an appearance of anger, in storms and tempests, in famines and earthquakes, in diseases and deaths, for they can be governed in this way and in no other. They make a virtue of their dread, confounding it with reverence, and offering it as a claim to favor. They revenge on man their fear of the Deity, in tortures innumerable, and of every conceivable variety. They wish to be feared, to be worshipped with awe and trembling. They claim the blood of a thousand victims to gratify their cruelty, and to increase the terror of the multitude, which is to them the most acceptable worship. They wish to impress upon others that they have power supreme, and that life and death are at their disposal.

We have said that there is a connection between the appetite for fermented food and drinks and the faculty of suspicion. The latter is excited to an intense and morbid degree by drunkenness; for all spirituous liquors are the result of fermentation. The appetite for intoxicating drink is provoked by cowardly apprehension. Some people take it before mounting the rostrum, to give them courage—not because they are modest, but because they are cowardly. Some take it to strengthen "faint heart," which "never won fair lady," and to grow mad, that they may be admired for their bravery. Some take it to make them soldiers, when it is safer to go forward than to run. Some take it to enable them to go through with their labors—not because they are industrious, but because they are lazy, and *Necessity* tells them that it "must be done." Some take it to drive away "the blues," to drown care, and to stupify sensibility, because they have not the courage to face adversity, and do not dare to suffer. But never does this yielding to fear give preponderance to courage: it excites madness, which is another name for cruelty, and the mere mockery of the courage that is wanting; and always does the appetite for fermented things increase the power of that very passion of which it is the slave.

The inebriate lives in the very atmosphere that engenders suspicion—the putridity of his own breath—in which the blow-fly, the crow, and the hog, with all their cowardly apprehensions, might be deluded into the idea of safety, as in the presence of something dead. In such a charnel-house, how could it be otherwise than that he should have "the horrors"? Suspicion, Cowardice, and the appetite for fermented food and drink, excite each other more and more. The consummation is a tragic scene, in which each plays a conspicuous part, with Cruelty at their head: the title of the tragedy is, "*Delirium Tremens.*"

All madness is cowardice and cruelty combined, as exhibited in the insane, and in the history of the drunkard from beginning to end. Who does not know of the cruelties inflicted upon wives and children, and the destruction of every tender and merciful feeling in the human heart, by an indulgence of the appetite of which we are speaking?

There is something natural in the fondness of the analytical Frenchman for substances in a state of decomposition. As he is always in the process of fermentation and ebullition, it is appropriate that he should make external matters and things correspond, and that he should have an appetite for tainted meat, and a taste for wine: and if we have a correct version of his history, he has proved himself suspicious, cowardly, and cruel. We see a strong resemblance to the vulture in the preceding portrait,

Marat, who, on suspicion only, and because he was excessively cowardly and cruel, caused multitudes of his countrymen to be arrested, imprisoned, and guillotined. His ambition was to become a terror, and to inspire cowards with awe—the only reverence

they are capable of—and to be thought powerful and brave in proportion as he was faint-hearted and cowardly. The countenance of Robespierre is that of a scavenger, full of apprehension, meanness, and cruelty; it resembles that of the young gentleman accompanied by the vulture, at the beginning of this chapter. The dog that loves carrion, and smells of it, is always wanting in pluck; and, to make up for the deficiency, he lives on garbage, and seizes the things that he will be thanked for devouring. A resemblance to such an animal, as well as to the vulture, is seen in Robespierre; and a resemblance to this or any other of the variety of scavengers, fits a man to be a rag-picker, rather than a president or a king.

There is such impudence in human nature, or rather in the want of it, that people of the character we have been describing pride themselves upon their suspicion, as if this were the evidence of superior penetration and wisdom. The want of confidence in others which arises from fear, is self-confidence, and this is pride. It is cowardly to have no faith in the future and in things unseen, and to shrink back into the past as the only reality, and thus to remain infants. It was the "reign of *terror*" when France was a nation of infidels; but what they are now, and what governs them, we do not say, except that they are as fond of baubles as children are:—

> "Fantastic, frolicsome, and wild,
> With all the trinkets of a child."

It is as cruel as it is cowardly to doubt a future existence, to rely only upon the past, and to believe only in reason and the evidence of the senses; for it seeks to destroy—it aims at annihilation. The French are like the frog in the well, that jumped three feet forward every day, and fell back two every night; for when they have been stimulated to take a step forward, they wish instantly to return to the past. The reason is this: the stimulus that urges them forward is that which excites cruelty and madness—the remedy which is sought by Fear to soothe its sufferings, and by Skepticism to exalt its pride.

CHAPTER XVIII.

There are vulgar people who are fond of tracing in the human face a likeness to the "calf," as we should infer from their frequent application of this epithet to juveniles of their own species. We would inquire of them if this individual looks as if he had been reared on milk, and were now going in search of some? If this be so, it is proper that the *heir* should be after him, though following like an humble petitioner who despairs of establishing his lawful claim. The preceding is a handsome young man, and evidently English; and the English, without distinction of age or sex, are known by the general appellation of "John Bull." But in this young gentleman, whose chin indicates a greater degree of precocity than his mouth and eyes, no person who has sat at the domestic board, where "calves' brains" are served up, can fail to be interested. There is delicacy in the expression of his face, along with an obtrusive bluntness. The degree of obtuseness in the features indicates just that degree of obtuseness in the intellect that entitles the possessor to the allegorical title that is applied to him. He owes nothing to instinct, and knows nothing at all until experience has taught him. He is like a calf in the *blindness* of the little instinct that Nature has given him; or in being subjected to the spontaneous action of his feelings and desires in a manner that causes him to act ridiculously. He is loud in his demands: when he wants anything, he shows that he can not be denied; and as to denying himself, that is entirely out of the question. He can not even wait; he will knock his brains out if what he calls for does

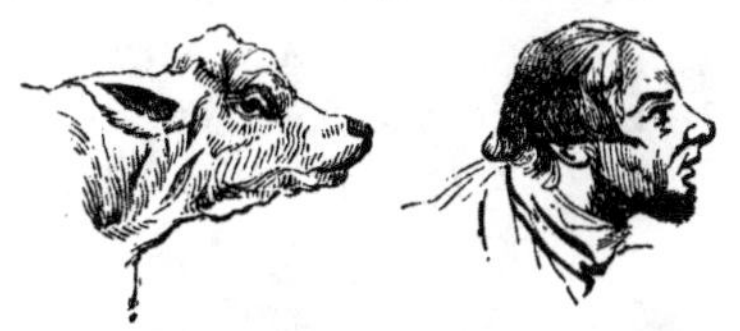

not come speedily. The reason is, he is deficient in instinct and in the faculty of self-control; and his large submission yields to the sway of his intense desires, instead of yielding to the government of others. His wants are of the nature of necessities, and therefore it is that they govern him, and govern his parents also. He is called self-willed, when the truth is his passions rule him, and he is perfectly submissive. But there is a sterner necessity than desire, and to this he must come at last. It is *punishment!*—oh, horrible!—yes, punishment wlll make him submissive to the yoke. Better late than never. Reader, if you doubt of this being an exact description of young Englishmen, observe for yourself, and you will be satisfied that we are right.

Let us now take a glance at the parents—the John Bulls. Here is the face of an Englishwoman, and it is seen how

much she resembles the cow; annexed is a portrait of Hume, and we see how much he resembles the male animal. Who can not discover by this countenance that the mind ruminates? You can almost see the regurgitation, and the process of preparing the food for more thorough digestion. Whoever sits down to the perusal of his pages will rise up edified and prepared to labor. To the traits first mentioned, which exist in the mature Englishman as well as in the youngster, may be added these: large economy (you see it in the double chin, and it is large in historians); great strength (you see it in the obtuseness of the features, and of all the members of the body); and large love of enjoyment (you see it in the lateral projection of the outer corner of the ridge of the eyebrow). The English are remarkably economical in domestic affairs; they are content with small profits, for they husband everything; and in political economy, circumstances considered, they are superior to all others. They can show larger double chins, more resemblance to the cow and the ox, better husbandry, and more economy in every respect, than any other nation. They are also strong and powerful, like the ox. This is indicated by a certain obtuseness of features that is a medium between grossness and effeminacy. They are the very opposite in this respect of those who resemble the horse. Refinement takes away from that unity which is the foundation of strength. All the refinement which the Englishman can receive will not make him effeminate. Such is not the case with the Italians, who, as will be shown in the next chapter, resemble horses; they have never yet recovered from the effeminacy which was induced by the civilization and refinement of their ancestors. The vigor and grasp of intellect which characterize the English are like the strength of the ox when he exercises it in draught, or in pushing with the horn.

But though the obtuseness in the features of the English, and the refinement in those of the Italians, indicate opposition in character, this opposition is like that which prevails in music—it is the opposition necessary to harmony: and there is, in reality, a remarkable affinity between the English and the

Italians. There is also an intimate relation between the horse and the cow: the latter steals from the former, and values and saves what the former throws away. The interests of the one harmonize with the interests of the other, but they do not therefore like each other over and above well, and it would be a perfect absurdity to harness them together!

The love of enjoyment is another thing in which the English prove their right to the appellation of John Bull. It is this which gives them the air of quietude so like the cow. They are indebted to this for the principal share of the gentleness and gentility that they are possessed of. It is this which is so pleasing in the Englishwomen, and which constitutes their principal charm; they are pictures of serenity and domestic comfort. In the love of enjoyment there is the taste for whatever is exquisite — as the flavor of fruit, the fragrance of flowers, the softest tones of music, like those of the Æolian harp, the most delicate tints, like those of the rainbow, &c. Everything beautiful in the English character is connected with this; and everything delightful in their works of art, in their literature, in their institutions, and in their homes, may be referred to it. It places them in a beautiful relation to the Italians, as it places the cow in a beautiful relation to the horse.

If the young Englishman presented at the beginning of this chapter was reared on milk, on the opposite page is certainly a specimen that is fed on beef. You have only to deprive the Englishman of the exquisite love of enjoyment above referred to, and the roughness, obtuseness, vast strength, and want of refinement of both the moral and intellectual perceptions, stand forth bold and prominent. The "mad bulls" of England are famous the world over, and they are the personifications of a certain class of Englishmen; but the one we have here is not mad. He may be an Italian converted into a Briton — a horse into an ox: he is simply gross, sensual, imperious, domineering, heavy and strong, stolid and obtuse, ungracious and wanting in sense of propriety! He answers very well to one of the varieties of Englishmen as given by Spenser:—

"The miller was a stout carl, deep of tones,
Right large he was of brawn, and eke of bones;
With shoulders broad and short—a knob or gnarr—
There was no door but he'd heave up the bar,
Or break, by running at it with his head;
His beard, as any sow or fox, was red!"

The ox is the very personification of repulsiveness, indicated in the size and strength of the spinal marrow, and by the extraordinary strength imparted to the muscles of the back. Emerson says of the Englishman, that "the axis of his eyes is united to his back-bone." We understand by this that he is quick to see whatever he does not like, that his eyes are the sentinels of his repulsiveness, and that with repulsiveness he guards his eyes. The same shrewd observer says: "The Englishman is remarkable for his pluck. He shows you that he means to have his rights respected. He knows just what he wants, and he means to have it. He is sure to let it be known if he is not served to his mind. Still he is not quarrelsome. Among the twelve hundred young men at Oxford a duel was never known to take place. His self-possession is not pugnacity; he does not wish to injure others—he is thinking only of himself!" This is a description to the very life. Even the mad bull has no animosity, or desire to injure anybody: he only wishes to gratify his headlong disposition, the instinct of which is in his horns.

It is the Englishman's title to the epithet of John Bull that makes him so fond of beef, and the influence of this kind of food upon him increases the resemblance. He wishes his national character to be that of a carnivorous ox; and hence the badge of his nationality, which he chooses above all others, is a *lion*. And the resemblance between the bull and the lion is very striking. The broad, deep, and powerful chest; the deep, reverberating sounds that swell from it; the grave and noble aspect of the countenance; the loose skin and wrinkles of the neck and face, giving the appearance of dignity and old age; the length of the body, and the strength of the back-bone; the long tail, with the tuft at the end of it; the brawny extremities and the matchless strength; the extraordinary size and thickness of the neck; and, in the bison, which is a kind of ox, the shaggy mane which covers it—all proclaim the right of the English to idealize their national symbol into a lion—especially as John Bull himself, who is the person intended to be represented, is carnivorous.

The liking of the English for horned cattle, their liking for the flesh of these animals, and their likeness to the animals themselves, may be illustrated by the following description, drawn by Dickens: "The blessings of Smithfield are too well understood to need recapitulation; all who run (away from mad bulls and pursuing oxen) may read. Any market-day they may be beheld in glorious action. Possibly the merits of our slaughter-houses are not yet quite so generally appreciated.

"Slaughter-houses, in the large towns of England, are always (with the exception of one or two enterprising towns) most numerous in the most densely-crowded places, where there is the least circulation of air. They are often underground, in cellars; they are sometimes in close back-yards; sometimes (as in Spitalfields) in the very shops where the meat is sold. Occasionally, under good private management, they are ventilated and clean. For the most part, they are unventilated and dirty; and, to the reeking walls, putrid fat and other offensive animal matter clings with a tenacious hold. . . . In half a quarter of a mile's length of Whitechapel, at one time, there shall be six hundred newly-slaughtered oxen hanging up, and seven hundred sheep—but the more the merrier—proof of prosperity. . . . . and it's—

'Oh, the roast beef of England, my boy,
The jolly old English roast beef!'

"Mrs. Quickly says that prunes are ill for a green wound; but whosoever says that putrid animal substances are ill for a green wound, or for robust vigor, or for anything or for anybody, is a humanity-monger and a humbug. 'Britons never, never, never,' &c., therefore! And prosperity to cattle-driving, cattle-slaughtering, bone-crushing, blood-boiling, trotter-scraping, tripe-dressing, paunch-cleaning, gut-spinning, hide-preparing, tallow-melting, and other salubrious proceedings, in the midst of hospitals, churchyards, workhouses, schools, infirmaries, refuges, dwellings, provision-shops, nurseries, sick-beds—every stage and baiting-place in the journey from birth to death!"

There is a trait in the Englishman and the ox so extraordinary, that it deserves to be taken particular notice of: it is submission. The sign of this faculty is the loose fold under the throat, and in the ox it is the dewlap. This name reminds us of the rich pastures of John Bull, in which the sign of submission laps the dew while the bull grazes. The submission of the Englishman is graceful in the extreme, for it is perfectly natural to him. The dew of his youth is upon it—and he is remarkable for the memory of his childhood. His submission to his sovereign is of a piece with his submission to parental authority; and as he was taught the one by punishment, he needs not that the other should be enforced. Monarchy rests more securely in England than in any other country, for it confides in the submission that is universally felt and recognised. It is no usurpation, and has therefore nothing to fear. They are as free as the people of a republic, and even more so—for, as Authority and Submission are on the best possible terms with each other, the duty to obey and the right to command are united in the same character, and it is easy for the people to be *one*. John Bull is a single individual, or the entire people, whichever you please: the description that is applicable to the one is applicable to the other. In their relations with other nations, they are like the youngster first described—selfish, imperious, governed by their own desires, submissive to their own wants, yielding to nothing but necessity. When they set their heart upon anything, diplomacy to prevent their getting it is mere mockery. If they are convinced at all, it is against their will; and—

"A man convinced against his will,
Is of the same opinion still."

The only argument that can avail with them is *force*, but of this they have naturally more than others, and it has been strengthened with them by exercise. Still it is necessary to give them "change in their own coin," or to "answer them according to their folly, lest they be wise in their own con ceit." However, it is a good rule, "Answer not a fool ac cording to his folly, lest thou be like him."

According to Physiognomy, the faculties of will lay in the cerebellum, along with the passion which Gall assigned to that portion of the brain. These, in a sovereign like Henry VIII., and in the animal to which he bears a resemblance, are im-

perative beyond measure, and their external indications are so large as to attract attention. A "bull-neck" suggests the idea of a tyrannical disposition, or of irresistible desire, and is never spoken of in the way of compliment. To the faculties of love and will in the cerebellum the neck is bowed by Submission, and they are made more tyrannical than they otherwise would be; they cause that the individual should act upon the principle that "might is right." John Bull shows a remarkable obtuseness of the moral and intellectual perceptions when the rules of morality are applied to himself; but when he takes the position of an umpire—in which case his perceptions are less under the influence of the faculties in the basilar region of the cranium, and more associated with exquisite discrimination or love of enjoyment—his perceptions are more refined. This is true of the person whose portrait is presented on the following page, and who, from his resemblance to the above, was well suited to cater to the selfishness, licentiousness, and cruelty, of that beastly monarch. Cardinal Wolsey and the king whose baseness he excelled should go together, as they did in sensual indulgence, and in the love of power, and in too literal resemblance to the animals they belong to.

When oxen draw together in a yoke, they lean away from each other, so as to be under the necessity of holding each other up. This is on account of their great repulsiveness—a trait which was mentioned as being a prominent element of the English character. It is an exhibition, also, of a sort of ox-justice—a pulling in opposite directions, in order to know which is the right way. Oxen never know the road; they are kept in it by pulling against each other; and they act precisely as if they were in a perfect state of dubiousness as to where they were going to, and as to what step they should take next. They see the two horns of a dilemma most distinctly, and prudently consider which they shall choose; and (a yoke of oxen being naturally repulsive to each other) the one inclines to the right horn and the other to the left. Between the two, if the yoke were not a strong one, it would be pulled asunder; and if a thong were not applied to them, they would not go forward at all. Precisely so it is with the English in all questions of law and equity, especially in a court of justice where the right of a question is a difficult point to be decided. The result is, that the parties upon the opposite sides are as antagonistic as possible; and the trial, with all the "gee-hawing," and yelling, and thrashing, makes excessively slow progress. If the patient in this case is not in respect to fortune as strong as a yoke, he is drawn and quartered, and the lumbering suit is stopped for the want of means to go on with it. With this peculiarity of the English we are so familiar, that we take no particular notice of it, and do not reflect but that it is as common to other people as to them. Of course, this spirit of litigation, growing out of antagonism, is a prominent trait in their descendants in this country; but it grows weaker, and is exhibited here much less than in England, and now much less than formerly.

It is the trait of character here described that makes the Englishman "as honest as a cooper's cow." He must know

"the right of the case" before he can pronounce judgment; he is particularly anxious to "take the right bull by the horns;" he endeavors to hold the scales of justice in impartial balance; his fellow-laborer is the man who opposes him, who counterpoises him by a weight of argument equal to his own. He loves to acknowledge a mutual dependence. If the love of truth did not bind him to his opponent, he would fall: hence he acknowledges a higher dependence upon truth than on man, as oxen acknowledge a dependence upon the yoke more than upon each other. He submits to truth as the ox submits to the yoke; his faculties of love and will are particularly submissive and obedient. Thus are those stern, rude, barbarian qualities mentioned in the last paragraph, turned to harmony with that delightful trait in the English character, the love of enjoyment.

Let us turn to this, and say a few words upon it before we part with the English. The quietness before spoken of as constituting a resemblance between the Englishwoman and the cow, conceals very often the viciousness referred to in Byron's couplet:—

> "If she will she will, you may depend on't;
> If she won't she won't, and there's an end on't!"

You are not to conclude that it is absent from the character because it is concealed, any more than you are to conclude that a cow will give down her milk, or will not kick over the pail, because she is seen chewing the cud so quietly. But there is a gentleness and serenity imparted by the love of enjoyment that may even *do away* with the objectionable feature that is expressed by the term "viciousness." In domestic life, in rural economy, and in everything connected with the love of enjoyment, the English are admirable; and they show a particular aptitude for everything Italian, or for those artistic things that are represented in the horse: and not merely do they appreciate these things, but they imitate and improve. As the horse has some super-excellent qualities imparted to him by the English, and is a great favorite of theirs, so art is fostered and improved, and has a certain quietude, softness, serenity, and exquisiteness, imparted to it in England; and in this respect it is happy there, though it lives a more charmed life in Italy.

CHAPTER XIX.

WE have observed that artists resemble horses. They are like them in the lines that compose the features, in the bearing of the body, in their gait and carriage, in the spirit which they manifest in their motions and thence infuse into their work, and with which also they inspire the beholder. The Andalusian horse, which we see represented below, is like an artist painting a battle-field, or a storm at sea. With his flashing eye he dashes the colors upon the canvass; starts at the

creation of his own imagination; holds, contemplates the scene with caution and pride, and then dashes on again! Courage and fear are equally mingled in him: his success depends as much upon one as upon the other, and both are indispensable. Like the artist, he takes in the whole at a glance, and carefully observes the details. And the artist—how boldly he dashes about the lines, like a horse in the battle-field; and yet how cautiously, lest the labor in details should not contribute to the harmony of the whole, and the project should be crowned with defeat! When all is right in the surroundings, how confidently he dashes into the midst—how full of fire; and yet how cautious, in the midst of confusion and smoke, to keep his place, to be governed by the rein, and to preserve the equilibrium between courage and fear! As he approaches the hour of his triumph or defeat, what great need has he of this union of opposites! What sadder spectacle of fallen pride than a horse tumbled on his back upon the field of battle? The failure of an artist is quite equal to it, to say the least.

With the horse, courage is inspired by caution, and caution by courage: for in the midst of danger from which it is impossible to escape, caution finds no safety but in courage; and as courage would rush into danger that might be avoided, it excites caution. With the artist, this mutual influence of caution and courage is exhibited in a super-eminent degree.

If you would see a strong resemblance to the horse, look at those who represent Nature on the stage, as well as at those who represent her on canvass. The sculptor is one who comes between the painter and the actor, and he, too, bears a strong resemblance to the horse. The Italians are a nation of artists and amateurs. The *dilletanti* are all Italy, and they may be classed according to the varieties of horses. We fancy that the reader will see a resemblance between the king of Naples (Ferdinand II., whose portrait is presented on the following page) and the variety which is there also given, in reference to which we should be warned not to put our trust in horses. He makes a fair show, and is wedge-shaped in front, but he takes a wide sweep when he brings up the rear. Time was when the horse had a Roman nose, and was exceedingly warlike; and he represented the Romans then, as he represents them now. Instead of the old Roman nose, which ruled "lord of the ascendant," we see now-a-days the "saddle-backed nose"

among the Italians as often as among other people, and attached to a horse as often as to any other animal. The Roman war-horse, that might well remind you of the slumbering lion, you can scarcely distinguish from the miserable cart-horse, with the ardor, the spirit, and the fire, driven out of him, instead of slumbering like the thunderbolt in the heavy cloud. This same horse becomes in after-times the clumpy beast of burden, and so it is with the Italian who is overburdened and poorly fed.

On the succeeding page, however, is the picture of an Italian female who loves to be useful — who does the much that her heart and strength prompt her to do, and no more. She is more noble than the Roman matron who reared her sons for war, for she applies the same elements of strength to the promotion of peace; and we may say that the animal that stands adjoining is more noble than the war-horse, and quite as independent. The aspect assures us of the good disposition, the willingness to labor, the confidence of good treatment, and the constant readiness for service.

The horse is a form of art. Symmetry is one of his peculiarities; and his motions, like the outlines of his body, undulate between straight lines and circles. *Action* is characteristic alike of the artist and of the horse. No judge pronounces upon the merits of a horse until he sees him in motion, or, to use his own phrase, observes "how

he handles himself." It may be said also that no amateur pronounces upon the merits of an artist until he sees how he handles his instruments, or sees his motions described on canvass or marble. The line of beauty insensibly perceived in the gait of a spirited, proud, dashing, but easy, graceful, and obedient horse, is the result of that perfect union of boldness and timidity before spoken of, together with an even balance between weight and lightness, and the symmetry which characterizes him. The affinity of the artist for the horse is therefore very great. Among other evidences is his habit of wearing the hair long, thus increasing his resemblance to the animal he so much admires. It is true also that woman, who is privileged to wear the hair long, is more symmetrical, more graceful, and in every way *more artistic*, except in boldness and originality, than man. She is also a passionate admirer of the horse, and skilful in managing him; and is herself the model of *that beauty* (see next page) which by the Italians, and by all who make pilgrimages to Rome, is sought for in the works of the old masters, and in the atmosphere of that delightful country.

The artist owes his artistic talent to an original genius infused into him from his earliest existence. How often do we hear it said that the man who is not born an artist can never become one! This shows that there can be no true art that has not its original in Nature, that does not agree with Nature, and that does not cite Nature as its authority. The child that is destined to be an artist is more a "child of Nature" than any other. In every movement of that wild one you see an inspiration of art; and the graceful, curveting, high-spirited horse seems moved also by inspiration. In Italian children, more than in any other, do you see those forms and those motions that waken in you the appreciation of art, and which cause you to start with pleasure and surprise, like an artist when he beholds a beautiful landscape, or like a horse, with a look of animation, when he comes to the brow of a hill, and sees a fine, beautiful country spread out before him. Laugh, if you will—but observe, and you will find that those sights which startle and animate the spirit of a horse are those which are the most interesting in the eye of an artist. Just such a curve in the road, just such a clump of trees, and just such a house, as excites the attention of a horse, attracts the artist, and he looks upon it as the result of an inspiration in the mind of somebody.

Inspiration is, indeed, the origin of art. Nature is a revelation, but it is only the higher faculties in man that are capable of regarding it as such; and art, which is inspired by this, is a revelation in a far higher sense than Nature is. The artful in Nature, as in the fox and the cat, is detestable in human beings. It is the province of the higher art to render subservient whatever is artful in the natural character. The faculties of imposture, intrigue, dissembling, and cunning, are converted by it into the love of responsibility, the love of concert, the love of ceremony (affectation), and the love of surprise. The horse manifests all these faculties in subserviency to art: the love of responsibility in carrying his master safely and proudly; his love of concert in galloping in rank and file, and in prancing to the sound of music; his love of ceremony in his graceful carriage, which is particularly manifested on ceremonial occasions; and his love of surprise in being startled at everything extraordinary — more from surprise than fear, though caution has much to do with it, and is one of the things necessary to an artist, as before observed. These faculties have a higher action in the horse than in other animals, simply because it is *a form of art*, and is subject to a kind of inspiration, corresponding to that of the artist. The dog shares in the pleasure of his master, and the cock is proud of himself; but it can be said only of the horse, that he

> "Shares with his lord the pleasure and the pride."

He is not free, however, as man is, to change the character that Nature gave him, except to a very limited extent. In so far as Nature has failed in making him a perfect form of art, he is capable of degeneracy. Horses sometimes "make believe." We have known them to feign lameness (though it is only the most miserable kind of horses that do this), and if their skittishness is not sometimes an affectation of fear, it is exceedingly like it. In circuses, horses are trained to this, and there it is certainly theatrical, artistic, and intended for effect. No other animal, not even the dog or the monkey, can play his part so well. The biting, the kicking, and the various equinal passions, are represented upon the stage to the very life; and here he is more admired as an actor than the clown himself, who, if he were so disposed, is too perverted to represent Nature perfectly.

Man is capable of making the higher faculties of art subservient to the lower, and by so doing he renders himself ignoble in the extreme. He is base, hypocritical, crafty, intriguing—everything that is included in the term "artful." Of this class are highly-accomplished rogues and villains. Such men evince extraordinary talents for art, and susceptibility of refinement; and it is by means of art thus perverted and profaned that they

succeed in their wicked designs—for art is pleasing to all. The indications of this evil disposition in them are the signs of the several faculties enumerated above, together with their resemblance to the horse. Not unfrequently they have classic features, of exceeding delicacy, like those of an Italian beauty; but in such cases the signs of the moral and religious faculties are wanting, and the signs of deception are larger than they should be.

To be possessed of superior talents for art is therefore dangerous. The talent for *acting* is perhaps more liable to perversion than any other. The danger in this case is from the faculty of affectation, which in its higher action is love of ceremony, or politeness. External politeness is made to exceed the internal; the rites of religion are more than the spirit and the power; the profession is better than the life; an appearance of sanctity is made the cloak of wickedness, and religion is made finally to consist of nothing but forms and ceremonies. In connection with this, the lowest class make an exhibition of themselves for the sake of gain. They feign deformities, infirmities, and calamities that have no real existence. They make "model artists" of themselves, and extend their hands for charity with such good success, that they are encouraged to ontinue their profession. To give a picture of the Italians, in illustration of the artful in contradistinction from true art, would require more time than it would be profitable to spend on such a subject.

One trait of the Italians, growing out of the thousand artifices they practise upon each other, is jealousy and distrust. Suspicion is said to be a characteristic of the Italians. It is so more from the prevalence of the artificial than from the strength of the faculty of suspicion. True art inspires confidence, for it changes the deceitful faculties into the very opposites. Who more than the sculptor and the painter love to give agreeable surprises? who more than Italian opera-singers illustrate the faculties of affectation and love of concert? By-the-by, there are sounds uttered by these Italian artists that remind us of the neighing of a horse.

Art raises man to the highest pinnacle of perfection. It includes education, improvement, regeneration, accountability —all that belongs to man as created in the image and likeness of his Maker. There is not a wider difference between e horse and the leopard, than there is between the artist in ne highest sense of the term, and one who is artful and designing.

If we were to define art, we could not do better than to say that it is a reflection of Nature. The mind of an artist is like a mirror: he throws back an image of the object that pleases him, that others may see it; for an artist sees more than others. He contemplates the scene, and the result is a reflection like the Daguerreotype — in which the Sun, not content with furnishing subjects for Art, affects the rival. Nor is this all. What the artist reflects is *creation*, and he therefore becomes a creator, taking Nature for his example. This is a higher kind of reflection; it is thought, reason, poetry, fancy, and imagination. It is the mission of the artist to see what others do not see, and then to reflect it, that others may share the pleasure and the inspiration. But art, by the exercise of reflection, is not rendered independent of Nature. The dependence is even greater than before, at the same time that the artist is rendered original, and is free to depart from the exact form of the objects of the senses. Fancy and imagination alone endow him with the largest liberty, and make him a very Proteus in the creation of works of art, surrounding him with

"Gorgons and chimeras dire;"

but poetry and reason, which are also creative, are bound by truth, and governed by the laws of order and harmony which Nature teaches. To depart from Nature, would be proof of a deficiency of the higher kind of reflection, and would condemn a man to the society of his own creations, which would be monsters, and not worth seeing.

As reflection includes reason, and is the essential of art,

the philosopher as well as the poet must be an artist. As the horse, too, is a form of art, he may represent the philosopher as well as the sculptor and the painter. The man who excels in either of the departments of art is deficient in neither of the talents referred to. In this portrait of a sage who combined them all in a supereminent degree, and who says also that the horse corresponds to reason or reflection, we observe a resemblance to that animal. We see it in the look, the air, the spirit that animates the countenance, as well as in the position and cast of the features. He reminds us of a horse that gallops long and free, with a distant object in view — ambitious, hopeful, confident, persevering — with his eye in the face of the sun, which is the object in the horizon toward which he is tending. The bold and successful discoverer in the unexplored regions of science and philosophy is well represented by a horse racing steadily over

a trackless desert, in which nevertheless his animation never fails for the lack of objects of interest. The noblest horse — the Arab or the barb — will best represent and most resemble the man of noblest reason; and if you add the wings of the eagle, you have a Pegasus that is the fitting emblem of the highest style of art, the result of the highest inspiration.

The philosophic mind, like the artistic, comprehends that "generals include particulars," and draws the outlines of his work before he enters into the details. As he progresses in the unfolding of Nature, or in transferring Nature to canvass, he "fills up the picture;" and his course is as much like that of the war-horse under the guidance of the warrior as it is like that of the artist. It is described figuratively at the commencement of this chapter. His bounds being fixed, the waves of thought are free; they have no power to burst into disorder and confusion; they are governed by Order and Harmony, which say to Reason, "Thus far and no farther, and here shall thy proud waves be stayed!"

CHAPTER XX.

One of the essential things in an artist, and in a work of art, is *unity of design*. In this consists the idea of beauty, which the artist perceives, and labors to produce. Without it there is confusion and discord, and consequently deformity and distortion. Harmony is essential to unity of design; and the crowning beauty is *symmetry*, because symmetry expresses unity and perfection, and hence purity — the very opposite of adulteration and mixture. The essentials of beauty are exhibited in the greatest degree in the human form, and in every department of art the highest perfection to which an artist can attain is the nearest approach to a perfect man which his subject will allow. We ascribe perfect symmetry to angelic beings, and wish that we were like them, which shows that unity of design is the principle in all things. What this symmetry indicates is what we should strive to be. It is the dictate of cowardice to suppose that—

> "Angel forms do often hide
> Spirits to the fiends allied."

The counterfeit of purity and intelligence is very like the original, but there are "counterfeit-detectors" in the science of Physiognomy as well as in other things. The "prince of darkness" may throw over his hideous shape some thin disguises, but he knows that they only who desire external beauty, without the internal, will be deceived thereby. But this, unfortunately, includes all, for we are so selfish as to wish to *appear* better than we are.

As the female is in form more symmetrical than the male, it is taken for granted that she is the last, best work of the Creator; and the qualities which we have ascribed to symmetry are attributed to her in a greater degree than to man. The artist derives from her his ideas of what is pure, perfect, and celestial. She is more fond of beauty than man—she is more congenial with it, and hence she is more beautiful. In our illustration of this we must not descend into everything—we must confine ourselves to our subject, which is the horse. In point of symmetry, woman has more resemblance to the horse than to any other animal—and her sympathies show that there is an internal resemblance as well as an external. She is particularly fond of equestrian exercises, and manages a horse admirably,

better than man does, where she has equal advantages, as is seen in Persia and in other countries where it is customary for women to spend much time on horseback. She loves the arching neck, and bending head, and finished outline, in a greater degree than man does, for her appreciation of the line of beauty in the horse is the necessary result of a higher degree of the same quality in herself than belongs to man. Are not the lady and horse above in admirable keeping with each other? do they not seem to breathe the same atmosphere, and to inspire the same spirit? Would you not place such a lady as that upon such a horse? is there not something kindly and responsive in their relations to each other? would not the horse feel the wishes

of his rider, as of an animating principle, without spur or rein? and would not the lady sympathize in every movement of the horse?

The lady here has the air of an equestrian more than the former, for she prefers a horse that requires "management," as she herself does, and one that moves as this animal does. Corresponding with the external resemblance, you can see that she

is intellectual, high-minded, independent, and goes straight forward; full of perseverance and determination; reaching forth to the future, not presumptuously, but clinging to the past; not jealous, but still ambitious that nothing should pass her on the road to fame.

If there is a form in Nature that may symbolize art, and furnish the artist with an ideal from which to trace the lines of beauty in creations of his own, that form is the horse. We discover the outlines of this animal most in implements of labor, particularly of agriculture. In chairs and sofas, or whatever is made to recline upon, we see the same form of beauty and of use. But in things made to correspond with the body in which the soul is lodged—as in vases that contain the substances that inspirit it, and as in architecture that is to the body what the body is to the soul, and as in dress that is the clothing of the external man as the form is of the internal—we see that the model of beauty and perfection in the mind of the artist is the human form. The arts which distinguish man from the lower animals are of the two kinds we have spoken of—resemblances to the form of the horse, and imitations of the masterpiece of creation. And as the works of art first mentioned are the appurtenances of a man, along with the vessel that contains his food and with the house and clothing that contain his body, we see why the horse and the artist should resemble each other.

The horse is the standard of beauty by which to compare all forms of the animal creation. This is an honor, truly. It is rendered on account of the symmetry which he possesses in common with man. As things symmetrical are harmonious (on which account mankind are inclined to become one), the horse and his rider are remarkably fitted to each other, and present an example of "unity of design." Where the two had a special resemblance to each other, they would seem blended into one; and hence the centaurs, as represented in ancient works of art, had a more natural origin than the mere habit of the inhabitants of Mount Pelion spending a great portion of their time on horseback; for no one would think of uniting a man and a donkey, though the former should ride the latter for ever. Mount Pelion was in Thessaly, and the Thessalians were celebrated riders; hence men and horses were particularly fitted to each other, and might be represented as one by those who understood the principle of symmetry; and that they were called "Centaurs," or "Bull-killers," is further proof of this, for the Thessalians were accustomed to hunt the bull on horseback. When the Indians first saw the Spaniards on horseback, they saw them as centaurs; they beheld in the man and the horse a single creature, and experience was necessary to enable them to distinguish between them.

Parts that are symmetrical can not be separated without violence. Even when the spirit has departed, it is sacrilege to divide the body—much more when the soul, whose unity is indicated by that of the body, is present in it. It could not be permitted to man to commit so horrible a sacrilege as to break a bone of the body of our Savior. One feels that it would be a kind of profanation to break the statue of a perfect human form, and hence the immortality of a work of art:—

"A thing of beauty is a joy for ever."

Unity is something to rejoice in; it is the attribute of God: and man is created in his image, to be an artist, and to finish the Creator's most perfect work.

Let it be understood that art is no more "strained" than the "quality of mercy." There is room for its exercise when there is no skill in the chisel or the brush. Hence a person who is not *called* an artist may have more resemblance to a horse than one who is. The highest expression of art is the highest beauty to which he is capable of attaining. In this animal, which we compare with Melancthon, what an admi-

rable illustration of symmetry do we behold! and how this effect is increased by the appreciation of the line of beauty in the *action* of the animal—in his curveting, his flexure of the joints, his motion of the legs, his holding of the tail, his curvature of the neck, and last and most beautiful of all, his looking at himself to see the elegance of his form and the gracefulness of his movements! This corresponds to that which in man may be called *self-examination*—the highest action of the reasoning and moral faculties combined—from which proceeds humility instead of pride, true dignity instead of arrogance—so nearly do opposite faculties and their signs approach each other!

The horse, by his resemblance to the artist, is related to the sun (which pencils and paints), to every halo, to the rainbow, the morning dawn, and the thousand reflections from the face of Nature that charm the eye with the beauty of form and color! The sun's horses are fiery and fleet, and could never be driven without reins; and it has never entered

the mind of man to substitute asses in their stead. Oxen may be yoked to the moon, which ascends the horizon like a loaded wain, but the chariot of the sun must be drawn by horses. As the difference between the beauty of objects in moonlight and of objects in sunlight, so is the difference between English art and Italian. The former is soft and subdued, and has the air of stillness and repose; but the latter presents the strongest contrast of light and shade, and has all the characteristics of the garish day. It is one of the peculiarities of the horse, which we have often observed, that a shade in a broad sunlight is especially pleasing to him, and it is equally true that the cow enjoys herself in the moonlight much more than the horse.

The fire of genius, the glance that penetrates creation, the intellect that searches through all things and beholds high and low, correspond to the rays of the sun, and also to the horse, in the flash of his eye, and the bearing of his head, as he flies over the plain inspired by the love of freedom and by the will of a mas-

ter who breathes a noble spirit like his own. Is not this horse, that resembles Rammohun Roy, and that might pass for one of the horses of the sun, a fine example?

This splendid intellect, this noble soul, born and educated to the religion of Brahma, dispelled by its radiance the darkness of superstition. He laid noble plans for reforming the religion of his countrymen, and published a work "Against the Idolatry of all Religions." In one of his works occurs the following sentence: "The consequence of my long and uninterrupted researches into religious truth has been, that I have found the doctrines of Christ more conducive to moral principles, and better adapted to the use of rational beings, than any other which have come to my knowledge." He acquired a knowledge of Sanscrit and other languages, that he might acquaint himself with ancient and different religions; and having studied the Scriptures in Greek and Hebrew, he published a work entitled "The Precepts of Jesus the Guide to Peace and Happiness."

"In April, 1831, the rajah, accompanied by his youngest

son, arrived in England, where he was received with every mark of distinction and respect. In every kind of assemblage, religious, political, literary, and social, the amenity of his manners, his distinguished attainments, and his universal philanthropy, rendered him a welcome guest; and his advice was sought by the English ministers on topics connected with the future government of India. He did not, however, live to carry into effect the various plans for improving the condition of his countrymen, whose welfare he had so much at heart, having been taken ill while on a visit at Bristol, where he expired in October, 1833."

A very different ambition from that presented opposite is exhibited by these animals, *scrabbling* to get ahead of each

other. They are like their masters, or rather like what their masters were when they set out in the race — or rather (begging their pardon) they are themselves the masters, and their riders resemble *them*. It is always so with those who

——— "throw loose rein
Upon the neck of headlong Appetite" —

the animal gains the mastery. It is a low ambition that is indicated by such postures as these: it implies a doubt in the actors whether they will be behind or before, which can never be said of an artist, or of a man of noble ambition. The am bition of the man having nothing manly in it fails, while that of the horse keeps on. The horse and his rider on the right side resemble each other before, and they on the left side resemble each other behind. A jockey picks out such an animal to go to the race as suits him best, and that animal he resembles. People who run their horses for sport, and drive them poor and lame, and break them down, and work them till they fall down dead, are, like those two fellows on horseback, as cowardly as they are cruel; and the horses that are marked to be the victims of such have their tails cropped, that their torment may be enhanced by the stings of insects. The connection between cowardice and cruelty was explained in the chapter on the vulture; and the persons we are speaking of resemble carrion-birds, and their perverted horses have something of the same features. It is customary with such persons to cultivate crossness and cowardice in their horses by special training. They are fond of an impure atmosphere, and of fermented drink; and sweating race-riders in a dunghill, to reduce their weight, is an invention worthy of those who resemble vultures. They clip the tail of a horse to show that he has the talent for "clipping it down"—the chief value in their eyes. Out on such artists!

We have here presented a quiet little pony, that has a good

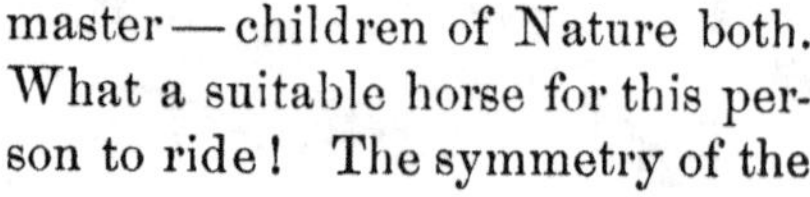

master—children of Nature both. What a suitable horse for this person to ride! The symmetry of the

pony is diminished by roundness, but in this it comports with the beauty of youth, as in the features of young Edward VI., who must have inherited this classic style of countenance (in which there is so much of purity and refinement) from his mother, Jane Seymour, rather than from his father, Henry VIII. Features like those just given have the promise of perfect symmetry when the individual has arrived at maturity: hence they perfectly satisfy the artist, as do also the outlines of a pony which indicate his fitness to be the pet and servant of a child.

The resemblance of certain people to asses is too frequently spoken of to allow us to pass this animal in silence. He has

a trumpet of his own, which he will blow if we neglect to speak of him. Shakspere has hit at a characteristic trait of the person who resembles an ass, in making the stupid fellow whom he disguised with an ass's head say:—

"Scratch my head, Peas-blossom. Where's Mustard-seed?" And to the question of Mustard-seed, "What's your will?"—"Nothing, monsieur, but to help cavaliero Peas-blossom to scratch." For, to tell the truth, the person who resembles an ass looks always as if he were sitting up to have his head examined, which, of course, implies the necessity of somebody "sitting up" to examine heads. He has as strong an inclination to one as to the other, for he wishes to "do as he would be done by." He is as much like the artist and the reasoner as the ass is like the horse, or as the brain is like the face, which means simply that they are *near* to each other—an illustration of the principle that "extremes meet." He is for making himself "thorough in the rudiments;" requiring eternally to settle the question whether there be such a thing as a foundation, before he will consent to look at the superstructure. His attention is occupied with the premises as the objects of chief importance, and hence he never gets beyond them. He will not look at reason, though you thrust it before his eyes; and though a fact as plain as the nose on a man's face be presented to him, he will deny it!

In contrast with this, we here present a man of lofty reason, who resembles a horse. And is not a horse like this, that looks like one of Aurora's, fit to resemble an astronomer, a bold and original genius, like Sir Isaac Newton, one who stands as it were in the centre of the solar system, and darts his rays thence, and comprehends all the relations and dependencies with the facility and perfection of a master? Would you not place such a horse as that on vantage ground? He looks as if he were standing on a hill, overlooking "the kingdoms of the world and the glory of them."

CHAPTER XXI

It is funny that a certain fowl should receive the good-natured diminutive which we apply to a small, pocket edition of the Turk, and to the country he inhabits. It is not always that a name is significant, but in the present instance it is peculiarly so, for "Turk" and "turkey" are as much alike as the characters to which they are applied; and we attach a dignity to the former, derived from a feeling of reverence, while to the latter we connect the idea of ridiculous familiarity. The turkey is too much like the Turk (who seems to be entirely unconscious of the position in which we have placed him) to be teased by an allusion to the individual to whom he bears so strong a resemblance. He has already be-

gun to strut, young as he is, and to exercise authority, but when he meets with a stronger than himself he is equally a pattern of submission. The sign of his extraordinary love of command is the muscular appendage at the top of the bill, where the sign of command is in the human face; and when the faculty is in exercise, this muscle is contracted, and when it is quiescent the muscle hangs loosely over the end of the bill. The activity of the faculty is accompanied with an exercise of attack—a command and a blow—the dicta, "Humble yourself, and be my slave!" This is the trait of character most remarkable in the Turk. He makes a slave of every person whom he can force to acknowledge the right of the strongest, and to all others he is submissive to the last degree. To gratify his authority, more than to satisfy his lust, he purchases a large number of wives, for wives in all countries are bound to "obey."

The sign of submission in the turkey is that fold of skin which everybody has seen hanging down under the throat, and which answers to the dewlap in the cow. The Turks are like the English in reference to both authority and submission, only that in the former these two traits are still more extraordinary. The government of a sultan and a religion propagated by the sword are natural to them, and they feel no jealousy toward republicanism, for the simple reason that their country is not the soil upon which it can grow. Toleration, therefore, may take root there, and Liberty may find a home.

If the eye be the "window of the soul," the spirit of the Turk must be fond of shadow, for not much light can enter its habitation through such windows as those. There is a certain drowsy dullness expressed in them, like what we see in the turkey, especially while young. It reminds one of windows smeared with dirt, through which midday is converted into twilight; and the young turkey has an air about him well suited to confirm the impression that it is night within, and that the inhabitants are sleeping. There is something in the nature of the Turk that draws the curtains over his eyes; perhaps it is bigotry: at all events he is very indifferent to light. Houses in Turkey, that make a grand show of windows at a distance, are found on approach to be bricked up in the places where light was supposed to be admitted. It is from this disposition in the Turk to make a show of glass without the reality, that makes his eye itself a sort of blind window. Certainly he is inclined to receive implicitly what Mohammed has told him, and to be as thoroughly hoodwinked as this hawk is that he holds on his arm, and about which he seems to be pronouncing a discourse.

But his eyes are held a while in order that he may see more clearly, and may use them to better advantage: external light and external objects are shut out, that he may have the light of truth, and may exercise his reason. When this shall be, he will bear a resemblance to birds of powerful wing, as the hawk and the eagle. The gradations from the turkey to the eagle are miserable, hard, and difficult. First, he will resemble the turkey-buzzard — then the stork— then the vulture—then the eagle. But the philosophy of this transition we can not stop now to describe. Suffice it to say that the quality of strength in the turkey is tough, grasping, and firm, and altogether like that of the eagle; and that strength and vigor of the same nature are characteristic of the Turk.

The poppy is to the vegetable kingdom what the turkey is to the animal, and the Turk resembles them both. The turban resembles poppy-leaves, and the head containing the seed is like that of the Turk. There is a connection between "Turkey opium" and the drowsiness of those eyes. As sleep is more appropriate to children than to grown people, the eyes of young turkeys are particularly sleepy; they have not waked up yet; and the same expression in the eyes of the Turk indicates that there is vast promise of something worth seeing for which the eyesight is being reserved. Opium is suited to the idiosyncracy of the Turk, and hence he can smoke it with comparative impunity; and children can bear this drug better than adults, for the simple reason that much sleep is natural to them. If there is a strong tendency to sleep, and the person is kept awake by pain, an opiate in exact proportion to the sleepiness does not act as poison; but if it is taken to *produce* sleepiness, or simply to subdue pain, it is deadly. If physicians and other people did but know this, how much suffering and death would be avoided!

The Turk and the turkey resemble the Arab and the camel. The Turk inclines partly to inhabit Arabia, and of course to rule there, for his love of command is as unbounded as that of the turkey. Yet he receives his religion from the Arab, thus acknowledging his inferiority—as the turkey, if he were endowed with reason, must needs acknowledge his inferiority to the camel, and at the same time desire to rule him. The turkey is slovenly in his eating, as the camel is; he "gobbles down" his food, and this manner of eating is to be observed in connection with the voice in the person who resembles the gobbler. The young bird peeps with his voice as well as with his eyes; and the same principle is true of the old bird in respect to gobbling, for the eyes are connected with the appetite for food, and they gobble also. The characteristic of the eye, the voice, and the appetite, is want of discrimination, and this is connected with the *love of command.* In respect to his voice, it is—"Hussle 'em out!" and his actions at the moment respond heartily to this sentiment; in respect to the eyes, it is—"Hussle 'em about!" a sentiment to which his movements, his display of feathers, and his whole body, respond; in respect to his appetite, it is—"Hussle 'em in!" and it is no sooner said than done.

This is the manner in which the Turk receives and delivers his sentiments. In respect to faith, he "eats what is set before him, asking no questions, for conscience' sake;" and what he eats he thinks is good enough for others, and he is sure to offer it to them; it is not the love of proselyting, or the love of command merely, but it it is partly hospitality, that prompts him to do so. In the young Turk faith is more blind than in the old; and the eyes, like the faculties of the mind, are peeping. In this portrait of the present sultan of Turkey, Abdul-Medjid, the eyes are of this description, resembling those of a young turkey. From such features we might expect a great deal if the eyes were open, and were not continually peeping after their own interests. The young turkey's voice peeps incessantly, and so do his eyes. Louis Napoleon's eyes are of the same character, except that they are carnivorous, and resemble more the eyes of a turkey-buzzard or a stork. Such eyes can have faith in the dreams of the alchemists, and can engage in a search for the philosopher's stone, confident of filling coffers with gold and of creating an inexhaustible treasury, as was the case with the individual last mentioned.

But let us glance at some of the more obvious, external resemblances between the turkey and the Turk. There is a great abun-

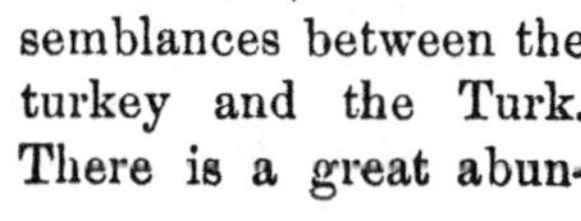

dance and looseness of dress, and freedom of all parts of the body, and thus a remarkably dowdy appearance, in the one biped as well as in the other. The sort of tippet that hangs from the breast of the turkey reminds us of something peculiar in the dress of the Turk, and the Turkish cloak and trowsers are amazingly in keeping with the feathers of the turkey when he displays them to the best advantage. We may call him a foolish bird, and say that there is no use to call him so, for that—

> ——"Pride steps in to his defence,
> And fills up all the mighty void of sense"—

and this is true of the Turk. But he is also too proud to be mean; he is honorable and sincere; he eschews cunning and hypocrisy; you see no cunning in either the turkey or the Turk. If he is in power, he bids defiance to all the world. It is only when his challenge is accepted that he acknowledges a superior. But he does not fight. The moment he is not the master, he is the slave. He has the highest possible respect for "the powers that be;" so that he has a certain "sublime port" about him whether he be the sultan or not.

Among the many excellent traits of the turkey we will mention only this, the instinct to cure disease. He is a doctor, and all the young turkeys that are born in a state of nature have to be dosed and drugged before they can

> "Wheel about, and turn about, and do just so,
> And every time they wheel about jump Jim Crow"—

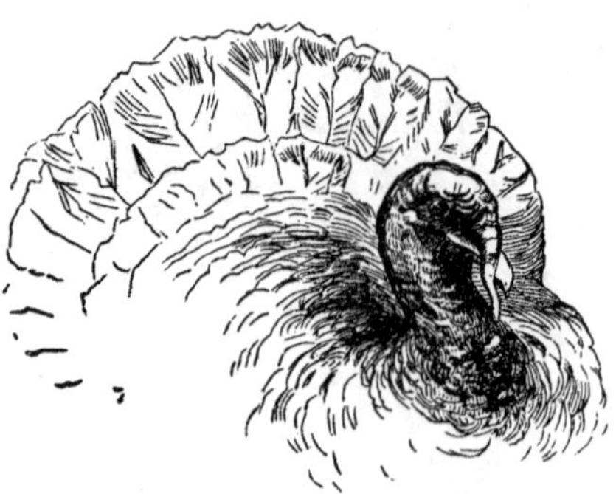

for this kind of exercise makes people sick, and the turkey practises upon the principle that an ounce of prevention is worth a pound of cure. The doctor we have on the opposite page is not a juvenile turkey: the "windows of his soul" are open; he is not a Turk, but he is like one, and wears a turban from a sense of what is becoming to him, or from natural choice, and he looks enough like the turkey to be said to have a strong family likeness to that bird. You may be sure that he is a good physician, that he has very great desire to be honored and to "render honor to whom honor is due," and that he is exceedingly honorable. That he is proud, and would make the cowardly slaves tremble, and that he is so ambitious of esteem that he is the first to set the example, or to do himself reverence, and that he is not afraid to solicit the honor he is entitled to, can not be denied; but he endeavors to merit the grand object of his desires, and that gives him an unusual degree of merit, so that those who see his good qualities overlook his egotism, and consider his pride and vanity as spots on the sun, that diminish nothing from the splendor of his beams. Who could expect anything contrary to this in the man who resembles the turkey, or, what is very nearly the same thing, the Turk? By wishing to resemble the great and honorable, he pays them a compliment, and himself too.

CHAPTER XXII.

THE turkey has a rival. The peacock can outvie him in splendor, but not in pride; in vain-glory, but not in ambition to excel. That the dispositions which are prominent in the peacock have their seat in the human breast, has been too often observed to require a formal argument in proof of the assertion. We shall therefore proceed to the comparison of certain persons with the peacock *sans ceremonie.* Whoever resembles this bird ought to possess qualities worthy of admiration, and also an extraordinary degree of the love of admiring and of being admired. No one need be told that in the tournure and entire air and manner of this lady there is an imitation of the peacock—the skirt flows behind in an ethereal beauty that is better imagined than represented in ink, and that will admit of no comparison but to the tail of the peacock; the neck and chest seem glistening with varied hues, as they turn to catch the rays of the sun in different directions; the head is worthy of a queen, and the eye is heavenly. This, at least, is the idea intended to be conveyed. In every part of the peacock there is something delectable; his flesh was as highly pleasing to the epicurean tastes of the Romans as

his external appearance is pleasing to the artistic taste of the most polished and refined.

Those who cultivate the appearance and manners of the peacock, possess the same traits of character—the same impulses, motives, and promptings—modified, of course, by the faculties that are peculiarly human. The beauty which surrounds them is an outbirth of an innate appreciation of the beautiful, together with the love of self; and hence they admire it with the fervency of self-love. In other words, they admire nothing so much as themselves: they are filled with vanity, and they believe that they are equally admired by others; or, if not, they desire to be, and they do all in their power to eclipse the beauty of every other object. They vie with each other for the reason that there would be no glory without conquest; but they are too conscious of their power, and admire themselves too much, to feel any great degree of jealousy for a rival beauty. Peacocks vie with each other, and there is a sort of self-love in this, for together they form a galaxy of stars, the glory of which is the property of each, so that each one may boast of the splendor of the whole as if it were his own. This is a degree of refinement of self-love, however, to which the literal peacock is incapable of arriving, and for this simple reason: in this degree of selfishness there is the opportunity and the demand that man should love his neighbor as himself. What a beautiful superstructure, then, may be reared upon a resemblance to the peacock! what a magnificent temple of humanity! But we shall see more of this by-and-by.

It is evident enough that there are very many people who resemble peacocks; but the resemblance in physiognomy which indicates the resemblance in character is not easily described. The most expressive things are the most inexpressible. Besides, it very frequently happens that the person who resembles the peacock loses himself in dress and equipage, like the peacock in the splendor and magnificence of his plumage. Nevertheless, there is to be discovered a similarity in countenance, particularly in the eye. In the following portrait of a Persian the resemblance is expressed, not only in the features, but in a look that is inexpressible, except by the idea that is conveyed of this magnificent fowl.

The fashion of that beard more, even, than the quantity, reminds us of the words, "Thou hast more hair on thy chin, than Dobbin, my fill-horse, has on his tail." What could be more peacock-like than the nose, the eyes, the softly-feathered head and even the beard spreading all around, like rays, and dyed according to the taste of the owner? And if so much can be conveyed in an engraving, how much more might be done with colors! The Persians, be it observed, are in the habit of staining their beards, and in one stage of the process it is a brilliant red, in which stage the vulgar class prefer to leave it. The Persians are, in fact, wonderfully like the peacock in character and externals. Whatever comes to us from Persia conveys this impression. Their fabrics, in the quality of their construction, and in the form and color of their figures, are like the head, neck, body, and tail, of the peacock, and outvie those of every other country: all things together, they are magnificent in the extreme. The Persians are delighted with positive colors, and with the bold, glaring, dazzling, glittering effects that are produced by them, in contradistinction from the neutral tints, which they have no taste for. They rival the peacock in the wide field which they demand for the display of their persons, in the splendor of their attire, and in everything that surrounds them.

In every country, those who resemble the peacock rival their beau-ideal in the circumference of their skirts, and in the train they carry behind them. The peacock elevates his tail, or depresses it, according to his caprice; and sometimes, when he lives in town, where he is a miserable bird, he trails it in the dirt: and so it is with those who resemble him. As to sweeping the ground with beauty that is fit to be elevated among the stars, it is indispensable to those daws that borrow the tail of the peacock in order to be fashionable, and have no power to elevate it. But the person who resembles the peacock should not defile his garments. He is worse than the pretender if he does, because he is capable of higher things. It is worse to profane heavenly things than to act the hypocrite; and the person who resembles the peacock, and understands the correspondence of its plumage, is capable of a lower degree of degradation, venality, and crime, than the person who does not.

The distinguishing features of the Persians are all included in their resemblance to the peacock. The fondness for extravagant display implies a love of riches, for the reason that these extravagances require wealth, and are termed rich and costly. Diamonds, gold, and gems, the property of the wealthy, form an essential part of this splendor and magnificence. The Persians have a passion for these things. The means for gratifying it can come by no natural process, but must be obtained by some diabolical incantation, or by the help of some "good genius that turns everything into gold." They are properly limited to a few; and when vast numbers have the desire for princely wealth and splendor, as is the case in Persia, they resort to dishonest, artful, magical contrivances, to gain their end. As a matter of course, all of them have the ambition to be courtiers, and to get as near to royalty as possible. Courtiers in Persia are very numerous, and of this class Mr. Fraser says: "Dissimulation and flattery are their chief study; their minds are occupied with intrigue, and their time in amassing, by the most flagitious methods, that wealth which their extravagance requires."

Poverty must necessarily accompany this extravagance and this unnatural production of the means of gratifying it. The Persians spend everything upon their backs, and therefore their wealth is superficial, and its influence is of short duration. Their income is never equal to their fondness for admiration, and falls as far below their love of splendor and parade as their heads fall below the rainbow in the sky, or as much as the noddle of the peacock is beneath its tail when the latter is elevated to an imitation of the rainbow. They run in debt, they borrow, they substitute tinsel for gold, they cheat, and they steal, all for the sake of "keeping up appearances." They prey upon each other; a display of wealth is a temptation to a stronger to come and seize it: hence they are divided between a desire of displaying whatever wealth they may be possessed of and a fear of losing it. They complain of poverty, at the same time that they make a show of the opposite, wishing to keep their neighbors in a state of dubiousness as to the real state of their finances. But their love of dazzling the eyes of beholders is so great, that the poverty they complain of is as sure to come as the glories which the peacock displays are sure to fall. It is only when "riches take to themselves wings and fly away" that they shine in all the lustre and beauty which the Persian so greatly admires.

——— "As birds
When mounted on the wing, their glossy plumes
Expanded, shine with azure, green, and gold,
So blessings brighten as they take their flight."

And the Persians would do nothing to lessen the brightness of those blessings which they so ardently crave. Says Chardin: "They are the greatest spendthrifts in the world; they can not keep their money: let them receive ever so much, it is immediately spent. Let the shah, for example, give one of them fifty thousand or one hundred thousand livres, in fifteen days it will all be disposed of. He buys slaves of either sex; seeks out for mistresses; sets up a grand establishment; dresses and furnishes sumptuously; and expends at a rate which, unless other means present themselves, renders him speedily penniless. In less than two months we see our gentleman commencing to get quit of all his finery: his horses go first; then his supernumerary servants; then his mistresses; then, one by one, his slaves; and, finally, piece by piece, his clothes."

Thus suddenly rises the tail of the peacock, like a halo of glory, and thus fades the glory from the sky when the pride that caused it has expended itself in the accomplishment of the grand design! And this is not regarded by the Persian as a misfortune, for it is natural to him. The rising and falling are in proportion to each other:—

"As well expect eternal suns and cloudless skies"

as that such a tail as the peacock possesses should be constantly elevated, or that such a fortune as the Persian delights in should be for ever in the ascendant. The base interpretation of the doctrine that "he that exalteth himself shall be abased, and he that humbleth himself shall be exalted," is exhibited in the Persian. Alternations of humility and pride are natural to him; but as his humility is the result of his pride, and as his pride is not based upon humility, he is too literal in his resemblance to the peacock, and is no illustration of the heavenly things which the beauties of the peacock correspond to. The splendor that surrounds him is born of prosperity and adversity, as the rainbow is born of sunshine and shower; and its height is in the brief interval between the extremes of each, as the hues of Iris are most beautiful when the mists are thin and the sun is descending. His delights are the product of the union of opposites; and as prosperity and misfortune are the mutual causes of his happiness, he has a sort of filial affection for them both. This is one of the reasons why he represents himself on the one hand to be poor and miserable, and on the other to be "rich, and increased in goods, and in need of nothing." He has no sensibility to disgrace: he can plead poverty as a recommendation to favor as easily as he can present beauty as a claim to it. He is as mean in his humility as he is arrogant in his pride. He is demoralized by the government more than by his own degree of the peacock propensity, for those who are in power have this propensity in greater excess than the governed. Says Mr. Fraser:—

"A minister or governor offends the shah, or is made the object of accusation, justly or unjustly. He is condemned, perhaps unheard; his property is confiscated; his slaves are given to others; his family and wives are insulted, perhaps given over to the brutality of grooms and feroshes; and his person is maltreated with blows, or mutilated by the executioner's knife. Nothing can be imagined more complete than such a degradation; nothing, one would imagine, could be more poignant than his anguish, or more deep and deadly than his hatred and thirst for revenge. Yet these reverses are considered merely as among the casualties of service, as clouds obscuring for a while the splendor of courtly fortune, but which will soon pass away, and permit the sun of prosperity to shine again in its fullest lustre; and experience proves that these calculations are correct, for the storm often blows by as rapidly as it comes on. Royal caprice receives the sufferer again into favor; his family is sent back to him, with such of his slaves as can be recovered; and his property, pruned of all dangerous exuberance, is returned. A bath mollifies his bruised feet; a cap conceals his cropped ears; a *khelut* covers the multitude of sins and stains, and proves a sovereign remedy for all misfortunes; and the whitewashed culprit is often reinstated in the very government he had lost, perhaps carrying with him a sentence of disgrace to his successor, to whose intrigues he owed his temporary fall."

Could such things exist in any other country than Persia, or be said of any other people than of those who resemble peacocks? The Persians are so insensible to disgrace, that "to give the lie directly is not deemed an insult. '*Een durough ust*' ('It is a lie') is as common an expression, used without offence from one Persian to another, as '*Gou khourd*' ('He has eaten filth,' equivalent to 'He has lied') is in speaking of another, even in the highest ranks." It is impossible that insensibility to disgrace alone could account for this: it is to be accounted for partly by the fact that lying is natural to them by virtue of their resemblance to the peacock, which implies a love for "false and deceptive appearances."—"Believe me, for, though a Persian, I am speaking truth," is a common exclamation to those who doubt their veracity. What is this but a profession that a Persian has a *right* to speak falsehood? And so he has, if he is to resemble the peacock literally. Who does not see in the heavenly hues and delicate fringes of that sweeping train something supernal, and does not transfer them in his imagination to a being far more worthy of them than this foolish, good-for-nothing fowl? The man who imagines that *he* is that person, and attempts to rival the peacock, deceives himself, and blazons a falsehood before the eyes of all who see him. He deceives himself and others with the idea that he is a superior being: thus he adds profanation to falsehood. If he can be guilty of the former, it is not strange that he will as readily admit that he is a liar as anything else.

Where everything is outside show, what can there be of worth within? How hollow-hearted, vain, fickle, and capricious, the people must be who resemble the peacock, and who do not convert this resemblance into a correspendence of the graces which the most exquisite beauty consists in! Lavishing everything upon external accomplishments, intent upon enlarging his dimensions, cutting a wide swell, and requiring room for his dress as the peacock does for his tail, the Persian must of necessity be heartless, coarse, and vulgar. He exerts his utmost to convert himself into the form of a bubble that is transparent, beautifully colored, and is sure to burst. Vastness and splendor are the thoughts that occupy him, and they vastate him of everything pure, refined, and noble. You can see the peacock strut in his legs, solar-effulgence in his body, and unbounded self-admiration in his eye. Such a body is formed to create a vacuum, and to draw everything after it, as with his tail the great red dragon drew down the third part of heaven, and the stars, in imitation, it may be, of the peacock!

The resemblance of the Persian ladies to their embodied divinity is as literal as that of the men. They are unscrupulous in painting their faces — using various colors for that purpose — and stain their nails with henna, and print fanciful figures on their persons by tattooing, besides setting the example of that kind of dress that is appropriated chiefly by females who are destitute of modesty and virtue. If the men are coarse and vulgar, the women are more so, for the perversion is greater. "They are utterly wanting," says the last-mentioned authority, "in all that delicacy of sentiment and language which is the charm of females in more refined countries; and, ignorant of what we consider propriety, they express themselves on all subjects with disgusting grossness." Their passion for external beauty is like that of the peacock: it is no proof of a love of that which this beauty conceals, and which it is intended to express. The peacock, with his beautiful plumage, is a vulgar bird, and is regarded with disrespect. The reason why the pheasant and the bird of paradise are not so regarded is that they make no display of their attractions, but wear them modestly, and thus gracefully, like one who is made more conspicuous by her beauty than she desires. In a bird that shows his feathers as if he were admiring himself in a glass, and were practising manners before it, the glancing and varying hues remind us of fickleness and insincerity. They indicate something unworthy of confidence, and which therefore it is not possible to feel an affection for. The peacock race are admired, but not loved. They are arrogant and overbearing when they have the ability to be so; and when they have not, they are as polished in manners, as lively and acute, as mild and courteous, as they are deceitful and treacherous. Such is described to be the character of the Persian court; and when we see the peacock displaying himself, we receive an impression of corresponding dispositions and qualities in the bird.

The peacock is beautiful in the extreme, and is regarded with extreme admiration. But the extreme of beauty is the most external; it is the least substantial, and the farthest removed from love, which is the centre; it has no sensitiveness, no tenderness; it is destitute of heart and soul; it is fading and transitory; it is driven forth to the outskirts; it is just upon the borders of Cimmerian darkness; and its "passing away" is represented in the extreme beauty of the extremity of the long tail of the peacock. What, then, must be the character of those who spend their lives in admiration of the extreme of beauty? Their souls are spent, wasted, in the object of their lives; and their lives are wasted; and they expire in darkness. Vying with others in dress and in mere brilliancy of eyes and complexion, admiring themselves supremely and seeking the extreme admiration of others, courting flatteries and delighted with adulation, they are the victims of those whose tastes are as superficial and whose professions are as hollow as their own; and in the specious appearance of love, purity, sincerity, devotion, and honor, they suffer an entire loss of them all.

If this be so, what becomes of the principle that external beauty corresponds to internal? If internal beauty shows itself in beauty of the outside, how is it that the Persians, the Circassians, the Georgians, and others that might be mentioned, are not better? Why was the beautiful marchioness de Brinvillier such a fiend incarnate? Byron has said, somewhat spitefully and somewhat truly:—

——"Your thief looks in the crowd
Exactly like the rest, or rather better;
'T is only at the bar, or in the dungeon,
That wise men know your felon by his features."

It should be observed, however, that in all these cases men are not guided by a knowledge of the signs of character in the face, but are captivated by the extreme of beauty, which consists of "false and deceptive appearances," and are such as are discovered in the peacock. Besides that, those who resemble this bird have great power of art, as those have who resemble the horse; and as the highest art is perfection, or the extreme of beauty, its perversion is the extreme of falsehood and deception. In all nature, the beauty we are speaking of is unsubstantial and idle—as in the rainbow, the flower, and the butterfly. A sunbeam glancing on water, or darting through crystal, is not the index of a soul; the greater the distance of an object, or the more extreme, the more deceptive is its appearance. We are sure to be taken by people at a distant view of them, or when they make their first impression upon us through the medium of some disguise; but we find afterward that—

"'T is distance lends enchantment to the view,
And robes the mountain in its azure hue!"

or, as to the disguises, and to be more particular as to the traits of character we discover—

"So the blue summit of some mountain height,
Wrapped in gay clouds, deludes the distant sight;
But as with gazing eyes we draw more near,
Fades the false scene and the rough rocks appear."

But we are very likely to ascribe the deception from this cause to the object itself, when in fact the object makes no pretensions to be anything but what it really is, and the deception lies in ourselves and in the circumstances. Besides, the object at hand may be far better than the "false scene" which we admired at first; but disappointment or pride may prevent us from acknowledging this, and thus many a worthy person is injured and abused to his face by those who admired him at a distance.

The exterior beauty which corresponds to the interior, and by which we can read the character, is something intrinsic, at the same time that it is exterior; whereas, the extreme of beauty that we are speaking of is extrinsic, superficial, or less than that, a mere gilding of the surface. By the interior we mean the soul, and by the exterior the body (including the signs of all the faculties), which is an index of the former: by the external we mean the hue and complexion, the garments, the manners, and the external accomplishments; and by the internal we mean something more excellent than the soul—something central, the index of which is the highest and most transcendent beauty. Thus heaven is within, and heaven is above. The sky, where the azure, the gold, and everything in the plumage of the peacock, are most displayed, is heaven, and heaven is within the soul: it is there that man may hold communion with God and with angels, and yet the dwelling-place of these is above, in the region of that extreme beauty which is paradise, in like manner as the soul is in the body. How sweet and wonderful! how intensely we realize it, and yet how incomprehensible it is!

The resemblance of the Persians to the peacock fits them for the highest perfection to which human beings can aspire. But they attain to the very opposite. "Pomp and ceremony are the delight of all Persians. They form, in fact, a part of the system of government, which is considered indispensable to the maintenance of authority. They term the gorgeous magnificence that surrounds their kings and rulers the 'clothing of the state.'—'You may speak to the ears of others,' was the reply of an intelligent native to an Englishman's remark on this subject, 'but if you would be understood by my countrymen you must address their eyes.'" So says a describer of the history and manners of the Persians; and we suppose that there is some connection between the substitution of eyes for ears, just alluded to, and the eyes which appear in the extremity of the tail of the peacock.

When the peacock displays his charms to the admiring spectator, it is easy to see in his stiff, formal, stately, and majestic aspect, the intention to astonish and overpower, and the assumption of a superiority that commands everything to bow before it. The perfect parallel of this is in the Persian court, as will appear from the following description: "The importance of individuals and of kingdoms is measured among them by the degree of show which is displayed, and of the attention which is exacted by their envoys. If an embassador assume great dignity, the nation he represents is believed to be wealthy and powerful. If he enforce deference, and resent the slightest neglect, his sovereign is considered a mighty potentate, and worthy of friendship and respect. Hence the diplomatic abilities of a royal representative are measured by the obstinacy with which he resists any meditated encroachments, or contests a point of form at his reception, rather than by the firmness with which he conducts a difficult negotiation, or the wisdom he exercises in establishing a treaty.

"The ceremonies of the court of Persia are, in fact, a subject of the most minute study and attention. When the shah is seated in public, his sons, ministers, and courtiers, stand erect in their appointed places, their hands crossed upon their girdles, watching the looks of their sovereign, whose glance is a mandate. If he addresses an order or a question, a voice is heard in reply, and the lips of the speaker move, but not a gesture betrays animation in his frame. Should the monarch command him to approach, the awe he affects to feel permits him not to advance until the order has been several times repeated; and these behests are always enunciated in a deep, sonorous voice, and in the third person —the shah saying of himself, 'The king commands'—'The king is pleased,' while his attendants usually address him as '*Kibleh Allum*' (the object of the world's regard!) and preface their reply by the words 'May I be your sacrifice!'

"When a foreign embassador arrives, the court assumes its most solemn aspect, and its resources are taxed to dazzle the stranger as well by magnificence as the exhibition of uncontrolled power. As he approaches the royal residence a deep silence prevails: the men stand like statues; the horses themselves, as if trained to such scenes, scarcely move their heads.

"The envoy is received in a small apartment by one of the principal officers of government, who, after a delay more or less protracted according to the honor intended to be paid, leads him to the hall of audience, where the sovereign, clothed in glittering apparel, sits on a throne covered with jewels. A garden, divided into parterres by walks, and adorned with flowers and fountains, spreads its beauties before the ample windows. Twice is the stranger called upon to bow before the king of kings ere he approach the presence, to which he is marshalled by two officers of state with gold-enamelled wands. His name and country are announced, and he is commanded to ascend. Arrived near the throne, the deep and solemn voice of the sovereign utters the gracious '*Koosh Amedeed!*' after which, retiring to his appointed place, he receives permission to be seated."

Before closing this subject let us look at it in its more favorable aspect. The beauty we are speaking of is paradisiacal. It is not for mortals to clothe themselves in the livery of heaven, except as the wedding-garment that is indispensable to their admission to angelic society. Like the bride, they must have made themselves ready before they can enter the heavenly mansion; there must be none suffering for the necessaries of life, much less must they obtain heavenly robes at the expense of bread and of comfortable garments for the poor. Admiration must be gratified in the beauties of the sky and earth, in golden sunsets, flowers, insects, birds, all things that Nature has provided for all, and every object that Art has created for humanity. The peacock and the humming-bird are fond of flowers, but the difference between them is as the difference between an animal characteristic and a human:—

"Self-love and Reason to one end aspire,
Pain their aversion, pleasure their desire;
But eager that its object would devour,
This taste the honey, and not wound the flower."

The peacock devours the object, and is therefore a dangerous ornament in a flower-garden. Not so a human being, unless he be totally depraved. The Persians are fond of flowers, not merely as ornaments, but as the signs of spiritual beauty, and as associated with feelings of humanity and refinement. They have a festival, of which the following is a brief description:—

"The feast of the vernal equinox, the new-year of the ancient Persians, retains its importance in the reformed calendar, in spite of religious changes. On the birthday of the young Spring, when all Nature rejoices (and in no country is the transition from the gloom of winter more rapid and delightful than in Persia), the shah, by ancient custom, proceeds from his capital, attended by the ministers and nobles of his court, and a large body of troops, to an appointed place, where a magnificent tent is prepared, having in it the throne of state. The ceremonies commence with a grand review; tribute as well as presents from the governors of provinces, from the officers of state, and from all who are entitled to stand in the presence, are laid at the feet of his majesty. A week is thus spent in feasting and joy." Where else in the wide world is "May-day" kept in such a style as this? There is a sacrilegious element in it in the form of royal selfishness, but we see in it a bow of promise for the Persians.

CHAPTER XXIII.

THESE two heads, the one of a celestial and the other of a terrestrial genius, convey to us the idea of congenial spirits. Judging from the expression and contour of the face, and from the similarity in

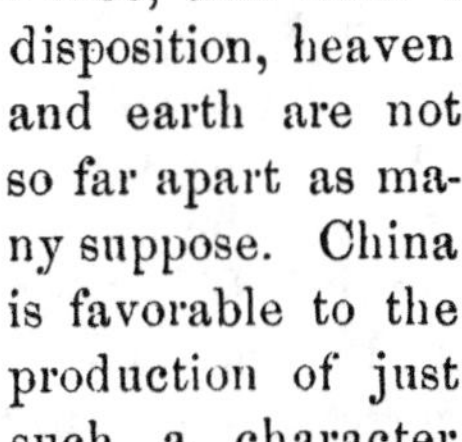

disposition, heaven and earth are not so far apart as many suppose. China is favorable to the production of just such a character

and physiognomy as we see here. The hog of that country, in the estimation of those who know how to distinguish a hog from a shark, is the perfection of beauty and excellence. The best point in the character of a hog is not a ravenous disposition, but simply a taste for anything and everything — an unbounded appetite, perfect digestion, and great tendency to grow fat. The hog-fancier is one who perceives the uses of the hog, and from these derives his knowledge of what the beauty and excellence of this animal consist in. We need not go far to find out the origin of our ideas concerning the beautiful: it is simply utility. When a person studies the points of beauty in a horse, an ox, a hog, a camel, a negro, an Irishman, a dancing-master, or any other living being, he will see that his ideas of beauty vary with the several uses to which they are severally adapted. The highest beauty is the highest use.

Now the comeliness of the Chinese is in remarkable agreement with that of the hog. Are not those half-closed, drowsy eyes, as seen in the portrait on the following page, a striking element of Chinese beauty? Can you not easily imagine that, exhibited in their perfection as they are in the softer sex, you might be smitten by them? The story of Narcissus becoming enamored of his own face on seeing it reflected in a brook, is not so absurd after all, for it is of eyes and features like their own that the Chinese, or any other race of human beings, are most likely to be enamored. The reason is, that there is one kind of beauty suited to one, and another to another, according to the country to which they adapt themselves, and to the uses they are intended to perform.

Let us do justice to the swine, and we shall see that he has points to be admired. If he has a taste adapted to everything, and an appetite that is not easily satisfied, he furnishes the most perfect correspondence to the intellectual taste and appetite of the Chinese, and their ability to digest and appropriate what they read, to become great with superfluity of learning, and of intellectual dimensions altogether unwieldy. We have heard of "learned pigs," and this term might be figuratively applied to the Chinese. The learning for which the pig has been distinguished is that of distinguishing one character or letter from another, and of picking out the blocks on which these are written, so as to spell words, under the direction, of course, of his master. This is precisely the kind of talent which is most remarkable in the Chinese. The eighty thousand characters in their language are nothing strange to them, but present an almost insurmountable obstacle to foreigners who would become acquainted with their literature. They regard literary acquirements as the sum total of intellectual greatness, and the man of letters is allowed a wide berth, not from dislike, but from his supposed capacities, and the great respect which is paid him. They designate the implements of writing (the brush, ink, paper, and marble) by a word which signifies the "four precious things."

But it would seem that this extraordinary literary appetite in the Chinese has its foundation in something more substantial. The celestials are the greatest epicures in the world, and, like the terrestrials, are rather indiscriminate in their choice of food—accepting as dainties rats, mice, cats, dogs, hogs, and a variety of unclean animals. Those great curiosities, the chopsticks, enable them to eat as hogs do; that is, by *throwing* the food into the mouth, a manner of eating that is to be observed in no other animal than the hog. If the hog had not the privilege of "pitching in" his food, he would not be a hog; neither would a Chinaman be a Chinaman if he did not use his chopsticks in eating. On this subject we quote the following from the French traveller La Place:—

"It seemed very doubtful whether I should be able to eat my rice grain by grain, according to the belief of Europeans regarding the Chinese custom. I therefore waited until my host should begin, to follow his example, foreseeing that, on this new occasion, some fresh discovery would serve to relieve us from the truly ridiculous embarrassment which we all displayed: in a word, our two Chinese, cleverly joining the ends of their chopsticks, plunged them into the bowls of rice, held up to the mouth, which was opened to its full extent, and thus easily shovelled in the rice, not by grains, but by handfuls."

Not merely as to the manner of eating, but as to the articles of food and the forms in which they are administered, do the Chinese resemble hogs. In illustration of this, we quote the following description from the same writer: "The first course was laid out in a great number of saucers of painted porcelain, and consisted of various relishes in a cold state, as salted earthworms, prepared and dried, but so cut up that I fortunately did not know what they were until I had swallowed them; salted or smoked fish, and ham, both of them cut into extremely small slices; besides which there was what they called Japan leather, a sort of darkish skin, hard and tough, with a strong and far from agreeable taste, which seemed to have been macerated for some time in water. All these et ceteras, including among the number a liquor which

I recognised to be soy — made from a Japan bean, and long since adopted by the wine-drinkers of Europe to revive their faded appetites or tastes — were used as seasoning to a great number of stews which were contained in bowls, and succeeded each other uninterruptedly. All the dishes, without exception, swam in soup. On one side figured pigeons' eggs, cooked in gravy, together with ducks and fowls cut very small, and immersed in dark-colored sauce; on the other, little balls made of sharks' fins, eggs prepared by heat, of which both the smell and taste seemed to us equally repulsive, immense grubs, a peculiar kind of sea-fish, crabs, and pounded shrimps. I had great difficulty in seizing my prey in the midst of these several bowls filled with gravy; in vain I tried to hold, in imitation of my host, this substitute for a fork between the thumb and the first two fingers of the right hand; for the cursed chopsticks slipped aside every moment, leaving behind them the unhappy little morsel which I coveted. It is true that the master of the house came to the relief of my inexperience (by which he was much entertained) with his two instruments, the extremities of which, a few moments before, had touched a mouth whence age and the use of snuff and tobacco had cruelly chased its good looks. I could very well have dispensed with such an auxiliary, for my stomach had already much ado to support the various ragouts, each one more surprising than another, which I had been obliged, *nolens volens*, to taste of."

We can not finish the description of the sumptuous habits of the Chinese, but enough has been said to show their resemblance in this respect to the hog. They may be also regarded as "hoggish" in that peculiarity of theirs, *the disposition to have everything to themselves*. This exclusiveness is assisted by large secretiveness, which is indicated in the expansion of the wing of the nostril, which sign is large in the hog, together with the sign of inquisitiveness, or the upward tendency of the end of the snout, constituting that peculiar form of nose called the "celestial." In the hog this particular form of the nasal protuberance is useful as well as ornamental. It answers the purpose of a prying curiosity, a

trait for which the Chinese are as remarkable as for their secretiveness. No doubt the Chinaman, judging from himself, attributes inquisitiveness to others, and this keeps his secretiveness in a constant state of excitement; and it is with great reluctance that he opens the gates of the celestial empire to earth-born foreigners.

The two faculties just spoken of give the hog and the Chinese a mining and delving disposition the very opposite of that which is implied in the appellation of the latter. They are for ever busy in obtaining the necessaries of life, except when supplied by others, and then they show extraordinary faculties of rest and sleep, as well as laziness. Earth is their mother, and they claim the indulgence of her lap and her fruitful rows of corn more than others of her children. They are wonderfully crowded together, and roll and tumble over each other in the struggle for a subsistence; for though their mother is planted on every hillside and valley, there are not rows enough for

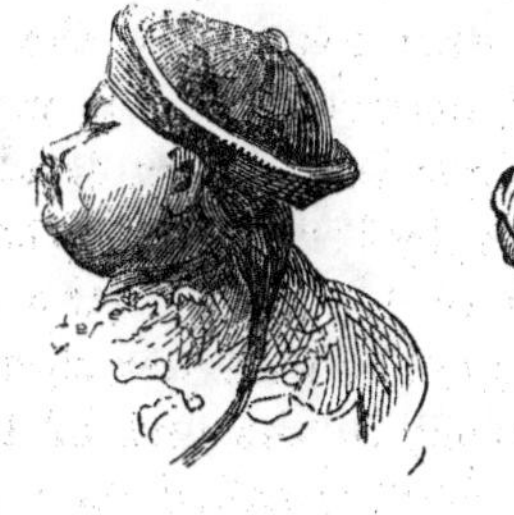

them all. The Chinaman has indeed many of the characteristics of the infant, and the infant is a "little pig." It would be easy to illustrate this, but we pass on to the signs of the Chinese and the hog loving the earth so well. One is, that they are both dirty. Says a work on China: "The great sin of the Chinese costume is the paucity of white linen, and con sequently of washing. Even their body-garment is sometimes a species of light silk, but capable of putrefaction. All the rest of their dress being of silks or furs, there is less demand for white calico or linen, in proportion to the numbers, than in any other country. They spread neither sheets upon their beds nor cloths on their tables, and the want of personal cleanliness has, of course, a tendency to promote cutaneous and leprous complaints." It should be observed, however, that scorbutic affections are natural to the hog, and it may be that in this respect the Chinese resemble him, though we can hardly suppose that his rolling himself in the dirt would tend to prevent it, as in the inferior animal.

The Chinese compare very well with the hog in respect to cruelty, tearing and rending, or whatever grows out of destructiveness and revenge, and the eating of garbage. The government of China is a wild boar: "The mandarin is preceded by a hundred executioners, who, with a sort of yell, announce his approach. Should any one forget to retire to the wall, he is severely whipped. On entering a city he can order any person, whom he chooses to have arrested, to be put to death, and no one can venture to defend him." As to the emperor, "when he goes abroad, all the people are obliged to shut themselves up in their houses. Whoever is found in his way is exposed to instant death, unless he turns his back, or lies flat with his face on the ground. All the shops by which he passes must be shut, and he never goes out without being preceded by two thousand officers, carrying chains, axes, and various other instruments of cruelty."

"Parents have the right to destroy or mutilate their children, thousands of whom are yearly exposed to perish in the rivers." They plead, in excuse for this, that they have not food for so many mouths, and the necessity of a living for themselves; and doubtless the sow, when she devours two or three of her numerous litter, may claim the benefit of the same apology. The Chinese "have one species of refinement on the score of skins. The young lamb *in utero*, after a certain period of gestation, is taken out, and its skin prepared, with its fine, silky wool upon it, for dresses, which of course require, on account of the small size of the skins, a great number of lambs to be thus 'untimely ripped.'" Who but people resembling the hog too literally would ever think of such a thing?

The Chinese and the hog are remarkable for subterfuge. They are excellent scavengers, as before illustrated. If one kind of food will not answer, another will: birds' nests, silkworm chrysalides, the tender shoots of the bamboo, things that nobody else would think of, are converted by the Chinese into food. They are willing, like beggars, to accept of anything. They are fond of disguises, and this fondness in the hog is gratified, together with his secretiveness, subterfuge, and inquisitiveness, when he rolls himself in a slough, and renders himself undistinguishable, or passes for a part of the plastic clay from which he was formed. The Chinese mustache has a filthy look, like something running out at the corner of the mouth, where the tusk of the hog makes its appearance, and is indicative of the same savage disposition. The Chinese and the hog are both characterized by very small feet; but whether the hog would render this peculiarity still more conspicuous, if he had reason, by compressing his feet, we can not say. He has certainly no disposition to

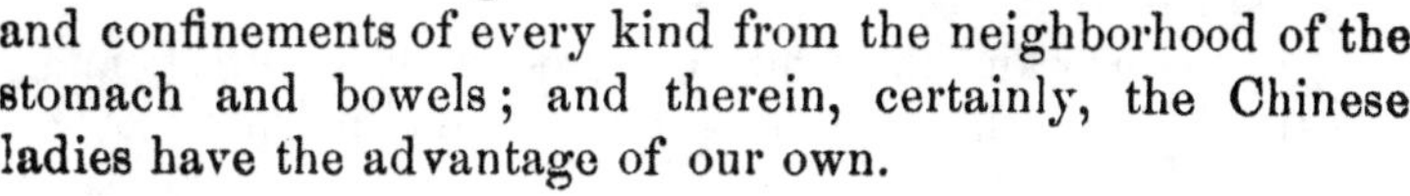

contract his waist, and the Chinese discard all ligatures and confinements of every kind from the neighborhood of the stomach and bowels; and therein, certainly, the Chinese ladies have the advantage of our own.

The hog loves a plastic bed, adapts it to his own mould, daubs the black pigment wherever his nose can carry it, paints in a very workmanlike manner the inside of his trough up to the very edge, an operation to which the softness and pliability of his snout are admirably adapted. In this respect he is not unworthy of being compared with the Chinese, whose fondness for working in clay, for moulding, glazing, painting, and leaving a stain, is well known. Both the hog and the Chinese exercise the faculty of moulding along with the faculty of protection, which makes them fond of trenches and strong walls, within which to ensconce themselves, and in this they show that degree of prudence which may with the greatest propriety be called "sconce." The hog treads the mortar, mixes the straw, digs the trench, from which he heaves up the wall; and the order which he observes, and the straightness of the line, show that he has an eye to a fortification—that he is capable, like an engineer, of laying out his plan, and of intimating what he wishes to have done. He is warned of the approach of a storm, and begins to look out for a squall, carrying straw in his mouth as his share of the materials for a primitive fortification, to make good his protection from the elements. Walking about with that peculiar air of self-importance that is ascribed to the hog, and which belongs to those who maintain a supreme right to the soil, he would yet prefer his sty or a mud-hovel to a palace, as a place to *live* in. In this they resemble the Chinese, who "endeavor to make a pompous appearance when they go abroad; and yet their houses are mean and low, consisting only of a ground floor." China abounds in canals and ditches, and the hog engages in such works of art as these, and loves to plough in the bottom of pools and stagnant waters for the means of subs'stence, in imitation of which the Chinese "cultivate the bottom of their waters, the beds of their lakes, ponds, and rivulets," and obtain from the mud such a variety of animal and vegetable food as entitle them to be ranked with hogs in the class *omnivora.*

As the hog and the Chinese agree so well in taste and appetite, and in the form, quality, and quantity of their food, it is to be expected that they would agree in corporosity. The added dimensions that come from a *deposition of fat in the Chinese empire*, might be illustrated by very numerous examples. "Those are thought to be most handsome who are most bulky," and it is worthy of observation and reflec tion that their gods, which embody their ideas of beauty and perfection, or of what is worthy of being admired, worshipped, and aimed at, have enormous stomachs, little feet, large ears, and small eyes, like the hog, and like themselves, only very much exaggerated. The hollow cheeks and meager aspect of many of the Chinese have hardly their parallel in the worst-conditioned and most perverted of hogs; but who does not know, if he will reflect upon it, that the Chinaman, like any other tea-drinker, tobacco-snuffer, opium-smoker, and what not, must be lean and shadowy—so much so, that you might almost rattle his bones? It is by virtue of his tea, which he keeps constantly over the fire and makes almost constant use of; and by virtue of his snuff, which he carries in a bottle that is seldom absent from his side, and ladles out with a spoon, to be snuffed up the nose; and by virtue of his opium, which, lying upon a couch, he spends hours in smoking—it is by virtue of these that he gives countenance to the idea with which he wishes to impress himself and others, viz., that he is *celestial.* It is remarkable that this claim is put forth by fat people, and by those who are epicurean in their disposition, rather more frequently than by others; but—

> "Were I as fat as stalled theology,
> Wishing would waste me to his shade again"—

and wishing to become celestial may have led the Chinese to the discovery of the use of tea; and in this they are more fortunate than certain of their emperors, who, in attempting to make themselves immortal, proved that the *elixir vitæ* was a misnomer. As to their opium-smoking, it is said that "a few days of this fearful luxury, when taken to excess, will give a pale and haggard look to the face; and a few months, or even weeks, will change the strong and healthy man into little better than an idiot skeleton."

Were we to mention all the points of congeniality between the Chinaman and the hog, it would swell this chapter to the dimensions they so much admire. We will notice in conclusion only this—a wonderful adaptation in respect to prowess, and disposition to the cultivation of the soil. Pope never made a greater mistake than when he said—

"The hog that ploughs not,"

for Nature has furnished this animal with a plough, and given him the ability and the disposition to use it. But we will bestow our compliments upon the Chinese rather than the hog. The annual festival in honor of agriculture speaks more for the honor of the Chinese than anything we have said of them yet. We quote the following:—

"Throughout the Chinese empire, agricultural improvement has in all ages been encouraged and honored. Ranking next to men of letters and officers of state, the cultivator of the soil is considered an honorable and useful member of society. It may be remarked here that, among the several grades of society, the cultivators of mind rank first; those of land are placed next; and the third station is assigned to manufacturers; while the exchangers of commodities or merchants rank lowest of all. A deep veneration for agriculture is inscribed on all the institutions in China. A homage to this primary art is still seen in the annual celebration by which the emperor makes a show of performing its operations. This anniversary takes places on the twenty-fourth day of the second moon, corresponding with our month of February. The monarch prepares himself for it by fasting three days; he then repairs to the appointed spot with three princes, nine presidents of the high tribunals, forty old and forty young husbandmen. Having offered a sacrifice of the fruits of the earth to the Supreme Deity, he takes in his hand the plough, and makes a furrow of some length, in which he is followed by the princes and other grandees. A similar course is observed in sowing the field; and the operations are completed by the husbandmen.

"An annual festival is also celebrated in the capital of

each province. The governor marches forth crowned with flowers, and accompanied by a numerous train bearing flags, adorned with agricultural emblems and portraits of eminent husbandmen; while the streets are decorated with lanterns and triumphal arches. Among other figures is a porcelain cow of enormous magnitude, carried by forty men, and attended by a boy who represents the genius of industry. At the close of the procession the image is opened, and found to contain numerous smaller cows of the same material, which are distributed among the people."

CHAPTER XXIV.

It is generally felt and acknowledged that the love for animals is closely allied to the love for children. When a man is convicted of a fondness for "pets," it is supposed that *petting* is one of the phases of his parental affection, and that he would pet his children in the same manner that he would his animals. It is taken for granted that an old lady who keeps parrots, or cats, or a lapdog, and shows them great attention, is simply exercising her faculty of "philoprogenitiveness," as the phrenologists would say, and that the degree of her fondness shows the degree of attachment she would have had for children if fortune had directed her affection in that channel.

It was before hinted that children are more nearly allied to animals than grown people; that Nature is the first parent of all, and that man has a foster-parent, by the name of Art, that instructs, refines, and purifies him, and thus distinguishes him from animals. This is reason enough why the love for children and the love for animals should be included in one.

But there is also in the mind of man a discrimination with regard to the several objects of parental affection. In childhood the resemblance to some particular animal is strongest, and wears off gradually, as the process of education advances; and as the fondness for pets implies that some animals are special favorites, and that others are not, of course there are a great number of *kinds* of children, and one person loves one kind and another another. Most persons, when asked if they are fond of children, can not honestly say "yes" without a qualification. They do not know exactly how to express their difficulty, not being aware of what the distinctions consist in; and hence one person says he is fond of children when they get largo enough to play; another says he is fond of infants; another says he is fond of children that have the air of a noble mother about them; another says that he is fond of them when Nature has given them features and expressions according to his own notions. It is on this principle that people are particularly fond of their own children, or that "every crow thinks her own young the whitest." Parental love seems often not to be developed until persons become parents; but the individual who is fond of all sorts of animals is fond of all sorts of children. This is true of those who have a sympathy for Nature in general.

As but few infants and young children resemble parrots, those who show a special fondness for these birds do so to the exclusion of an affection for children; they lavish all their love upon their pets, expend sums of money upon them, and if possible would cause them to inherit their fortunes. But those who see a great deal of beauty in little pigs, as thousands do, as is evident from their gazing upon them with admiration whenever they have an opportunity, and from their express declarations, find a multitude of children that they are fond of. When they look into the little pig-eyes of a child, their own eyes twinkle with delight and with a reflection from those; and when they look at its little porky cheeks, and at its little snouty face between, they wish to press those cheeks with their own, and to "measure noses" with that little turn-up nose, and to measure mouths with that little turn-up mouth, and it is ten to one if they do not gratify their desire.

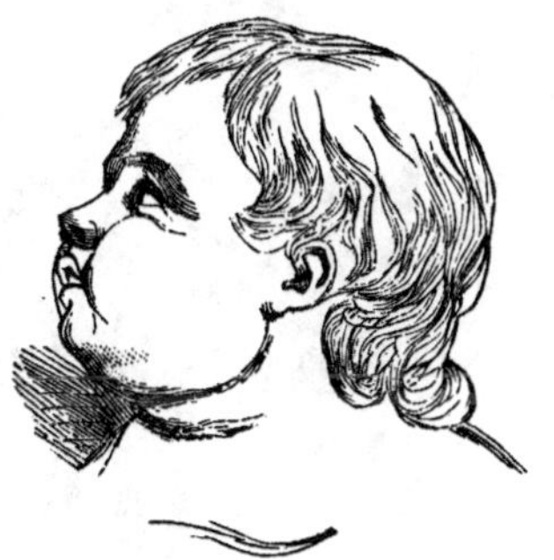

But the parental love of others refuses to descend to this seeming grossness: they could not caress a child like that represented above. Some little thing that resembled a puppy or a kitten would please them more, for they resemble dogs or cats, and from self-love they beget children in their own likeness, and from this principle they love them. They conceive children in their brains; these are their beau-ideals, and all others are the objects of invidious comparison and contrast.

There is in reality not much parental affection in the parents of children who are of the kind just represented. They are too selfish to extend their affection to anything that bears a likeness to themselves, for the more others are like themselves the more they regard them as rivals. They love only that which they receive, or have before received, or have the hope of receiving; and when they perceive that they have children (which was a thing they did not wish), they look upon it as a misfortune, and as something they must submit to because it can not be helped. The cultivation of family pride will go far toward making them content with their situation. Whatever is important in their estimation must come from themselves, must be derived from their own portliness, and must still be considered as a part of it, and there are no children in the world of the least consequence but their own. Their pride is enormously increased by an addition to their bulk, and they walk with an air of greater importance than before, and as if they were at particular pains to show themselves —The consideration that what they receive internally will add to their portliness adds also very greatly to their estimate of the high value and importance of eating. They are sensual in reference to everything which they receive, but sparing in reference to everything which they are doomed to part with; and if they give away anything, it is included in the debt which they pay to Nature, or is something useless.

The hog is an aristocratic individual, as is seen in the description of the person who bears a resemblance to him, and in various other hoggish dispositions that have not been mentioned. It is easy to see that the "Hermit of Belly-full" is hospitable to himself, and has no kindness to waste on children or on anybody else. He is partial to his own society, and dreads the approach of a guest, for he has nothing to spare—he has no more than he wants himself. He looks as if he were saying, "What have you come here for?"—as if he would say this to his first-begotten; and as if to the second he would say, "I've more mouths than I can feed already;" and as if to a beggar he would say, "I've nothing for you: get you gone, you dog you!" It may be that after dinner he will be good-natured, for the hog is good-natured when he is full, but this does not make him benevolent. Eating is his principal employment, and he spends a share of his time in measuring his dimensions by the quantity of air or water he is capable of displacing, for he blows like a porpoise, and rolls himself around, and views himself askance, and regards complacently the reflection which he sees in his broad mirror, which he keeps always in the dining-room and opposite his place at the table. The hog exhibits the same trait of character in his disposition to wallow out into a green pool, the surface of which shines like a metallic mirror, and there, with half-opened eyes, which show that he is not sleeping, to consider and enjoy himself. The man who resembles him does not *stand* before his mirror, but *sits down*, and congratulates himself on the results of his hearty appetite and his good digestion.

The hog receives attentions like a lord: they sit well upon him; and that high life is his natural element is evident from the fact that his eye has the expression of happiness and good cheer, when his wants are supplied without any trouble of his own. You may see, from the knowing expression of his eye, that he is "a pig in clover," for the knowledge of this fact gives his eye a wonderful deal of intelligence: he seems to see that his numerous retainers are bent upon making him happy, and his eye dances when he sees them dancing attendance upon him.

But who does not see that there is still more

meaning in that eye, if he can only get at it? To be well fed gives a man the appearance of benevolence. He can not find it in his heart to wish evil to those who wish him good; nay, he wishes them well for his own sake. This it is that is likely to be mistaken for benevolence in the eye of one who resembles the lucky hog we are speaking of. This happiness and good-nature, along with a determination to have what is wanted, expressed in the other parts of the countenance, favors roguishness, which is seen in those eyes more plainly, we might almost say, than the eye itself. You might fancy Francis Joseph, the emperor of Austria, with such eyes as those, taking the child first presented by the toes, one by one, and saying: "This pig says, 'I go get corn;' this pig says, 'I go too;' this pig says, 'I'll tell master;' this pig says, 'I don't care if you do;' this pig says, 'Queek! queek! can't get open gran'fer's barn-door!'" And the pig we see above answers to all these characters perfectly, with the addition that when he comes to the last he looks around for somebody to help him, expressing his desire to be admitted, and pointing with his nose to the place that he wishes to go to. He wants unlimited range, and has been so long pampered and indulged, that he has no thought of denying himself anything. We may say, speaking allegorically, that he is looking with his nose toward Hungary, which he associates in his mind with the hunger of that part of his countenance; and with his eyes toward Russia, asking assistance from that quarter for the gratification of his imperious desires. If there is any meaning to the word "piggish," as applied to human beings, surely it is applicable to the pig.

The animal we are speaking of has the appearance of being well dressed, which naturally accompanies good living: this takes place in anticipation of the dressing that will be given him preparatory to his receiving the title of "Pork." Nature demands this for her *protegé*, otherwise he would not be so smooth and sleek; and the doctors who do their share in the labor of "giving him a dressing," take shelter under the favorite motto that it is their business to help Nature in the accomplishment of her good intentions. It is vain for a pig to ask favor of a turkey, alias the Turk, for—

"Good mussulmen abstain from pork;"

but it is the most natural thing in the world for a pig to look to a goose for assistance, for the two are fitted to be companions; they have tastes in the same direction; they are in every way congenial, and can sympathize with each other heartily. Look at those eyes again: do they not look doatingly upon the fair, round form of the goose, alias the Russian? do they not say, "If you'll scratch my back, I'll scratch yours"? Are they not courting her for a helpmate, and telling her that she will make a good one? Ah! who has not felt what a world of expression there is in the eye of a pig? what winning confidence! what unity in all the infinite variety and phrases of feeling! all being included in one consuming, absorbing emotion, *self-love!*

Too great a degree of this affection eats a man up. It makes a beggar of him; it takes the starch out of his ears, robs him of his cleanliness, together with his dressy appearance, and clothes him with rags and tatters. The more clothing he has on the more poor and miserable he looks; and as it is the same with the hog, the dressing of this animal consists in scraping away the clothing he has on, as a gardener scrapes away dirt. For the illustration of these observations, compare the preceding hog with the one following. "What a fall is that, my couutrymen!"—and this in consequence of supreme selfishness, when the means for gratifying it, and for being made happy and good-natured, are taken away! He calls for help still; he is dependent on others. It is so with the person who resembles him. As the means of subsistence are gone from his head, he holds out his hat

to receive them at second hand; and he holds a staff in his hand to pick his way with, showing what dry picking the gutters afford him, and to signify how little supper he has to lean upon. His staff is an emblem of the "staff of life," which is the special object of his pursuit, and it impresses the mind with the idea that he is a pilgrim and a stranger, and is looking for something that he can't find. A well-disposed, benevolent individual would suppose that it was a "city out of sight," but it is merely what the coming hog is looking for and can't see till he has hit it with his nose, when instantly he seizes upon it with all the interest of a new discovery.

It may not be amiss to inquire why a person who is supremely selfish should be in so destitute and miserable a condition. It is simply this: his desire for everything, his greediness to eat all the world up, deprives him of taste and discrimination. This accounts for the want of taste in the hog: he would rob the very plants of their nourishment—

filch from the soil the decaying vegetables and the offal that had been placed there for the production of verdure. He seizes first upon that which is thrown away, as being that which is most likely to be lost if he does not get it; by this means he expects to acquire the world, for he knows that the soil is the origin of capital, as many a politician will tell you, and that the pennies make the pounds. The miser and the beggar are of this description: the two are often united in one. It is not in the sign of economy that their beggarly disposition is indicated, but in their resemblance to swine. The hog-formation is very commonly met with in the politician also. The beggar, with his hat in his hand, is electioneering for votes, and may not be aware that there is a hole in the bottom of his hat (we do not say *top*, for, like himself, his hat is inverted), for the votes to fall out of. His subserviency, submission, independence, and firmness, which belong to the top of his head, are turned downward, and that portion of his head leaks.

What an ashy hue, covering a fire of life that can scarcely glimmer through it, is seen in the eye of that hog! You can judge from the rest of the countenance that the eye of that beggar is the same. They are such eyes as glare upon you in nightmare, and are expressed by the term *spectral*. They indicate that there is appetite without taste; that the spectre is of the kind whose god is their belly, and who haunt those who pay reverence to the same deity. Soft, rich, luxuriant eyes indicate a great deal of taste, and less appetite: they are full of life and beauty, and in every respect the very reverse of those of the two beggars before represented.

The pig is never negligent of appearances, as we see in the last example, as well as in the preceding; and there is one thing that he has a particular regard for, and that is, the looks of his tail. In the chapter concerning the rhinoceros it was seen how Appetite, which resides in the head, gains the mastery of Insensibility, which resides in the tail; and it was seen that in the hog the former takes pride in showing that the latter is its servant, while in the rhinoceros the two are on terms of friendship with each other. The hog has the same sort of pride in his tail that the aristocrat has in his footman who rides modestly and proudly at the tail end of his coach; and the pride comes from the same source and in the same manner in the latter instance as in the former. The hog looks askance at his tail, and twists and flourishes it about, before he touches the morsel that is under his nose, as if he would ask permission to eat it (the tail being the older), and would at the same time twit the tail of his ability and determination to do as he pleased, and would also congratulate that member on its share of the bounty, and on having so lordly a master. The head, be it observed, is synonymous with appetite, and the tail with insensibility, as was explained in the chapter referred to.

However much an aristocratic pig may acquire smoothness by the shortening of his hair, and by giving erectness to his ears instead of to his bristles, he never loses the least scrap of his tail, unless by the hand of violence. In fact, the more he has the appearance of being dressed for the market, the more he figures with his tail, running through all the Arabic characters, from 1 to 9. Such a close calculator is he, that he never misses his figure, and it would never do for him to part with the member with which he does his reckoning, inasmuch as he reckons upon it so highly: as well might a noble lady part with her footman as he part with the evidence of his nobility; there is no keeping up appearances without it!

In the Chinese, who were proved in the last chapter to resemble hogs, this trait of character is exhibited to perfection. No Chinaman, who lays any claim to respectability, would part with his "pig-tail." It is natural to him, and he improves it by cultivation. His dressing his head in the manner of dressing a pig is a sign of consequence, and a consequence of high living or of high life; and in the degree that he does this he improves his pig-tail; he reckons upon it, he sets store by it, and would not part with it for love, though he might possibly for money. Love with the Chinese is not very strong, but it is made fleshly by the exceeding grossness which they share in common with the swine. This is proved by the disgusting fact that in Canton and its suburbs there are sixteen hundred brothels, each of which pays, for a monthly license to the police, two hundred dollars! Thus love and money are proved to be synonymous with those who resemble swine — a rule as applicable to one country as to another. The hog-formation is common to the authorities; and it is sometimes said figuratively of the hog that his proportions are aldermanic, but this does not prove that there are not moral qualities in the alderman to render the animal nature entirely subservient.

Speaking of the Chinese in respect to love, they are jealous of their wives, and pen them up as they do pigs, thus acknowledging that there is a relationship between them. Says Mr. Davis: "It is the fate of the emperor's wives and women o reside for ever within the walls of the palace; and, after his death, they are confined for life in a prison called the Palace of Chastity.'" As much as they wish to enlarge themselves, and to have "room and verge enough," they wish to cramp and confine their women, and show that above all others on the face of the earth they deserve the title of "lords of creation." Hence a woman is esteemed beautiful in their eyes in proportion as she is little, and a man is esteemed beautiful in proportion as he is fat and large. Hence, too, they cramp the feet of their women, which are the organs most likely to run abroad, and make them a great deal littler than Nature made them. As soon as a female is born, if she be of the higher class, her toes are doubled down under her feet, and tightly bandaged, so that at the period of maturity the entire fore part of the foot looks as if it had been amputated, while the sides and ankle are swelled to an enormous extent; and these feet, manufactured according to their science of pedology as applied to women, they call the "golden lilies," in allusion doubtless to the modesty of which the lily is the emblem, and which this lesson is intended to inculcate. If this is not hoggish, what other of the traits that we have enumerated may be called so?

As we progress with our subject we must refer occasionally to our text, "Man is an animal." That all men are not the same *kind* of animals is a clear deduction from the facts that have been presented, and it is fortunate that they are not. If the Chinaman resembles the hog, he must have a particular admiration and fondness for that animal: he must rest back upon it when he acknowledges his dependence upon Nature, and feels his relationship to his mother earth; and inasmuch as the hog is not a fit animal to be rode upon, he must rear himself upon its flesh. What the ox is to the English, the hog is to the Chinese. This appears from the fact that twenty-four thousand pigs are slaughtered daily in the city of Canton. According to our notions, a pig would be a strange animal to offer in sacrifice to a hero or to the gods;

but in the fifteen hundred temples dedicated to Confucius there are, among the animals sacrificed annually, twenty-seven thousand pigs! So high an honor as to be offered in sacrifice in company with sheep and lambs, or even alone, was never conferred upon the hog in any other country than China. So absurd a thought never entered the head of anybody less ridiculous than the Chinaman—but "no dispute about taste."

It has been already observed that the Chinaman has a taste of his own. It behooves him to make use of whatever external attractions are in accordance with it, and to make the most of these while young, for when he gets old he is excessively ugly, and his wife is no better looking than he. "Pretty little pigs—ugly old sow!" is especially applicable to China; but the pig-tail is so supremely beautiful, that the loss of minor beauties of complexion, freshness, and expression, are not missed. There is, however, a significance in the shaving of the head. It indicates that the individual is formed to receive impressions on the brain, and that the mind is cleared from brushwood, and prepared to receive seed into a virgin soil; or that it is like a sheet of fair paper, to be written upon; that it is, in short, an infant mind, plastic, faithful to the impression that is made upon it, suited to the study of letters and words, learning its lessons by rote, and following copy, or imitating, to perfection. Hence the Chinese should be scholars, and they who resemble them should be men of letters, and the hog himself should be literary. We should see the former surrounded with books and papers in orderly confusion, in the midst of his wealth and in the centre of his empire, having an eye to the whole, and ready to dispose of each particular object in its proper order, and according to the rule—

"Discord is harmony not understood,
All partial evil universal good"—

and the hog we should see surrounded with straw, in a cell that is thoroughly littered, where he can feel perfectly at home, and improve and grow fat, and enjoy himself, instead of living in dampness and wallowing in the mire.

It is a fact well worthy of observation that the men of most extensive learning have a resemblance to the hog. We could give numerous examples of this, but one will be sufficient—

that of Erasmus, who is seen to have the air and manner of the wild-boar. Appetite for intellectual food, which shall cause the mind, by growing, to become enlarged, corresponds to appetite for the food of the body; and as the hog has an appetite and relish for everything, and can digest everything that he has the least inclination to swallow, and never becomes disgusted or sick at anything that can be appropriated to the formation of

n animal, so it is in respect to the individual who resembles hog, and to the food that is capable of being appropriated o the formation of a human mind. The portrait on the preceding page is of Erasmus reading; and the boar looks as if he were in a brown study—as if he were consuming the midnight oil, or lard, or fatness, which is very likely to be wasted away by too great attention to books. Looking at the eye of that animal, you can hardly help imagining that he is reading by candle-light, and that supreme silence reigns around him—that he is reading the great book of Nature while she is asleep. He resembles the bear very strongly, and there is an important relation between the hog and the bear, as will be seen by-and-by.

CHAPTER XXV.

It is not so easy to idealize the bear into an eagle as to change the bull into a lion; but the polar bear (see page 203) is sufficiently powerful of himself, and would have the advantage over the lion of being a *truthful* emblem of a great and powerful nation. When the lion shall eat straw like an ox. the polar bear may be our national ensign. The United States should stand confessed the "Ursus Major," the object of universal interest, the "polar star" of Freedom throughout the world.

With the exception of man, the polar bear is the brightest example of conjugal attachment which the world affords, and parental love is here more beautifully and wonderfully exemplified than in the eagle. What nobler emblem, therefore, of the character of his government, or what more appropriate badge of his nationality, could "Brother Jonathan" require? Next to this, or perhaps we should say before it, we would choose the Indian, with his bow and arrows.

There is a relation of *harmony* between the hog and the bear, and this implies opposition as well as similarity, and this opposition must be maintained. The king of Naples resembles that kind of horse that has most resemblance to the bull; and here we have a specimen of a Yankee who resembles most that kind of bear which bears the strongest resemblance to the hog. Th Syrian bear (which this is) approximates very closely to tl wild-boar, and is as ugly in disposition as he is in looks. You recognise in him the child-hating savage that Indian

mothers hold up as objects of terror to their little ones. Yankee mothers do so too; and if you should look in their faces you would see that mixture of cunning and cruelty, that unfeeling mockery, that thoughtless insensibility, which you see here.

The polar bear is the very contrary of all this. He has both the ability and the will to maintain his rights, and therein he is worthy to be honored. As male and female, in their mutual fondness for their offspring, which is based on their mutual affection for each other, they present the most perfect emblem of a true government that the world affords. They are governed by their young, for parental love rules them, and it is this which influences their cubs; and so a republic is governed by the weak and dependent more than by the great and strong. The "Russian bear" (by which we mean the Russian government) is the very reverse of republican, for it resembles a hog, and a hog resembles a goose. Russia takes its cue from China, and in connection with the fact that the Chinese wear queues, or pig-tails, it should be observed that the emperor Paul adopted the pig-tail, and introduced it into the army. His courage and military display were peculiarly Chinese, except that they partook more of the nature of the goose than of the hog.

There are three personages of whom the distich is true—

13

"Great is thy power, and great thy fame,
Far kenned and noted is thy name"—

two of them called "Nicholas," and the other the bear that is now pretty well understood to be a bug-bear. Whether the son of Paul, who represents the Russian bear at present, inherits the formidable qualities of his father, is not yet fully decided. The bug-bear rushes suddenly from under cover, and cries, "Boo!" which is a very common practice with the hog.

We must, however, keep to our text, which is the resemblance between the bear and the Yankee. This resemblance, as before observed, is particularly strong. As truth perverted is worse falsehood than any other, and as hypocrisy is more infernal than any other kind of wickedness, so that kind of bear that is perverted into a near resemblance to the hog resembles the meanest sort of a Yankee, than whom there can be no greater impostor on the face of the earth. Than such a one there can also be no more unprincipled tyrant, or, in other words, inconsistent republican, to be found. A sneaking, under-ground miner, descending lower than the hog—delving for sordid gain—pandering to the strongest—is such a resemblance to bears, that disgrace the name of their species, to be found on the western continent?

As the resemblance to the hog often shows itself in an extraordinary literary appetite, we are not surprised to find that the ursine sloth (which, according to natural history, would be more properly called the susine bear) has a decided resemblance to the literary loafer. The specimen on the page following is a rare character among the native Indians, and yet he has an existence even there. You may recognise him in that peculiar lip, which bespeaks the ambition for distinc-

tion; in that peculiarly-shaped nose, which indicates the ability to run itself into the ground; and in that general resemblance to the long-lipped bear which indicates extraordinary laziness, and the disposition, and thence the necessity, of

sharing in the prey that is taken by the more courageous and noble of the species. The same dispositions, if they did not follow so closely upon the hog as to produce a literary turn, and were not so ursine as to produce an indisposition to physical exertion, would make the petty despot, lording it on his own domains, like the autocrat of Russia on his, supported and kept in power by the labor and indulgence of others.

One of the marks of degeneracy in the bear and in the Yankee is a peculiar flat-headedness, the result of too near an approximation to the hog. This indicates "a flat," in the ordinary acceptation of the term, when applied to character. Here is a Yankee loafer that is allowed to belong to the class

to which this particular designation is applicable. Bearishness is conspicuous in every limb and feature, and in the very

look, but it is like the old-fashioned bearishness which is indigenous to the Old World mingled with that which is indigenous to the New. His appetite, you may be sure, is enormous, and makes a particular demand for pancakes. His resemblance is to an old-country bear, one that carries him a good way off from our immediate sympathy: yes, the Thibet bear is like him; they two look enough alike to be brothers. Which is the greater loafer it would be difficult to tell.

The Flat-head Indians, by-the-by, are an example of what is indicated by this peculiar form of the physiognomy. By increasing the flatness, they illustrate the self-satisfaction which is characteristic of folly. Their resemblance to the bear is quite remarkable, and so is that of every other tribe of American Indians. The Yankee resembles the Indian in whatever constitutes a resemblance to the bear, and too often in those things which constitute a resemblance to the hog. The Indian has small hands and feet, and therein he differs from the bear, but between him and the Chinaman a striking similarity of features and expressions has been often observed. This is invariably the case with the meaner sort of Indians and the same class in China. The principle of degeneracy in this case is a loss of distinction between the hog and the bear—a sort of fusion and amalgamation of the two—and this takes place, although the Indians and the Chinese never see each other.

Above is a characteristic Indian face—and it is seen to have a great deal of Yankee expression in it. The grizzly bear is the variety that claims the honor of this comparison. There is nothing of that leering, sneaking, dishonest expression which there is in the foreign bears and in the countenances that resemble them, but a straight-forward, hungry, mind-his-own-business expression which it is gratifying to meet with in a savage of such extraordinary prowess. In California there is a tribe of Indians, called Root-diggers, whose track is so like that of the grizzly bear, that it can only be distinguished by the size. The ball of the foot is more deeply indented in the ground in consequence of their treading more heavily on that part of the foot, like an animal. They are thought by some to be a link between man and brute, as if it were possible for such a link to exist. And why is this? It is because their resemblance to the bear has degenerated into that of the hog. They subsist entirely on roots and acorns, refusing flesh, and having no knowledge of agriculture. The only article they are capable of manufacturing is a basket, so tightly woven as to hold water; and this is invariably conical, so that when they set it down they must make a hole in the ground to receive it. This reminds us of the Chinese cap, and of the form that is characteristic of the Chinese architecture. They make themselves holes to crawl into by sticking bushes into the ground, bending them over, and placing dirt upon the top; and there they live like hogs. They propagate their species at the season proper to animals, and have the smallest degree of parental love, as they have not the least of the conjugal. They converse more by the motions of their bodies than by words, and seem to know scarcely anything. They spend most of their time upon their haunches. They are naked and exceedingly filthy. Their arms are short and stubby, the bone from the shoulder to the elbow being long in proportion to the forearm, the hand bearing no small resemblance to a paw, and the whole arm bent and inclined inward, like the hind feet of the bear. Their faces are ugly, and vacant of anything human except in so small a degree that it is scarcely to be perceived. In short, they illustrate perfectly the principle that confounding the resemblance of the bear with that of the hog is the lowest degradation to which it is possible to attain.

If we were going to have a sermon on that subject, it could

not be more appropriately given than by one who resembles a bear, as it must be supposed that such a one would have a better appreciation of the subject than any other. The person who resembles such a bear as this must have a tongue, and be able to use it. He will paw about his ideas over the heads of his audience, until he has magnetized them into a sound sleep! He is no "flat," as you can see at a glance, but to

be at the opposite extreme is almost as bad:—

"His speech is a fine sample, on the whole,
Of rhetoric which the learned call rigmarole."

You can not doubt of his ability to do justice to pork and beans, and that he would prefer dumplings to pancakes:—

"The large, round dumpling, rolling from the pot,"

is the signal for extraordinary preparations. The reason for his head being so round is, its perfect sympathy with his stomach. The bear that resembles him in this and other respects is a Bornean, and one that killed himself with kindness, in the benevolent labor of endeavoring to satisfy appetite.

An Indian is capable of compensating in a single meal for a fast of several days, and of voluntarily abstaining for a week in anticipation of a bear-hunt; for hunger stimulates destructiveness, and goads him to desperation. He needs a bastinado like this to compel him to kill the bear, for the bear is his divinity in form, his beau-ideal, the very perfection of that savage nature which he delights in.

"The pursuit of these animals," says a writer on natural history, "is a matter of the first importance to some of the Indian tribes, and is never undertaken without much ceremony. A principal warrior gives a general invitation to all the hunters. This is followed by a strict fast of eight days, in which they totally abstain from food, but during which the day is passed in continual song. This is done to invoke the spirits of the woods to direct the hunters to the places where there are abundance of bears. They even cut the flesh in divers parts of their bodies, to render the spirits more propitious. They also address themselves to the spirits of the beasts slain in preceding chases, and implore these to direct them to an abundance of game. The chief of the hunt now gives a great feast, at which no one dares to appear without first bathing. At this entertainment, contrary to their usual custom, they eat with great moderation. The master of the feast touches nothing, but is employed in relating to the guests ancient tales of feats in former chases; and fresh invocations to the spirits of the deceased bears conclude the whole. . . .

"As soon as a bear is killed, a hunter puts into his mouth

a lighted pipe of tobacco, and, blowing into it, fills the throat with smoke, conjuring the spirit of the animal not to resent what they are about to do to its body, or to render their future chases unsuccessful. As the beast makes no reply, they cut out the string of the tongue, and throw it into the fire. If it crackle and shrivel up (which it is almost sure to do), they accept this as a good omen; if not, they consider that the spirit of the beast is not appeased, and that the chase of the next year will be unfortunate."

But the Indian must give way. We call the English "John Bull;" in return for the compliment, we think they

should call us "Neighbor Bruin." The largest rivers, lakes, bears, and Yankees, are to be found here. The American

who looks across the water for his ideas and other commodities will resemble the European bear, which has more of a swinish look and disposition than our own; or he will resemble the grizzly bear in the "Zoological Gardens." The American black bear, in the degree that he approaches the pig, is less noble than some of the other varieties, but his look is tha of a genuine Yankee notwithstanding. The foregoing is a regular "Down-Easter," and the animal that looks like his shadow is an old-fashioned New England bear. Dress "Brother Jonathan" (of whom this is an accurate representation) in Indian costume, and you could almost swear that he was an Indian, and that intercourse with the pale faces had turned him white.

There is a style of American face superior to this: it is that which is most commonly met with in the capitol of the nation; and there is a variety of Indian face that corresponds with it. The Americans with this cast of countenance are of the grizzly variety; they are hard to kill, and, under severe provocation, when their revenge is roused, they are fearful enemies to grapple with. The temperament is melancholic, and therewith mild and gentle, but exceedingly powerful. The Indian, like the bear, spends his life in the woods, is taciturn, dark, gloomy, and retired, and by nature a perfect savage; but by distinguishing these traits from those which are similar in the hog, we have them represented on a higher plane, as in the variety of American character just referred to. This resemblance is seen in the gait and posture as well as in the face.

But the polar bear, represented on the following page, with his fine Indian counterpart, resembles a nobler race of Americans still. These are they who represent greatness, the pillars of the constitution, with clear, cold intellects, touched only by moonbeams, that have no power to dissolve them. They represent truth, uninfluenced by fear or favor. With less of clemency, tenderness, and forbearance, than the last mentioned, they are nevertheless the guardians of these, and as such they loom up in the distance, cloud-capped and dismal, and —

———"like giants stand
To sentinel enchanted land."

And yet under that cold exterior there is the lava of love; under that snow-white mantle there is a warm heart that can not endure a nearer approach to the sun; beneath that countenance, "emotionless as the sphinx," there is the well-spring of sympathy and good feeling:—

———"The gloomy outside
Contains the shining treasure of a soul,
Resolved and brave."

The cavern, overhung with ice-crags, which he makes his home, is the guard of domestic virtue; obtained with difficulty, it is secure from danger, and the love which conquers all things preserves the treasure which it obtained by toil and suffering.

The strength, bravery, faithfulness, and parental affection of the polar bear, are so interesting as to be familiar to every reader; but for that very reason we

may venture to quote the following in illustration of the noble virtues that may be set forth, or at least symbolized, by a savage monster, being those very traits in the animal nature upon which should be reared the superstructure of American character, and hence of American institutions. We would remark here that the courage of the white bear is essential to his other good qualities:—

"Of the ferocity of the polar bear, Barentz gives a striking proof. In Nova Zembla they attacked his sailors, carried them off in their mouths with the utmost facility, and devoured them in sight of their comrades. A few years ago, some sailors in a boat fired at and wounded one. In spite of his receiving another shot, he swam after the boat, and endeavored to climb into it. One of his feet was cut off with a hatchet, but he still pursued the aggressors to the ship. Numerous additional wounds did not check his fury: mutilated as he was, he ascended the ship's side, drove the sailors into the shrouds, and was following them thither, when a mortal shot stretched him dead on the deck.

"But even this formidable animal is not without its good qualities. It is a faithful mate and an affectionate parent. Hearne tells us that, at certain seasons of the year, the males are so much attached to their mates, that he has often seen one of them, on a female being killed, come and put his paws over her, and rather suffer himself to be shot than abandon her.

"While the Carcase frigate, which went out some years ago to make discoveries toward the North pole, was locked in the ice, early one morning the man at the mast-head gave notice that three bears were making their way very fast over the frozen ocean, and were directing their course toward the ship. They had, no doubt, been invited by the scent of some blubber of a walrus that the crew had killed a few days before, which had been set on fire, and was burning on the ice at the time of their approach. They proved to be a she-bear and her two cubs, but the cubs were nearly as large as the dam. They ran eagerly to the fire, and drew out of the flames part of the flesh of the walrus that remained unconsumed, and ate it voraciously. The crew from the ship threw upon the ice great lumps of the flesh of the sea-horse which they had still remaining. These the old bear fetched away singly, laid every lump before her cubs as she brought it, and dividing it, gave to each a share, reserving but a small portion to herself. As she was fetching away the last piece, the sailors levelled their muskets at the cubs, and shot them both dead; and in her retreat they wounded the dam, but not mortally. It would have drawn tears of pity from any but unfeeling minds to have marked the affectionate concern expressed by this poor beast in the last moments of her expiring young ones. Though she was herself dreadfully wounded, and could but just crawl to the place where they lay, she carried the lump of flesh she had fetched away, as she had done others before, tore it in pieces, and laid it before them; and when she saw that they refused to eat, she laid her paws first upon one and then upon the other, and endeavored to raise them up. When she found she could not stir them, she went off, and when she had got to some distance she looked back and moaned. Finding this to no purpose, she returned, and, smelling round, began to lick their wounds. She went off a second time as before; and, having crawled a few paces, looked again behind her, and for some time stood moaning. But still her cubs not rising to follow her, she returned to them again, and, with signs of inexpressible fondness, went round pawing them and moaning. Finding at last that they were cold and lifeless, she raised her head toward the ship, and uttered a growl of despair, which the murderers returned with a volley of musket-balls. She fell between her cubs, and died licking their wounds."

CHAPTER XXVI.

This man resembles an Indian (foreigner though he be), and it is plain that he resembles both the Yankee and the bear. There is something in the look of the eye (a kind of Indian squint), and something in the cast of the nose and lip, and the angle of the mouth, and in the hair, that shows a remarkable agreement with the accompanying bear, which is

one of the grizzly bears in the Zoological Gardens. Watch those eyes narrowly (the bear's eyes), and you will see something roguish in them: *that* is Yankee roguishness. It is coupled, you see, with a wonderfully honest expression in the other parts of the countenance, and with a *tout ensemble* that excites your sympathy, and prepares you to be taken in. Your first impression is that he is in a deplorable situation, and that he would not deceive you for all the world, and you are ready to give him as good a bargain as he asks. You feel assured that he is sufficiently self-sacrificing to take up with "a living profit," and to live on porridge in order that you may be supplied with all the articles of luxury and refinement that you desire. He makes you think that, being in want of the necessaries, he parts with his things at a sacrifice; that you would very greatly oblige him if you would consult your own interest; or that you are a very benevolent individual, without any eye to selfish advantage—whichever you please: and the result may be, that you will exchange necessaries for luxuries, and be in want of the former while he enjoys them both. There is a great disposition in people to put confidence in the bear, but he is generally known to be more treacherous than he looks. Again we say, study those eyes, for they are a study: do you not see that they "reckon" and "kind o' calculate"? They are full of study—there are volumes in them.

The Yankee says frankly that he "guesses," for like other people he attaches merit to his peculiarities. It is "speculation" that you see in those eyes, both the bear's and the man's. You can discover in that man's countenance that his head is full of plans and projects. He would make a good representative in Congress, for it is such like people that are sent there. The bear represents the American people, and it is very proper that their representatives in Congress should be bears in various ways, as they are proved to be. They look like the preceding animal when they are thinking of the "loaves and fishes," but they are "ravenous as bears" when it comes to a demonstration of the principle that "to the victors belong the spoils." But this too literal resemblance to the bear is illustrated chiefly in personal and sectional interests, while the "affairs of the nation" call for a resemblance upon a higher plane, where the moral and intellectual faculties predominate over the animal.

The older the Americans grow, the more they look and act like bears, provided the animal nature is not kept under by cultivation and refinement. Observe how much the foregoing bear resembles, in posture and in everything, the remnant of old people who come under the denomination of "revolutionary soldiers." In the manner of standing there is something original; it looks like standing to make a speech of four hours' length; it is Websterian, is it not? The walk is equally singular; it is a kind of "Indian trot," a gait which the green Yankee has fallen into as if it were natural to him. The Indian female here presented is an example of it; and the following, which is the grizzly bear in motion, exhibits the gait in its original perfection. It is evident, too, that the "Indian dance" and the "bear-dance" are very similar; and Yankee dancing differs very little from either, as illustrated by Darley in the portrait of Ichabod Crane taking part in a dance, in which the position of the arms and the motion of the nether extremities are worthy of Bruin.

The Indian is seen generally looking down; he walks with a limberness of the knees; he sets down the whole foot at once, but rises upon the toe when the foot leaves the ground: he turns his toes inward, and his fingers outward when he

rests his hands; and in these and other ursine resemblances the modern native American is his inferior. But as noble a superstructure may be built upon this basis as upon any other, and before we get through we may say "a nobler." Here is the face of an Indian, a Chippeway warrior, that resembles the grizzly bear, while it exhibits the signs of benevolence, probity, and justice, with prudence and discretion. His name, Meta-Koosega, or Pure Tobacco, compared with the names of other Indian warriors, is expressive of rare virtue and excellence;—and should you meet him in the forest, you would not doubt for a moment, on looking at his face, of his willingness to smoke with you the pipe of peace. There is something in the temperament and contour, the gait and carriage, and in the general expression, that constitutes a striking resemblance between the Indian and the bear.

It is well known that the parent-bear and the cub are very much attached to each other. The passion of parental love in the former is indicated by the length and elevation of the loins, of which the polar variety is the strongest example. We have read that a bear, having lost her cubs, has carried off pigs from a sty, and adopted them as her own—which was most natural, considering that there is so much affinity between the hog and the bear, and that parental love in the latter is so very strong. The length and vigor of the loins in the squaw, indicating the same quality of parental love as in the bear, is very great, and it is known that the Indians have many times stolen children from the whites and brought them up in their own way. On the following page is the portrait of a female who was reared by Indians, having been captured by them in infancy; and we see how completely she is metamorphosed into a resemblance of her foster-parents.

14

The change appears to have been inimical to beauty, perhaps because it was too sudden, or because the materials were not of the right kind.

Parental love in the bear is reciprocated by an almost equal degree of filial affection on the part of the cub. In the young Indian the affection for parents is very strong. The whole race of aboriginal Americans—that are worthy of the name—are celebrated for their love and reverence for their forefathers and the graves of their ancestors. Filial affection, which reciprocates parental, causes the cub and the Indian child to be more fully formed than others at the same age, and to be early developed but not precocious, in order that they may do as much for their parents as their parents have done for them. This mutual strength of parental and filial affection has the mutual love of the parents for its foundation and no other; and this foundation is stronger in the Indian than in any other savage in the world, and stronger in the bear than in any other beast. The poignant grief and suffering of the Indian when his wife and children are taken from him by the malice of an enemy, show the strength and nobleness of his nature, and how excellent a foundation for a superstructure of civilization and refinement is a resemblance to the bear. As the conjugal relation is the origin of all others, so conjugal love is the basis of all the domestic and social affections, and all the relations of life are dependent upon these. Brother Jonathan, therefore, in his resemblance to the Indian and the bear, has a more glorious destiny than any nation in the world, and it is only a degeneracy like that of some of the Indian tribes into a resemblance to the hog (which is the very opposite of the bear in respect to conjugal, parental, and filial affection) that will destroy him.

Be it observed that filial love is appropriate to the child, though it reciprocates parental affection and is like parental love in relation to second childhood, and that it preserves childhood and develops manhood at the same time. The bear, the Indian, and the Yankee, agree in this: they exhibit a remarkable degree of forwardness at the outset, and at the same time an uncouthness of figure and gesture that is in ludicrous contrast with the shrewdness of the intellect. The early development of manhood, and of the bodily and mental strength appropriate to it, together with the preservation of childhood, and the consequent backwardness and immaturity, are illustrated in Daniel Webster (a portrait of whom is presented on the following page), Henry Clay, and very many of our public men, as well as in the Indian. How often do we see the "overgrown boy" in the person of some distinguished individual, a powerful orator, a wise counsellor, a great statesman! A person not experienced would call him a "country bumpkin," a "greenhorn," and various other names, expressing the infantile side of the character, without taking a view of the manly one.

The genuine Yankee, who presents the true *type* of the American character, has no local habitation, but, like the Indian, is diffused everywhere over this North American continent. It is a mistake to suppose that he originated in New England: the national peculiarities were first developed there, but the Yankee is a production of every state in the Union, and his characteristics increase in intensity in proportion to his wandering habits and to his occupation of the territories of the red man. In Oregon, Texas, California, and New Mexico, he is more a Yankee than ever, and his new provincialisms show his love of being separate and distinct from all others. He is as intent upon creating a nationality of his own as we should suppose it possible to be if the Indian were not a stronger example of the same disposition. But in a mining country those who resemble bears are more liable to run into a resemblance to the hog than in any other, as is

evident from the greater resemblance of the Indian tribes in those regions to the latter animal than to the former. Where the bear is noblest, there the American may be so, and there also he is most liable to perversion. Where Indian civilization was greatest, there Indian degradation is lowest, and so it must be with the white men who occupy their places.

Of all simpletons and fools, the Yankee charlatan and impostor is the shallowest and most disgusting. In the possession of slyness, affectation, and imposture, he resembles the Indian; and these, combined with a roaming disposition, acquisitiveness, and the love of traffic, make the "Yankee pedlar," famed for taking everything in exchange, and thus for the variety of his goods. Now the Indians whom we have known from our childhood are those who wander about peddling moccasins, besides brooms and baskets made of wood, split, and splintered, and stained, and who receive in exchange provisions, clothes, and money; and though they

appear so very demure, they are very fond of practical jokes, which they perpetrate with great gravity — a peculiarity in which the Yankee partakes as if it were natural to him. The latter resorts to "tricks in trade" with as much sobriety as the Indian — with the seriousness of one who is engaged in a lawful calling. If this is proof of any relationship between the Indian and the Jew, the white American will also, in the course of time, prove himself to be the same lost tribe that the Indians are supposed to be.

Why is it that "Brother Jonathan," when he is "driving a bargain," whittles a stick? and why is it that he drives the stick into the ground when he comes to the conclusion that he has "a Yankee to deal with"? This is a question that a philosopher might be puzzled to answer. Be it observed, however, that the extemporaneous mechanic is engaged in whittling out an arrow; that he points it, and is prepared to shoot it, like an Indian — when suddenly he discovers that, for the lack of coolness, or in consequence of the shrewdness of the person he has to deal with, he has "run the thing into the ground" — a misfortune which he commemorates by driving down the stick, and marking the spot where it happened

The Indian is a hunter: at all times and under all circumstances he is found in some search or research, either profound or superficial, and this gives him that thoughtful, meditative look, which it is so difficult to penetrate. In this he is like the Yankee on the one hand and the bear on the other. The look we are speaking of is often mistaken for a proof of something extraordinary—as if the person could search for nothing of less importance than the philosopher's stone, when the truth is he can not search for anything, not even for a flea, without the same expression of mysterious learning. To most people such faces are impenetrable, for the simple reason that they indicate the ignorance of the mind in regard to the mysteries that it is engaged in penetrating; but this, we perceive, is a proof of the *want* of knowledge, and it may relate to trifles as well as to matters of consequence. The Indian receives much greater credit for wisdom than he deserves; and one of the peculiarities of the Yankee is his uncommon sapience in matters that he knows nothing about. It is his business to hunt, and nothing is found that he himself has not discovered. If you tell him anything new, he expresses no surprise, but professes to have known it all before, and still wears that sage expression which indicates that he is penetrating still deeper into the same subject. Be he never so ignorant, his hunting disposition makes him wise in politics and in the affairs of the country generally, and you can hint at nothing in divinity or law, or in ancient or modern history, that he is not familiar with. As this is from a propensity of his that must needs be gratified, it requires only the removal of hypocrisy by honesty, and self-love by benevolence, to make him in reality what he claims to be.

We have been struck with the excess of the Yankee peculiarity described above in the character of the Indian—in one who is penetrated with a literary ambition. He wishes to fire everybody with the idea that he is a wit, a poet, and a scholar. Nothing disturbs his equanimity, nothing surprises him. He listens to everything you say as if he did not hear, and looks as if he might enlighten your ignorance beyond measure, if it were not for the vulgar astonishment that would be excited, and the attention that he wishes to avoid. But he is one of those whom prudence forsakes in consequence of

> "Vaulting ambition that o'erleaps itself."

He "attempts to live by his wits, and fails for want of stock," and then is discovered his true genius, which is his ability to "run his face" for whatever literary capital may be necessary to acquire him fame — till he runs himself out!

The bear looks always as if he were intent upon the object of pursuit. In his solitary wandering he is not tempted to turn aside except to revenge himself. His instinct demands to be let alone, and he concedes the same privilege to others. In these respects the Indian and the Yankee agree with him perfectly. The sense of individual rights is very strong *in them* as well as *in him*. They will not be trampled upon; they will not pay tribute, nor render involuntary service; the country they live in must be their own; they must be able to wander far upon their own lands; they must possess a right in the soil, a *home*, so that each one may say—

> "This is my own, my native land!"

The Indian is ennobled in the estimation of the white American for the possession of those qualities which the latter discovers in himself; and the bear is honored by the unconscious imitation of his peculiarities. When you meet him, if he is not pressed with hunger, he turns aside and allows you to pass on your way, for he recognises his own individual right and yours, and he expects you to recognise your own and his: but if you are so cowardly as to fire a ball into him from a distance, he turns upon you with the most tremendous rage and fury; and as this can be of no service to him unless he can come in contact with you, it is proof of his courage, and that his disposition to mind his own business is not caused by fear. In this the Yankee is his imitator as well as in other things, and it was well expressed, at a time when it was being illustrated, in the words—

> "Yankee Doodle is a lad,
> He's honest, kind, and civil;
> But if, again, you make him mad,
> He'll flog you like the devil!"

The last person referred to may simply mean the bear; for, like the bear, the Yankee is courageous; he gives the enemy

a cordial welcome; he is bound to fold him in his embrace; he advances in the face of danger; the more he is wounded, the more he rushes upon the deadly weapons; the stronghold he takes by storm; he assails with the desperation of a "forlorn hope;" he struggles in the very embrace of death—

> "Foiled, bleeding, breathless, furious to the last,"

he meets death joyously, whichever may be crushed in the embrace. It is such anger as only he who resembles the bear is capable of, that says—

> "O that my tongue were in the thunder's mouth!
> Then with a passion would I shake the world!"

The war-whoop of the Indian is something peculiar, and the loud shouts of the white Americans when they storm a battery is probably from the same cause.

The bear has the highest appreciation of luxuries and delicacies, and is at the same time in desperate hurry to devour his food. He searches the woods and plains for vegetables of a fine flavor, such as berries and fruits, and climbs trees and exposes himself to the stings of a thousand bees for the pleasure which the taste of honey affords him. As rough and rude as he is, he is contented with nothing short of nectar and ambrosia; and there are no people in the world so fond of sweets as the Americans, both the red men and the whites.

The index of this exquisite taste is the richness and lustre of the eye, all those qualities which are included in a *pearly appearance*, whatever be the color of the iris. This sign is perfect in the bear, though on account of the smallness of his eye it is not generally observed ; and as to the eye of the Indian, it is sufficient to say that there is none so beautiful as his. As of everything beautiful, the more you look at it the more you admire it. The power of fascination is chiefly in the eye, and when beauty exerts this influence it commands a tribute that is not always deserved.

The charmers called "psychologists," "mesmerizers," and other names of the same import, have the quality of eye referred to, and a strong resemblance to the Indian. The portrait at the beginning of this chapter is very like that of the chief of psychologists, whose face appears at the commencement of his works on that subject. Such eyes contribute very much to the magic power that is ascribed to eloquence —that of "persuading people to believe in the existence of something that never was and never will be." The Yankee has such persuasion in his eyes when his object is to "bargain, lease, and convey." The eyes called "eloquent" are truly dangerous, because, like eloquence, they monopolize belief, and prevent the intrusion of a doubt.

But it is not the intention of Nature to deceive. A pearly richness and lustre of the eye indicate exquisite taste in reference to food ; and in proportion as the mind is elevated it indicates refinement of taste in dress, buildings, furniture, manners, literature, eloquence, and in everything of which taste may be predicated. It indicates *refinement*, but it may be "refined cruelty," "refined roguery," and "refined deceit," as well as "refined sensibility," "refined manners," and "refined intellect." As in reference to food, taste is related to what is good, or fit to be eaten ; and so in individuals and in art it is related to excellence, to virtue, purity, and goodness, or to whatever is deserving of love ; but there is sweetness in poison, and the like quality is not unfrequently discovered in men and women of base passions, of whom it is said, "The poison of asps is under their lips."

If there is anything in the eye of the American to distin guish it from others, it is the quality we are speaking of. Let the eyes of the New-Englanders speak for themselves. The Boston ladies deserve to be celebrated for the beauty of their eyes, which are like those of the Indian. As their ancestors were the earliest inhabitants of the country, their eyes are more beautiful than those of Americans in general. They are equally remarkable for the richness and delicacy of everything in which they have an opportunity to display their taste. Their clothing is silk, and vies in lustre with the eye. The Americans are not slow to acknowledge the exquisite taste of the Indian costume, and of everything ornamental which the rude art of the Indian is capable of producing. In steamboats, and whatever else is new, the Americans show more taste than the Europeans.

CHAPTER XXVII.

If our idea be correct, the "Russian bear" will turn out to be a goose. We make no reflection on the mental capacity of that distinguished personage, but shall not cry his favor so much as if we had not discovered the resemblance just alluded to. Here is a person, the emperor Paul, who has been introduced to the reader twice before, and each time as one of the

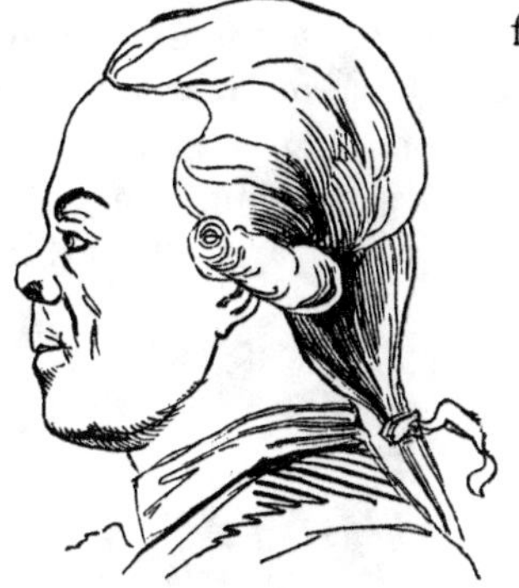

"greatest geese" that was ever hatched from a golden egg. It appears that his mother, Catharine II., was ashamed of him, and wished to pass him over "in favor of his son Alexander, whom, in her will, she appointed to succeed to the throne." The latter individual (see next page) seems to us to have no small resemblance to a duck (a bird that in its essential points differs very little from the goose); and that he was looked upon by his grandmother as a duck, while his father was regarded as a "goosey," is quite an argument in favor of our science.

But all geese are not deficient in intellect. A gander saved an ancient city from storm, for geese were great at prognosticating storms, and they are the same now that they were then. The Russians are equally "up to snuff," and it was very gooselike to set Moscow on fire to save it from the French — gooselike in two senses, for it required a foolish noddle to suggest the idea, and it turned out to be a capital expedient. Many a bright idea has its origin in a goose's brain — for truth is simple, and is better suited to the simple-minded than to the sophistical. As there is "but one step from the sublime to the ridiculous," so there is but one step from reason to common sense, and it is expressed in the word *expediency.* The Russians are full of expedients, for, like the goose, they have large subterfuge.

The hair growing down in a point in the centre of the forehead indicates the fiery action of subterfuge, as the pitching downward of the forehead itself over the top of the nose and the inner angle of the eye indicates the watery action of the same faculty. The one is the choleric and the other the phlegmatic mode in which this faculty exhibits itself. Though the burning of Moscow was disastrous to the French, it showed the character of the Russians, and illustrated the principle that "it is a foul bird that litters its own nest." This is true of the goose, and it is the result of expediency. This same faculty leads to backbiting, to the undermining of character, to tattling and

slander, to burning out men's eyes, and to whatever else Subterfuge might be supposed to engage in. The goose salutes you with the only means that is left her to vent the slander

of her serpent-tongue, a hiss, and she runs at you from behind with a serpentine movement; and the least objectionable of all the manifestations of this faculty is her fondness for gabbling. This was the character of the female progenitor of the three princes whose portraits are given on this and the preceding pages, the last of whom is the grand-duke Constantine, a younger son of Paul, whose tyrannical government of Poland is well known. Though we have treated them as subjects for charcoal sketches, they should, to have justice done them, be treated in a more elaborate way. But as there is a law of antagonism between fire and water, so also there are two actions of subterfuge, the one intended to extinguish the other. When one is in excess, the other is necessary to counteract it; for as of those two elements so of these, "they are good servants but hard masters."

The goose is a sort of feathered swine, as much like the Russian as the hog is like the Chinese, who are therefore similar. She forbids you to trespass upon her territories; encroaching on others, she discovers that encroachments are being made on her rightful dominions, and is slow to back out from those which she herself has made. When she has once taken possession of a field it is almost impossible to drive her from it, and the more you try the harder it is, for she has a propensity to go against obstacles, as is illustrated in her flying against the wind. Of course, then, she has a wide range, which implies a wide territory, but she is also attached to home. She is not to be disfranchized, and she snugs herself up by the side of other geese so closely, that there is no danger of their not keeping together, or at least within hailing distance; and each one interdicts the other from violating any of the rules of mutual help and protection. He (or rather *she*, for there is not much manhood in the character of the goose) is always troubling herself about the affairs of her neighbors, and therefore the flock is kept within bounds and they keep each other in order, of which we have the most perfect illustration in the flight of wild geese, for each one has to be at his post to attend to his neighbor, and in giving orders they all pipe at a time. They are fond of ordering each other to hush and mind their own business, but this is done with an eye to the general good; or, rather, this is the result of each one's attending to his own personal safety by shielding himself under the wing of the rest, and ordering them to take care of themselves, to mind their eyes, and

to follow his example. Of course, then, the goose is no fool: the only fool in the flock is the one that, like the emperor Paul, minds other people's business without knowing sufficient to take care of himself, and who accordingly goes ahead, takes the responsibility, and is thrust forward by the wiser ones who know the danger, and who treat him as the *odd* one, and exclude him from the honor of being included in the general estimate of geese. The goose proper, in all the traits enumerated above, is the precise counterpart of the Russians.

To descend from the body politic to the body corporate, the goose is very warm-blooded; he is fond of ice and snow, and of a vigorous climate, which remind him of his feathers, and make him gather his clothing more snugly and warmly around him. The Russian is fond of his ice-hills, which he manufactures especially for his convenience and for the pleasure of curling his legs under him and lying low; and he is fond of plunging into snow, as into a bed of down, and of muffling himself in furs, and of travelling in a cottage. This is his method of sojourning. The goose is so well provided with comfortable clothing, that by others she is supposed to have "enough *and to spare*"—and when she is "tamed," as it is called, or brought under the influence of their wills, she thinks as they do. Plucked of his feathers, the gander loses his noble instincts; he feels oddly; he is not even a weather guide; he wanders about, with "his nose turned up to the wind," but he is not able to prognosticate a storm, he is lost, he acts as oddly as he feels, and has the appearance of a "perfect goosey." The Russian who resembles this specimen of a goose goes thinly clad, is destitute of foresight and sagacity, and, with the power in his hands, would insist on every other person wearing thin clothes and being as great a fool as himself. This, again, was the emperor Paul, whom, the reader perceives, we are strongly tempted to "pick at" and to reduce to the condition of "a bird without feathers." This would be "making a man of him," according to Plato's definition; but as we are not Platonists, we will turn him over to the disciples of the philosopher to finish.

The fox lives on the sagacity and foresight of the goose, and therefore he has an abundance of both; but there are foolish geese that have lost their feathers, and are strayed away, and have not the spirit even to hiss or spit fire at their oppressors; and it was probably some cowardly fox in the habit of making mutton of such geese as these that lost his tail in a trap, and then proposed to his neighbors to adopt the same fashion. We have no doubt but that the nose of that animal was a snub and "turned up to the wind," and that he had a look similar to that of the goose, as the wolf has a likeness to the sheep, and that therefore he was perfectly sincere in the proposition; and that for that matter he might be regarded as a cockatrice hatched from the egg of a goose. Such is the character of a certain one among the Russians who will figure "positively for the last time"—we can not say when.

CHAPTER XXVIII.

Here is a person who, if he be not very much mistaken, has the air of a swan. In him it looks like an affectation of grace and dignity, but in the swan we admire it exceedingly. Without it the bird is both ugly and uncouth. It must consequently be something admirable, and for this reason it is the object of hypocritical imitation. It is the character of a devotee that gives this expression of countenance, accompanied with this position of the head. A devotee may be a votary to himself or a votary to some religion. "What a perfect air of self-complacency!"—you are ready to exclaim, on looking at a person with an expression of countenance like the above. It is even more than that: it is an adoration of something of which himself is both the centre and the circumference. He is, in his own estimation, *a saint*, and he expects, when he has given sufficient proof

of his sanctity by mortifications of the flesh, to be canonized by the vulgar. He is the victim of blind superstition, and of violence inflicted by his own hands. *Silliness* is the characteristic of the man who goes to an extreme in his resemblance to the goose, but *insanity* characterizes the man who bears a like resemblance to the swan. By this we mean a *literal* resemblance, and not that of which the goose and the swan are the representatives. In those who are inclined to insanity more than to idiocy, there is an affectation of grace and dignity, and a hypocritical sanctity, which says, "I am holier than thou"—accompanied with a condescending modesty, that seems to say: "You could not expect me to let down my dignity, but I will nevertheless condescend to speak to you; but I am a person of high rank and noble blood, and it becomes you to take care how you make too familiar with me; and presently I shall expect you to kneel down and do me reverence, for higher beings than you pay their obeisance to me. Should you displease me, you might feel my vengeance!" They suspect themselves to be endowed with certain Divine attributes that others are not aware of, and that it is necessary they should present these glaringly before the world, that they may no longer have an excuse for their ignorance and neglect.

"But what has all this to do with the swan?" Why, to tell the truth, the swan is, in his own estimation, a grandee of the highest order. You see it in that dignified bearing, by the side of which the pomp and pride of the peacock sink into insignificance. He is the very personification of complacency; he is perfectly at his ease; all things are as he would have them. He looks into his pure, white breast, reflected in the placid bosom of the water, and finding there nothing to displease him, he is "settled upon his lees," and floats in downy voluptuousness like a spirit in a snow-white cloud, not doubting but that he is as much an object of devotion to others as he is to himself. He carries his head in such a position that he may not lose sight of "his humble self." He is constantly the servant of himself so long as he lives, and with such assiduous care and attention he lives long. The vestal flame is kept constantly burning, and the stars their vigils keep in devotion to the swan, who, floating all night upon the water, fancies he is floating among them. He places his hand upon his heart (figuratively speaking all the while), and asks the world to witness its purity, the sincerity of his intentions, and the heaven within his own bosom. And indeed he is the symbol of heavenly felicity in the human breast, and of that purity and devotion that are made for each other, and that constitute heaven, wherever they may be.

But he is the symbol also of the very opposite, for the qualities which he represents are commonly perverted. From his stainless breast, and from that realm of purity which his form describes, extends something like a serpent with a serpent's head, and this, unless it be turned to look at the shadow reflected in the wave, and to explore the depths of that celestial love which makes its home with the innocent and pure, is the serpent full of cunning and malignity, of sensuality and pride. Then it is, as when we see him on land, that the swan loses all his grace and dignity, and is no longer beautiful, but snakelike and repulsive. Thus it is with the man who was formed to be a votary, and forsakes truth; who abandons the purity that is the object of devotion, and that is also the native element of the devotee. And he who can turn his eyes away from the innocence of his childhood and the principles that were planted in him by the Creator, and then look upon the malignant passions that have taken their places, and can call these good, is one who has deceived others until he has deceived himself, and is in a fair way to become insane.

One of the symptoms of this malady of the mind, from its incipient stages to the degree of confirmation, is "using vain repetitions as the heathen do." The devotee who is a self-worshipper acquires for himself the name of sanctity, not only by his sanctimonious bearing in the performance of various rites and ceremonies, but by "taking the name of God in vain;" and when his delusion has gone so far as to cause him to forget himself, there flow from his mouth volleys of oaths. An individual like the one figured at the commencement of this chapter has an air that may pass for reverence during the devotions of a congregation, as when the people rise for prayer, or that shall indicate his ability to swear like a pirate. The transition from a devotee to a "high buck" is an easy one. But in whatever stage of transformation he may be, "vain repetitions" will characterize him. You shall see this sanctimonious air tinged with a smirk in the person whose calling is the repetition of a cry several times a minute during the day from one year to another. He is the very person to act a conspicuous part in the display of sudden and miraculous piety. You can hardly repress the spontaneous ebullition of "Old hypocrite!" the moment you set eyes on him. But words are human, and what you condemn in him is the vain repetition of them, by which they are converted into "by-words," and you would not be profane because he is. The mendicant devotees of India make a sacrilegious use of language all their lives, for a "by-word" is that which is often repeated. *Mockery*, too, is characteristic of profanity. In persons whose business is the repetition of the same words from morning till night, as in beggars and those whose mode of selling partakes of the character of begging, you see *mockery* written in every part of the countenance. Repetition is a mockery of reason and humanity, for reason needs only to hear once in order to understand, and humanity needs only to hear the cry of pain in order to relieve it, and to fill the needy with bread. The repetition that is vain and hypocritical deafens the ears to the voice of real necessity, and to the voice of humanity, which commands respect like the voice of God. Words are precious pearls that are not to be cast before swine; but they who cast them out as dust of the street, and, most of all, those who make *sacred* words thus common, mock those whom they deceive, and they mock at the weakness and the sufferings of poor humanity. Mockery, and a caricature of benevolence and honesty, are legible in the faces of those who accost the passers-by with an invitation to purchase; and even the newsboys, young as they are, have enough of this expression of countenance to distinguish them. The extreme of this degradation and abuse of words is babbling insanity.

All this is the result of a perversion of those qualities which constitute a resemblance to the swan. It is therefore the very opposite of what we discover in true devotion. The swan is grace and dignity "to the very life." As there is no parade in that graceful carriage (for we must look to the turkey and the peacock for parade), so there is no organ of pretension — no medium of professions — or, in other words, no voice. His course through life is quiet and noiseless, save the slight sound of the ripples that break upon his breast. The devotee who is truly devout makes no professions: his life is pure, and it speaks for itself; it shows also the quality of truth, as the whiteness of the swan shows the purity of the element that bathes him. He teaches by example; he observes the precept, "Use not vain repetitions as the heathen do," but whispers, "Our Father who art in heaven."

It may have occurred to the reader that in India, where the characteristics we have described as belonging to the devotee are carried to an extreme, is to be found the greatest national resemblance to the swan. This is a fact that may be easily confirmed by observation. But the Indians resemble serpents as well as swans, and for the reason already stated. They exhibit the swan in his more disagreeable aspect. Infernal rites and ceremonies, hypocrisy, incoherency, violence

inflicted on themselves or others, are the characteristics of them all.

That sacred stillness which betokens reverence for truth, a disposition to listen to it, to obey it, and thereby to teach it in the most effective manner, or to exhibit it "to the very life," is perverted in the enjoining of stillness in the presence of those who consider themselves privileged to make a noise, and of reverence toward those who arrogate to themselves peculiar sanctity. You shall see the vestal virgin, whose soul is the heaven of tranquillity, and whose life is one of unobtrusive benevolence; and by her side the self-worshipping devotee, who is full of professions and hypocritical cant, and whose life is devoted to offering up sacrifices on the shrine of his selfishness. He wins bribes from the rich, but the poor who have nothing to give must appease his vengeance with their blood.

> "What smooth emollients in theology
> Recumbent Virtue's downy doctors teach!"

but these are for the rich only, who are willing to pay for flattery with the blood of the poor. Devoted humanity is silent under wrong, silent even to the false devotion that condemns it "as a sheep dumb before her shearers"—not because it has no redress, but because it is willing to be sacrificed in testimony for the truth, which is the greater good. But like the dying swan, that is fabled to breathe forth its life in enchanting melody, is the martyr in the hour of death. When he can no longer teach by example, he can teach as one inspired; and the swan, if the ancient fable be founded in nature, is his appropriate symbol even to the last. The phœnix, that was consumed in flames and rose again from its ashes, was this very bird, or one, according to the representations, exceedingly like it.

CHAPTER XXIX.

"What! a man look like a frog?" It is even so: you see the resemblance, or you would not ask the question. In the one figure the Frenchman is recognised, and in the other the frog. You say, perhaps, that "the first is an exaggeration, and that therefore it can not be taken as a proof of any special resemblance." Your premises we admit, but the

inference we draw is the very reverse of yours. If the exaggeration were not one of the characteristics of the Frenchman, you would not recognise the likeness. Yes, monsieur, you display astonishment at our boldness; but if you were not considerably like the frog, the exaggeration of your peculiarities would destroy the resemblance altogether.

We see, then, a reason for the Frenchman's *penchant* for frogs: it is like that of the Arab for the camel, the Englishman for the ox, the Chinese for the hog, and the Indian for the bear; and, as it is a poor rule that will not work both ways, his fondness for the frog as an article of diet is a reason for the resemblance. The organs which were the result of the life of the animal, and through which the life manifested itself, enter the stomach of the Frenchman, and thence into the circulation, to nourish and build up the body; and hence it is evident that the reptile we are speaking of becomes part and parcel of the Frenchman himself. This is as it should be, if, as we imagine, the race of Titans who were changed by Latona into frogs, are the race now called Frenchmen! It was in revenge for their refusing water to her and her children; and so they are metamorphosed into the likeness of an animal that lives in water, and has a plenty of it.

The French should be judged by their own philosophy: they say that the mind is a function of the body, or a secretion, or in some way a production of the brain and other material organs. Therefore, if they build up their bodies with those of frogs, they must strengthen and nourish their souls from the same elements! We believe that there is a correspondence between the soul and body throughout, and that the former responds instantly to whatever enters into the composition of the latter. The influence which the qualities of the frog, so highly esteemed by the Frenchman, must have upon the disposition and manners of the consumer, and even upon the higher faculties of his mind, is easily inferred, and is confirmed by even a hasty glance at his physiognomy. Which is the more sociable and noisy; which the more constantly engaged in *tête-à-tête;* which is the most lithe in all his members, and fond of versatility, and of hopping about, the Frenchman or the frog, we leave to natural history to decide.

There is as great a variety of Frenchmen as of frogs, and love of variety is the characteristic of them both. The wonderful disposition of the frog to change his shape, and his astonishing capacity to do so, are scarcely to be distinguished from the same disposition and ability in the Frenchman. This is effected by various inflations and puffings out in this direction and in that, especially in the region of the neck and shoulders. Fashion changes man into as many shapes as those of Proteus—without, however (at least in the case of the Frenchman), destroying the proper and legitimate indications of the character, and the resemblance to the frog. The Frenchman displayed here is an unmanly character; he resembles a female; and it must be confessed that the French follies we are now speaking of are exhibited more in women than in men. The French are like women in their looks, their actions, their judgment, their unwillingness to be governed, and their inability to govern themselves—their love of change, their love of order, and of turning things topsy-turvy—their disposition to go to extremes, their ability to become more cruel and more infernally wicked in every respect in the degree that they are capable of being better, than those who are *bona fide* and unequivocally men.

There is the fable of the frog that endeavored to swell himself to the dimensions of an ox that stood cooling himself in the water. The ox, for aught we know, may have been a huge island, and the frog may have considered that the water was all his own, and that the ox had no business there. There is certainly a great degree of similarity and contradiction between John Bull and his fashionable neighbor the Bull-Frog!

"M. Thiers asserts that there can be no dispute as to the high position France holds, especially in her silk manufactures (at the 'World's Fair,' in London). He was struck with the fact that France is pre-eminent in all the articles of luxury, which none but the wealthiest can buy; whereas, England excels in the productions usually consumed by the middle and poorer classes. Thus democratic France works for the rich, and aristocratic England works for the poor."

We see, therefore, that in the case of the frog and the ox there was no occasion for any jealousy on the part of the former, nor for any contempt on the part of the latter, but that they were well suited to each other, and that it was fortunate they were near neighbors. The ambition of the frog to swell to the dimensions of the ox was no vain ambition, for the works of art that contribute to the gratification of taste and to spiritual elevation are equal to those more substantial productions that contribute to the necessities of the body. It is beautiful that aristocracy and democracy should be friends; that they should help each other; that the frog should not swell himself so much for his own gratification as for that of the ox; and that the ox should not draw so much for his own benefit as for that of the frog.

As the Frenchman is lacking in manliness, it is right and proper that the French-*woman* should possess it, and that the feminine quality that she is deprived of to make room for the manliness, should belong to him. It is as easily seen that the Frenchwomen are uncommonly masculine as that the men are feminine. There is more true heroism in the characters of Joan of Arc and Charlotte Corday than in all the *men* of France that have ever lived. Madame Roland would have governed France more wisely and more nobly than that country was ever governed: but it so happens that in countries where women have none of the qualities of statesmen they are made queens, and where they are possessed of these qualities they are made to stand aside and give place to tyrants. The Frenchwoman presented on the following page should be contrasted with the Frenchman preceding: in dress and everything she is less feminine than he; she has very much the appearance of the cow, because of the relation between the English and the French, and yet she is thoroughly French, and has a strong resemblance to the frog.

The outer integument of the Frenchman has a wonderful

tendency to be puffed out: pads, bustles, balloons, and airy nothings, show the nature of the aspirations by which he expects to make his greatness equal to his desires. What it is that his soul lives on, aside from the breath of popular applause, it would be difficult to tell: it is as great a mystery as the life of a frog, that seems to live on air. Ambition is the ruling passion of the Frenchman; he spreads his sails, and fills them with his own breath, for he can rarify small praise into an immense volume, and it is his business to rarify and refine. Like the frogs in a pond, each one endeavors to be heard above the rest, though the bull-frog orator is loudest of them all. Yet it is remarkable that when one strikes a note the others join him, to the end that they may be heard to sing in concert by the outside listeners.

But as everything which is not loved for its own sake soon begets weariness and disgust, change is earnestly demanded: revolution must come, though it overthrow what is worthy of being loved and cherished; and ere long the new fashion will become old, and the old will become new again; and thus one change will follow another interminably, as whim or caprice may dictate, showing that stability is not the thing desired or sought after. The Frenchman says, as an excuse for plunging into a revolution, that he wishes disturbances to be over, that he may "attend to his business;" and there is truth in this, for he wishes one commotion to pass, that he may enjoy another: his very life is commotion.

But frogs are a happy people, and so are the French when the men they choose for rulers resemble frogs, and not alligators. Marat and Robespierre resembled vultures; but others, more common and less cruel and cowardly than they, resemble lizards, animals that rule by the power of the tail, as was described in the chapter concerning the rhinoceros. In the face of Louis XVI., here represented on the right, there is a very strong resemblance to the frog, and everything that is moral and much that is

noble to confide in, with nothing to distrust; but in the likeness to the left, that carries an impression of a relationship to the crocodile, there is something forbidding and formidable, which a man should give heed to. Look at the eye and jaws of that crocodile, counterpoised by a tail that may at

any moment take upon itself the functions of the other extremity; and look at those feet that are formed to go backward or forward, according as the supreme power shall be transferred to one extremity or the other—and say if there is anything in the physiognomy of that animal that you could confide in?

The *intellect* of the Frenchman is in keeping with his disposition and with the activity of his bodily organs, and is a further proof of his resemblance to the frog. He "jumps at conclusions," and this requires that he should have a wonderful degree of instinctiveness, or an intuitive perception of things. He does not reason, for reason requires prudence, deliberation, and proceeds step by step; whereas, instinct never delays, or makes a false step, or puzzles its brain about anything. The Frenchman is most truly himself, most prosperous, most happy, when he trusts entirely to Nature; but when he attempts to reason, he is sure to go wrong. In giving the frog an instinct to "jump at conclusions," Nature has provided a yielding element for him to fall into, lest he should break his bones; and this provision is all the more important, inasmuch as the frog has but a very general idea of where he is going to leap to, and when he makes a plunge it is a "leap in the dark." There is the same beneficent provision for the Frenchman in all that concerns his interests. When he jumps at conclusions it is at the practical, and the practical is always susceptible of modification and change; like water, into which the frog plunges himself, it accommodates itself to the individual; and *it is in this* that the Frenchman's passion for alteration and variety is intended to receive its full gratification. But when the conclusion that the Frenchman jumps at is *theory*—when he aims at first principles—when he endeavors to trace effects to causes—it is a leap in the dark still, but it is not into the water, but against a rock, and he knocks his brains out! It is the nature of his mind to go from mind to matter, from causes to effects, from God to the material universe; and therefore if he takes upon himself to go contrary to this, he says that Nature is God, that effects are causes, that the soul is from the body, and that principles are the results of experiments, and have no existence, no eternity, no authority, except as men may choose to establish them for their own convenience. Thus the Frenchman's simple faith, which is the practice of truth, or a life of charity and good works (the very strongest expression of confidence in the principles by which these are prompted), is wrecked, and he resembles a toad with a tail, an alligator, or an animal in which the distinction between before and behind, forward and backward, is not easily determined. When the Frenchman reasons *à priori*, it is instinctive, and he reaches the conclusion, though he jumps at it; but when he reasons *à posteriori*, he reasons *à priori* still, and mistakes this for that: the rock on which he splits is Nature in place of God.

The instinctiveness which is so remarkable in the Frenchman implies exceeding confidence in the intuitions of his own mind, and in the dictates of Nature. This is more beautifully illustrated in Montaigne than in any other writer that we know of. But the French philosophers in general have suffered a serious perversion by following with the rest of the world in the path of Bacon; or rather, in *thinking that they are doing so*, when they are in reality going in the very opposite direction. They have too little independence to be faithful to their own instincts and to the principle of Descartes — too little not to adopt the inductive method of investigation, when it is the fashion of the age to do so. The Baconian Frenchman, when he thinks of reasoning, starts (as everybody else does) from the basis of his own mind, and thus acknowledges its superiority over the mere facts of science; but, what is strange, after acknowledging this, he goes to matter for the cause of the mental phenomena which he exhibits in the investigation. He is no more required to investigate causes than a frog is required to go backward; and he no more needs a knowledge of them, further than flows into him by intuition, than a toad needs a tail!

It is a law that an animal should correspond to the element he lives in. Land is stationary: animals that live upon it can maintain a permanent position, and it is nothing strange for them to go backward. Water and air are progressive; animals that live in them are in constant motion; and for the locomotive powers of a fish or a bird to carry him in any other direction than forward is a very strange thing indeed.

The animal that lives in water or air, and seldom touches land, must "go ahead," and it is his instinct to do so; therefore if in any case he turns tail foremost and goes backward, he is guilty of the grossest absurdity and violation of Nature's laws, and when we look at him we see that he is a monster, destitute of symmetry and proportion, with forms and shapes that indicate dispositions unworthy even of an animal—traits unearthly and infernal. Thus it is with the lobster, an animal more hideous than any that lives on land; and thus it is with the serpent, the alligator, &c., though less than with the former, because, as they live partly on land, they are not capable of so great perversion.

"But what is the application of this to the Frenchman?" For the person who resembles a frog to go backward, is to change into the nearest resemblance to that animal that can be found among animals of the retrograde variety. Of the French infidels and atheists, some resemble the Surinam frog (a frog with a tail), some the cameleon, some the lizard, some the alligator; and the greatest of them all (if Voltaire be the greatest) resembles a lobster, as may be seen in the expression of the eyes, and, though less, in the scenery of the face. The Frenchman being instinctive and by nature practical, lives in the external, in the sensual, in the material and the gross, and considers that if there be any evidence besides the "evidence of the senses," there is at least none equal to it. But the mere objects of sense are filthy, for the simple reason that matter is essentially dirt, and that it is only the supremacy of the spiritual (in which beauty resides) that can make it pure. The sole reason why a flower is not dirt as much as the soil from which it grew is, that it signifies a spiritual beauty, of one kind or another—love, friendship, or some pure sentiment; and unless an individual perceives this, his observation of a flower as an object of sense is on a par with his observation of soil, of a bug, of a worm, of a snake, or any vile thing on the face of the earth. It is no affectation in the Frenchman to lay the stress that he does upon the "evidence of the senses," for he sees as much beauty in the vilest reptiles as in the most delightful birds; nay, he takes most pains in examining, painting and describing the former: and the most loathsome swellings and diseases do not disgust him, but on the contrary he delights in examining, representing, and describing them, and invents extraordinary methods of perpetuating and holding them up to the admiration and wonder of the world. He exhibits this character of grossness and sensuality in paintings, and in every variety of art, to a greater degree than any other nation. He is full of "unclean spirits, like frogs," that were seen in the Revelation "coming up out of the bottomless pit." Here is one of them (a Frenchman in caricature), and the man who is composed of frogs like this must be an illustration of the principle that "the whole is like the parts that compose it." The frog has those things about him that the Frenchman admires: *warts*, bearing a likeness to buboes, blotches, and chancres; besides puffings and swellings, having the appearance of tumidities from disease or from excessive grossness. Also the critical acumen in reference to sensual objects, and the taste for natural history, manifested by the Frenchman, are exhibited by the frog (and usefully too), in clearing the garden of grubs and bugs, and leaving the more beautiful things comparatively untouched. But as bad as it is to be sensual, and to bear too literal a resemblance to the frog, it is worse to attempt to reason, or to go backward, when the idea in the mind is that the objects of sense are essential, primary, superior, the most important, and therefore the causes of all things. Was there ever anything so stupid as that shrug of the shoulders, and that leaden gaze, and that motion toward a twigging of the nose, which is exhibited by the Frenchman when he is called upon to know anything or to believe anything beyond the evidence of his senses? Yes: the frog preceding is very like him and quite equal to him in that; and he is himself ten times more stupid and insensible when he puts "the cart before the horse," the "effect before the cause," and declares

solemnly that reason has an office to perform, and that by means of it he knows something that he did not know before, viz., that the horse is pulled along by the cart, and that what people have supposed to be the effect is in reality the cause! He resembles the alligator, and the alligator is a stupider animal than the frog, and far more unfeeling and infernal. The frog in him took leave of absence for a while, in order that he might seek out fitting companions, and when he returned he brought such things as lizards and lobsters with him to share in the government of the domain. Thus is illustrated the saying: "When the unclean spirit has gone out from a man, he walketh through dry places, seeking rest and finding none. Then he saith, 'I will return to the place from which I went out;' and when he has returned he findeth it empty, swept, and garnished. Then he goeth and taketh with him seven other spirits worse than himself, and they enter in and dwell there; and the last state of that man is worse than the first."

CHAPTER XXX.

THE expression "mercurial Frenchman" is a familiar one. A metal moving about like water, instead of being crystallized and having a base to stand upon, is no exaggeration of the extraordinary mobility of the people referred to. Attempting to lay your hand on a globule of mercury is like attempting to lay your hand on a frog—you light on emptiness; and in like manner you can never get the better of a Frenchman in an argument, for he occupies no place in particular, and you can not calculate where he will jump to. It is a general rule, however, that the frog will jump into the water, as the deepest and most important element; and in like manner the Frenchman will jump to scientific facts, as the deepest and most important truths. As these are pliable, and he can make them what he pleases, it is impossible that you should trace him, except by the mud which he stirs up from the bottom, which soon obscures him entirely! Supposing even that you have him in the field where the rules of rhetoric are laid down, you lay hands on vacuity when you think he will stay still. This is not his fault, but yours; but if he takes to his scientific facts, and from these reasons against reason, assuring you that these are the central truths and the causes of all others, argument is at an end. As the frog goes to its natural element, so goes he to his own place, as the safest *for him.* Like an infant in the posture that is best suited to his condition, he regards only the objects of the senses. The *ipse dixit* of Science, from which he is begotten, puts an end to all dispute. The umpire in this case, who appears in the form of a bull-frog, swells about the throat till head and shoulders are mingled into one, and he appears like a monster with eyes in the upper part of the chest; and all in the endeavor to utter a croak that shall be deeper and more oracular than any which preceded it. However much you desire to get a sight at him, you are doomed to disappointment, for he has sagacity enough to know that the expectation that is aroused by a voice like that would never be realized.

To mention all the varieties of Frenchmen in connection with the varieties of the frog would be an endless undertaking. There are frogs of a sanguinary disposition (constituting the entire population of a pond of which the water is cut), that muster into a regular army, the master-spirit of which is a frog of wonderful ambition and reckless of blood. Two armies of this description meeting each other leave thousands of their number dead on the ensanguined field. Compare the leader of a noisy army of frogs with the picture called Bonaparte, and with others that might be mentioned. Then there are dirty frogs, that live in mire, and know not the use of water, but are covered with spawn and slime; and to match these there is a class of Parisians that excel in filthiness. Then there are clean frogs, beautifully colored and speckled, that do not even injure the spring-water that they live in—frogs that you really love to take in your hand whether you be Frenchman or not; and the like of these make Paris a cleaner city than any other in the world. Then there are frogs with yellow skins and beautiful golden eyes, that hop about in the sand, true to their instinct which requires them to live in an element that is shifting; and these are they who talk of stability in the government, and build their houses upon the sand. Then there are toads "ugly and venomous," that "live upon the vapor of a dungeon," by which their brains are rendered prolific—toads who never change their habits, and who are therefore unmitigatingly disgusting in both dress and manners; and to go with these there are Frenchmen who disfranchise themselves, who are not reckoned among frogs, but are alternately

sent to the galleys, banished, or imprisoned. Then there are tree-toads, who take the hue of the times in which they live, and who are more elevated in feelings and sentiments than the frogs who surround them, and who redeem the character of the toad, and offer encouragement and example to the lowliest and the most degraded. Were it not for the Frenchmen whose voices make such sweet melody as these, in contrast with the chattering and croaking of the remainder, the multitude of frogs would sink in the depths of sensualism, to rise no more. Then there are frogs that we skipped in their proper places, such as put their heads together above the surface of the water, entangled with spawn and sea-weeds—

bandits that disappear on the appearance of a spectator the moment he can say "Jack!"

The talent for caricature, for which the French are distinguished, has its origin in the love of exaggeration before spoken of. As it is contagious, we plead guilty to the same offence. The French know how to take these things; and besides, as a general rule, it is a sufficient compliment to represent a man as he really is. A man is in general what he chooses to be; and hence the danger of offence is in describing him as he is not. The French love to have their qualities exaggerated, and therefore it is that they deal in compliments as well as in caricature. They have little inclination to be dissatisfied with what is said of them; for when they are "blown" they are ready for blows, and a blow from a stone does them no more harm than a blow of wind. For the same reason, when a Frenchman is able to dress himself as he chooses, he can pass for whatever he likes:—

> "Through tattered clothes small vices do appear;
> Robes and furred gowns hide all!"

With such a *tournure* as he alone has the art of producing, he does not ask even the mantle of charity to be thrown over him. He is fond of wit, and a good joke is never at his expense, for he has more instinct and less sensibility than others. He plays with heads as a child with a rocket, and a revolution is genuine sport—to all but those who say, like the frogs in the fable, "It may be sport to you, but it is death to us!"

Apropos of this, the French being remarkably like children, and having a great deal of instinct as animals have, are wonderfully fond of fables; and there is a fable which relates that once upon a time the frogs became wearied of their monotonous existence, and prayed to Jupiter to send them a king; whereupon the god sent them a *log*, which killed many as it fell among them, and made such a splashing that the rest were awed into stillness; until, finding that it had no longer any power of doing them harm, they became impatient—abused, insulted, and leaped upon it, and accused Jupiter of sending them a *thing*, and at the same time demanded of him with deafening clamor that he should send them a king that was animated, like themselves, only a great deal more so; whereupon Jupiter sent them a *stork*, that began immediately to devour them with an appetite that threatened to exterminate the race. This is the sum and substance of the fable, and it is particularly applicable to the people who resemble frogs, as much so as if it had been written to describe them. Æsop must have been inspired to have prophesied so correctly, and to have understood the character of the frog so well. The log will do very well to represent the rule of those Frenchmen who, after the distinction necessary to a revolution, allow the people to do as they please. The stork will represent the rule of one who absorbs into himself the will and functions of the people, and interprets them as he sees fit. The former is like a log, because the Frenchmen who are particularly concerned in it are of the variety that resemble alligators, the most refined and elevated of whom have the character of cameleons; and the latter is like a stork, because the person who exercises it resembles that bird: like the crow, vulture, and other carrion-birds, the stork is cowardly; but he has a show of courage; he is not boldly but cunningly revengeful. His faults are primarily his fondness for carrion and for every species of filth and nuisance,

his cowardice, also his love of snakes and reptiles — for though these are regarded as high virtues in the bird, as making him an excellent scavenger, and the receptacle of things so vile that even the vilest of human beings reject them, yet they are the foundation of the most despicable traits in a human being. The lazy and vicious are very fond of whatever relieves them from the trouble of labor and cleanliness; and this is the reason why the stork is held in such high esteem in Egypt, Holland, and many other countries, and why the Mohammedans even venerate him. As he is fond of frogs, it is but right and proper that frogs should be fond of him, particularly when they add to the cause of their liking him his disposition to relieve them of all trouble of governing and disposing of themselves. His fondness for frogs may be shown in this: "Bellonius informs us that storks visit Egypt in such abundance, that the fields and meadows are white with them, and that the natives are pleased with their arrival, as the birds deliver them from innumerable swarms of frogs, and also devour serpents." The "grave air and mournful visage" of the stork constitute one of the resemblances to the person of whom the following is a portrait (Louis Napoleon). The Marabou stork is the bird we have chosen to stand by his side. For a description we quote from a writer on natural history: "In its habits this bird bears a close resemblance to the white stork of Europe,

but becomes still more familiar, and, in consequence of its larger size, renders more essential service in the removal of carrion, offal, and other nuisances. This important office like the adjutants of Calcutta, it shares with the vultures; and both birds are universally privileged from all annoyance, in return for so meritorious exertion of their natural propensities. They seem to be constantly attracted by heaps of offensive substances collected in the villages and towns, which they devour without scruple, and in immense quantities. . . . Nothing seems to come amiss to the voracious appetite [of this stork]; for when carrion is scarce, it attacks reptiles, small birds, and even the lesser quadrupeds (as mice), which it usually swallows entire." From this it appears that no very great danger is to be apprehended from such birds, except by frogs, and animals that are more weak and cowardly than themselves. "When excited, they elongate their necks, and stand at their full height, menacing with their large bills, which are, however, too light to inflict any serious injury, even had the birds courage enough to attempt it."

Having spoken hastily of King Stork, we will give a brief description of King Log. There are certain frogs whose greatness appears in the grating of their voices. As it is not natural for instinct to reason, these, by setting themselves up to be reasoners, and by reasoning backward when it is their instinct to go forward, degenerate into lizards of the larger variety—*large*, because it is their ambition to be so, as indicated by their voice, and by their habits of swelling and expansion.

Opposite to these there are tree-toads, with fine, soft, musical voices, and with a disposition to shrink into the substance of the tree that they are perched upon, at the same time that they desire eminence—as much, even, as the frogs last mentioned desire a grovelling situation, and to be distinguished. The Frenchmen who resemble tree-toads, by adopting induction as the rule of reasoning, degenerate into a resemblance to the cameleon, the most harmless and beautiful of lizards, as the tree-toad is the most harmless and beautiful of toads. Who can look at the following portrait of a Frenchman, and not say that it is a genuine "character," a distinct *genus*, drawn to the life? Would you not know by those feet and hands that he had wonderful powers of clinging to whatever ne takes hold of? That right arm has the peculiar thrust that is observed in the right fore-leg of the cameleon, and it is evidently grasping the contents of his pocket. That left arm has the very same character that is observed in the corresponding member of the quadruped. That left leg—how admirably it imitates the left that sets itself down on the limb of the tree! and the right, how like in character to the one that forms the basis of support, and insures safety to the cameleon! and even the coat-tail adds amazingly to the resemblance, in the manner of its descent from

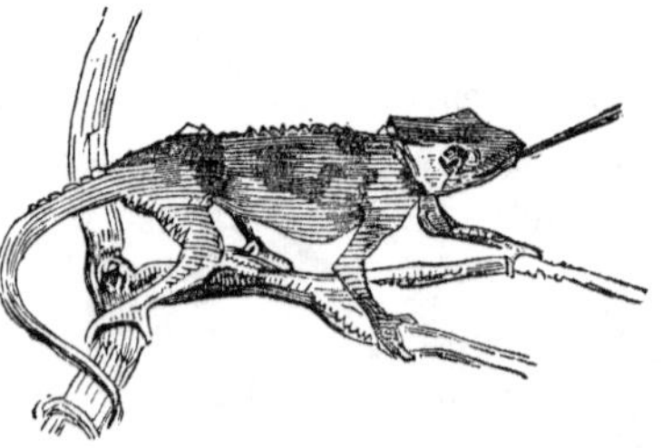

the back, in its length, and in the support which it adds to the posterior aspect of the right extremity. But when we ascend to the head, the likeness is no less remarkable, and still more interesting. In the peculiar angle and curve of that forelock the individual has embodied some striking trait of his character—an endeavor, it may be, to resemble the cameleon in the artistic disposal of everything belonging to him. The top and back part of his head, together with the forelock, turning up on one side and down on the other, are imaged forth in corresponding points in the head of the cameleon. The nose, too, has the very curve, and the very expression of stubbedness of disposition, together with the love of eminence and accommodation, in the proportions, that are rudely set forth in the nasal organ of the inferior animal. And that eye, was there ever any like it save in the cameleon? Does it not seem as if it would look this way while the left eye looked the other? and as if it would look upward while the left regarded the earth? Precisely so; and in this he bears as close a resemblance to the cameleon as in other things. It is well known that the cameleon has the power of moving the eyes in opposite directions, up and down, and toward all points of the compass, just as if he were two animals instead of one. Descending from the head to the chest, we see in the form of the latter, in the whole length of the vest, in the swelled and in the girted portion, and from the top to the groin, the evidences of a disposition in this particular Frenchman to borrow his fashions from this favorite pattern of the qualities of mind and heart that he is inclined to cultivate. There can be no doubt of his abilities and disposition to change his colors to suit the times and circumstances, to blend in with that which most predominates, and to turn that coat of his as often as the exigencies of the case may require; and of course this implies the ability, if not really the disposition, to bear a scolding tongue, and not merely to survive under it, but to take it good-naturedly, and to thrive and prosper, and to speak a good word to the neighbors in favor of his amiable spouse.

The moral qualities are swerved from their proper and legitimate action by the influence of the animal faculties when the latter predominate, as was shown in the peculiar action of justice consequent upon the bovine qualities of those who resemble the ox. "Pulling and hauling" is the sum of proceedings in the English courts, and oxwhips are applied lustily, accompanied with shouts, in which "gee" and "haw" are the conspicuous words, equivalent to *pro* and *con;* and it is curious that oxen, like John Bulls, are directed to pull to the right and to the left at the same time, as is evident from the repeated command, "Gee-haw!" Hodge is quite certain of being obeyed when he utters such an order as this, and he delights in the increased labors of his oxen in their endeavor to pull away from each other, for they are "performing an immense amount of labor"—the grand thing which he proposes to accomplish. In respect to justice, John Bull and Monsieur Frog are the very antipodes of each other. Natural historians inform us that the ranunculi have a singular mode of administering capital punishment. Two stout fellows place themselves on each side of the offender, and crowd upon him until they have crushed him to death. In like manner, French justice places the accused between two parties; and these, instead of inclining to separation, are disposed to agreement: both parties conspire to condemn, and agree to "go halves" in the division of the spoils! If a king or a deputy is so unfortunate as to come to trial, the people rush upon him *en masse;* there are none to defend him, and his death is the explosion that scatters them in wild disorder, to concentrate again at the Tuileries, or some other place, where they revenge the death of their former victim upon their leader. They are essentially democratic only on this principle, that "where the carcass is there the eagles are gathered together." We have seen it suggested that the eagle which the French republic displays aloft is a Gallic bird, and may be nothing more nor less than a gallinaceous fowl.

CHAPTER XXXI.

We have lingered on the verge of one part of our subject, longing for the eloquence which it would seem calculated to inspire, and find that we are likely never to go on unless we content us with plain English, like that which has already served us. That subject is the resemblance between the Irishman and the dog; and the eloquence which we craved (without knowing exactly what we were waiting for) is "Irish eloquence." This is so prominent a trait of Irish character, that if the resemblance

alluded to exists, it must be characteristic of the dog. And so it is. Listen how the loud sound of the watch-dog booms through the air at night, and how the welkin rings with responses from

> ——"mongrel, puppy, whelp, and hound,
> And curs of low degree,"

in imitation of guns, thunder, and the rolling eloquence called oratory! On all sides round echoes the "war of words," in which *accent* and *emphasis* play the conspicuous part, the sounds being jerked forth like the report of a rifle; and the merest squib of them all is as ambitious of being the "big gun" as the one that may justly lay claim to that distinction. Is not this a description of Irish eloquence? Has not the Irishman *pathos* also to express his bereavement? and does he not hold his "wakes," in which he rivals the dog in wailing, as at other times he rivals him in debate and oratory? He seems to howl and bay the moon, as if the wavering stars would shed more tears, and the chaste Diana, the patroness of thieves and vagabonds, would be melted with sympathy at the tale of his sufferings: not to say that the Irishman is a thief and a vagabond, in a worse sense than that he is exacting, and that he gives himself up "to license unrestrained," and with a feeling of abandonment to be the prey of pickpockets, grief, beggary, and intemperance. We speak now of the "common run" of Irish, and they are like the "common run" of dogs that "take after them," and that are thieves and vagabonds without qualification.

The Irish, take them as they come over, are remarkable for holding you by the button while they inflict upon you what they have to say, or (if they are so fortunate as to be merchants) what they have to sell; and they are distinguished for pertinacity in begging, or in "beating down;" and, certainly, if they are so elevated as to be purchasers instead of beggars, they have a right to be impudent, though it is somewhat difficult to distinguish buying (as they practise it) from begging! The Irishman's mouth waters for everything he sees, and he is the "greatest tease," in every sense of the term, of anybody we know of, with the exception of the dog, who, it must be expected, will follow the fortunes of his master. "Like master like man" is a trite saying, and as true as it is trite. Compare the Irishman and the dog in respect to barking, snarling, howling, begging, fawning, flattering, backbiting, quarrelling, blustering, scenting, seizing, hanging on, teasing, rollicking, and whatever other traits you may discover in either, and you will be convinced that there is a wonderful resemblance.

The son of old Erin wastes his breath in sighing for the past, and fails in his efforts for the future because he has no heart in it. He has ardent wishes, but it is for the old, for everything hallowed by the tender associations of bygone days. Yet these refer to some wished-for good in the future. What he hopes and anticipates is, the return of the good old times of learning and hospitality, of domestic affection and neighborly love, which characterized his ancestors. Noble traits were these, and it is the deep consciousness of the same affections in his bosom still that links him to the past with a tie that bleeds and suffers with everything in the present and the future that essays to rend it.

In our opinion, we have alluded to the finest trait in the Irish character — a susceptibility to an exquisiteness of pleasure or of pain, which comes from an extraordinary degree of consciousness. The cords of affection in his breast are endowed with the highest degree of sensibility, and for the reason that they do not utter themselves but in tones of the most thrilling pathos, and therefore it is too that they refuse to be broken. They attach him to the past, to the objects of his first love, and the necessity of change rends his heart. But there is a way in which he can submit to the operation of having the ties which bind him to his kindred and country rent asunder, and his heart taken from him as if it were a fungous excrescence — and that is, to be made *drunk*. Alas that he should have fallen into the sad necessity of being made insensible, that he might suffer himself to be torn from all that his heart holds dear — from wife, and children, and home, and the relics of his ancestors! What is left of the Irishman when you take from him his household gods, and his tender susceptibility of pleasure and pain? He is a miserable imitation of the Frenchman (see next page), both in the frivolity and hilarity which are the first effects of intoxication, and in the loss of sensibility, and the sundering of domestic ties, and the recklessness of old associations and of the feelings of others, which are the inevitable result of his potations repeated and persevered in. He becomes a fatalist as much worse than the Frenchman as madness is worse than folly, as whiskey is worse than wine, and as insensibility that is induced is worse than that which is natural. He prates and babbles, and is full of the ambition of being an orator, and is in every respect as miserable a caricature of the Frenchman as the perverted American is a miserable representation

of a Chinaman, and as the degenerate Italian is a miserable impersonation of the Englishman. It will not do for the Irish to resemble frogs, nor for dogs to resemble Frenchmen. The

consciousness of the Irishman adapts him to domestic life, to which the dog is suited; and the instinctiveness of the Frenchman adapts him to communism, like that of the frog, or those wonderful examples of instinct the bee and the ant: and an attempt to reverse the order of things is destructive to both. France is a bad atmosphere for the Irishman; and let the man who resembles the dog, or is a descendant of the Irish, not be ambitious to "learn French." If you find him so, you will also find him snappish, ambitious of being a politician, and of distinguishing himself as an orator; and in default of these he will be for ever applying the "lash of scorpions" to his nearest neighbor.

> "Close at my heels the snappish cur
> With yelping treble flies" —

will be applicable to him. French dogs are the least amiable of their species, if we may judge from what Dickens says of them: . . . . "And here are sheep-dogs, sensible as ever, but with a certain French air about them, not without a suspicion of dominoes, with a kind of flavor of mustache and beard; demonstrative dogs, shaggy and loose where an English dog would be tight and close; not so troubled with business calculations as our English drovers' dogs, who have always got their sheep on their minds, and think of their work, even resting, as you may see by their faces — but dashing, showy, rather unreliable dogs, who might worry me instead of their legitimate charges if they saw occasion — and might see it somewhat suddenly." The genuine Irishman — the one who is worthy a birthplace on the Emerald isle — resembles that noblest of all dogs, the Irish wolf-dog, and more the dog of St. Bernard and the Newfoundland dog than the scavenger-dog of the city and the great variety of whining, barking, howling, snarling, snap-

ping dogs that, like Irishmen, are scattered the world over. The man who in feature and expression resembles those nobler animals just mentioned, is more seen than heard; he has feelings too deep for utterance; he is linked to the past by the tenderest associations; his love is pure, concentrated, of the strongest kind, and therefore eternal, looking to the future for the consummation of what is already begun. He is the very opposite of the Frenchman, and the farthest remove possible from the vacillating, tyrannical, cruel, faithless, hypocritical, beslavering Irishman, who illustrates the saying of Pope:—

> "Of all mad creatures, if the learned are right,
> It is the slaver kills, and not the bite!"

Those nobler Irishmen are found at home, for their hearts are there; and if they are compelled to leave their country (not "for their country's good," as certain Englishmen are who are sent to Botany bay), you hear them use the word "home" as synonymous with their country, when they refer to the land that gave them birth; that is marked everywhere by the hallowed shrines and footprints of their ancestors. They have true eloquence, the very opposite of that haranguing, brawling, litigating, campaigning, brazen eloquence of the "common Irish," who, in reversing their original character, outdo the peculiarities of the French. Their words are the language of genuine feeling, but they are generally silent, for the love that burns in their bosoms is a holy flame. Their eloquence is the very essence of harmony and pathos, and every word they utter may be treasured as an embodiment of love, a sacred memento of the heart from which it came.

Thackeray, in his "Irish Sketch-Book," speaks thus of Irish gentlemen: "I have met more *gentlemen* here than in any other place I ever saw—gentlemen of high and low ranks, that is to say—men shrewd and delicate of perception, observant of society, entering into the feelings of others, and anxious to set them at ease or to gratify them." This is in consequence of the exquisite susceptibility which we call *consciousness*, but when he adds, "of course exaggerating their professions of kindness, and in so far insincere," we behold the tendency toward "puppyism," or a resemblance to those dogs that fawn, first upon their masters and finally upon everybody, especially upon those from whom they hope to receive favors; and in the last stage of all they become "toadies."

The same writer says: "In regard to the Munster ladies, I had the pleasure to be present at two or three evening parties at Cork, and must say that they seem to excel English ladies, not only in wit and vivacity, but in the still more important article of the toilet. They are as well dressed as Frenchwomen, and incomparably handsomer. . . . . . In the carriages, among the ladies of Kerry, every second woman was handsome; and there is something peculiarly tender and pleasing in the looks of the young female peasantry, that is perhaps even better than beauty. . . . . The hair flowing loose and long is a pretty characteristic of the women of the country; many a fair one do you see at the door of the cabin, combing complacently 'that greatest ornament of female beauty.' . . . . I never saw in any country such general grace of manner and ladyhood."

Were we to choose the animal that would most resemble this description, we would choose the most beautiful in the world, and that would be the *King Charles spaniel* (see next page). The still consciousness; the deep feeling and sympathy of those eyes, in which there is more eloquence than words can utter; the quiet, the gentleness, the grace; the exquisite cultivation and refinement, of which those very long, pendent ears are the tokens; everything about the dear creature that speaks of tenderness and love, of domestic happiness, of exquisite appreciation and sensibility, of sensitiveness to unkind treatment, of forgive-

ness, of meekness, of inoffensive innocence, of a disposition to live in peace and harmony with all mankind — remind us of woman in that refined society that is included within the domestic circle, and has its origin from domestic virtue.

Saint Patrick is said to have driven all the toads and snakes out of Ireland, and we might add lizards included, for these are a medium between the two. But, in expelling them from the land, he may have caused them to transmigrate, and to appear again under the mask of the native inhabitants! "Bloody Irishman" is a term applicable to the Irish in general, but particularly to that variety that resembles the bull-dog. "Kill" is a word attached to half the places in Ireland — Kildare, Kilkenny, Killarney, Kilkerny, etc. It should be

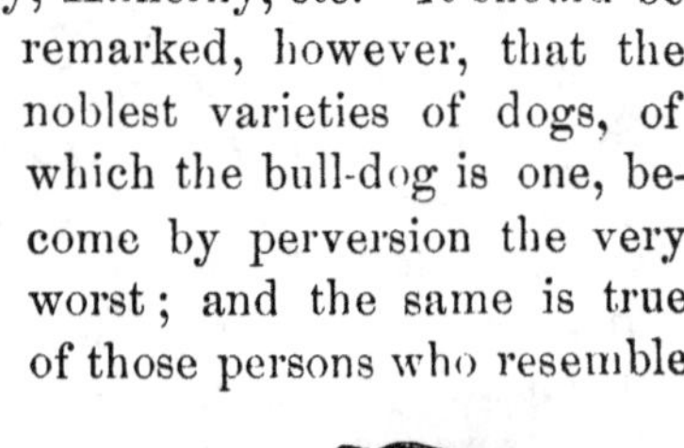

remarked, however, that the noblest varieties of dogs, of which the bull-dog is one, become by perversion the very worst; and the same is true of those persons who resemble

the nobler varieties of dogs. They are either remarkable for their stanch integrity and tenacious adherence to the principles of honor and uprightness, or they are noted for their tenacity of purpose, right or wrong, and in pursuit of their victims are like Spanish bloodhounds; or they answer better still to the description of Cerberus at the gate of hell. The man who resembles the shepherd's dog is by perversion converted into a resemblance to the wolf. His affection for sheep, or in other words for innocence and virtue, is converted into the appetite for mutton, or the desire to seduce and to devour that which it is his duty to protect. He has in his face a look of innocence, like that which he lives upon, but which he changes into its opposite. He is the "wolf in sheep's clothing." He looks "sheepish," in a sense that can hardly be distinguished from "wolfish," and when he looks with admiration upon unstained beauty in the opposite sex you can see in him an "evil eye" like that which is discoverable in the wolf, or like that which makes the dog look "as if he had been stealing sheep." The dog, if he be worthy of the name, is "death" upon the wolf, and this is particularly the case with the Irish wolf-dog, who *resembles* that animal as much as he hates him. This is just the difference between the genuine coin and the counterfeit: the more the latter is like the former, the more vile and worthless it is, and the more it is opposite to the true. Hypocrisy is the very opposite of the goodness which it affects, for it is the perversion of truth, which is falsehood, and the perversion of virtue, which is vice. But though the wolf-dog and the wolf resemble each other and resemble the sheep, the one has a mean, cruel, cowardly expression of countenance, and the other has a magnanimous, mild, courageous expression, that wins your confidence. And so it is with the "Shepherd of the sheep" and with the "wolf in sheep's clothing." The "sheep," we are told, are able to distinguish between one and the other.

The dog is a very great wit, and exceedingly fond of sport and game. He shows his waggish disposition in the manner in which he plays with you and with other dogs. He appreciates the joke you play upon him if it be a good-natured one, and surprises you by the disposition he has to reciprocate it, and by the tact he displays in making you the subject of laughter. He is alive to fun and frolic — not playfulness merely, like that of the cat, but something absolutely droll, ridiculous, and absurd. The parallel of this to the disposition and talent for which the Irish are most celebrated, is at once perceived. The lowest, the most ignorant, the most stupid, are not exempt from a peculiar kind of smartness, a certain keen perception of the ludicrous, and a readiness in making apt replies; and there is not a dog but has the same appreciation, and the same facility of expressing it, so far as a dumb dog can express his ideas of things. The tolerance with which a Newfoundland or a dignified old mastiff regards the gambols of a puppy, who makes bold to jump into his face and pull him by the tail, is not mere forbearance, but is, if we may judge anything from his actions and the expressions of his countenance, in consequence in no small degree of the gratification of his "wit and mirthfulness."

This talent for wit sharpens the Irishman's slander, as is evident from the nature of his satire; and it is similar with the dog, as is shown in his worrying and teasing poor animals instead

of doing simply what his master bids him. It is easy to set him on, but hard to call him off, and precisely so it is with the "plaguey" Irishman. There is a wonderful tenacity in this love of teasing, which is the counterpart of the Frenchman's fondness for caricature; and the poor victim, thinking the dog has "the wrong pig by the ear," is fain to cry,

"Bloody murder!" and "Leave go!" The dog, we know, cries some time after he is hurt, showing the continuance of the pain, but the hog ceases shouting as soon as the dog ceases his persecutions. Ergo, the dog, like the Irishman, is a tease and a torment. This is a character, in fact, that it seems impossible for the Irishman to get rid of, for when he tries his best to please he is still vexatious. "What torments these Irish servants are!" is frequently heard from those who have not been the subjects of their satire. They are as proverbial for their ridiculous mistakes as for their wit, and this is the more strange as it seems to be a contradiction in character. But it is according to the principle, "They who take the sword shall perish by the sword," and the same is true of the French. These "Irish bulls," as they are called, are not from lack of shrewdness, but from a want of instinctiveness the trait that is peculiarly natural to the French; and it is in consequence also of that imperative, headlong, impetuous disposition which the bull-dog has in common with the bull, and which the Irish have in common with the English. The lack of instinctiveness is shown in the awkwardness of their motions. Their imitations of the French, which are mere perversions of their own characters, increase this opposition and render it all the more conspicuous. They are like beetles—

"Against the traveller borne in heedless hum,"

or like the pumpkin that you can not keep out of your way, but are always

tumbling over, bringing you into the same blundering, awkward condition with themselves. If the Irishman were not distinguished for this, there could be no food for his wit, for he could not place you in a ludicrous position in his own mind without placing you so externally. This is true of all persons who have an extraordinary sense of the ludicrous. It is on this principle that the French, who are the fittest subjects of caricature, are themselves the greatest caricaturists in the known world.

Among dogs, the commonality, which aspire to the condition of toads, and to that of frogs in stagnant pools by the roadside, love to dig in the dirt, to roll in it, to splash through the mud, and esteem it a luxury to have a pig-pen, or a snug, warm kennel to harbor in. Among the Irish, the commonality take to dirt-digging more naturally than to anything else; they are dirty in their persons, and admit their pigs in the mud-cabins which they themselves occupy. They are good servants if you deal harshly with them, as a master does with his dog; but the moment you are disposed to be familiar with them they are all over you, jumping against you, and laying their dirty paws upon your clean clothes, as if you were no better than they. You are loved by them quite as well, and they are quite as happy, if you teach them good manners: but the true way to restore to them that sensibility, delicacy, sense of propriety, tender affection, and exquisite susceptibility of enjoyment, which is their rightful inheritance from their ancestors, is, to treat them as if they were possessed of these qualities, and thereby to set them the example. The man who wounds the feelings of his dog, will soon have a dog as hard and ungenerous as himself; but the man who treats his dog as he should, will have a faithful servant, who will say, "Go on, master, I will follow thee to the last gasp, with truth and loyalty."

CHAPTER XXXII.

"ARRAH! come on, now! I'm ready for ye!" is as plainly expressed in the attitude of this Irishman as in that of the dog, and it is perfectly natural to both; but the attitude indicates more the posture of affairs inside than is expressed in words: there is a provisional clause in the defiance, which, if it were written, would read thus—"if you are not too strong for me!" The cowardly disposition exhibited in the manner of looking, of standing, and of grasping the *shelalah*, is not to be mista-

ken; and it is in the attempt to look and to feel courageous that it is most betrayed. If Paddy were not a coward, he would not arm himself with a club as a preparation for a successful resistance, much less would he use this cruel instrument to attack with. Cowardice and cruelty are inseparable, and the proof of the one is proof of the other. The cause which operates to produce these two traits, as explained in the chapter concerning the vulture, is brought to bear powerfully upon the Irishman, who drinks to drive away the feeling that he is a coward; then to screw up his courage to the point of defending himself; then to make him pitiless, abusive to his friends, cruel and desperate; then to drive him to madness, and to fancy himself rich, generous, and lordly, as he has the inclination to be; then to shut out the phantoms of wretchedness from his sight, and to drown himself in oblivion; and finally to struggle feebly against the ghastly messengers that come to torment him in the hour of dissolution.

As the dog has a predisposition to be fond of carrion, and has a large chest for the exhalation of carbonic acid gas, it is natural that the Irishman should have a leaning to fermented liquor, and that his chest should be large, enabling him to dispose of a great quantity of excrementitious gases by exhalation, and thus adapting him to the evil habit he is inclined to. Under these circumstances, if the Irishman is temperate, it is a rare virtue. His countenance expresses the greatest possible degree of sobriety, which betokens a trustworthy character, in which is included courage, prudence, honesty, faithfulness, integrity, and nobleness. If in this portrait of an honest dog there is not something sufficiently human to deserve all this, there is at least perfect sobriety, and a resemblance to a true-hearted and honorable gentleman. Gentleness is a virtue; and the dog, if he be well bred, is a gentleman, because he is naturally rude; while the cat, being natu-

rally quiet, can not have the virtue of gentility ascribed to her. The least degree of intemperance is a breach of politeness; it is synonymous with rudeness; while sobriety includes all those qualities that are ascribed to people of the most polished and refined manners. The dog represented on the preceding page is a Scotch terrier. You can see in his countenance undaunted bravery, and a sturdy opposition to all sneaking and meanness, to all cruelty and cowardice, and to all seeking after fermented liquors and fermented food — to all the traits which are manifested in the rat, and of which he has none. He hates the rat, as a thing engendered in filth, which he despises, and as possessing traits the very opposite of faithfulness and courage; and hence he kills the rat, but does not eat it; he is intent upon its destruction, but has the strongest aversion to devouring it. He is not cruel: he does not tease people, nor bark and bite, and worry poor animals. He is not cowardly: he is never seen cowering, or dodging, or skulking, or sneaking along the gutters, looking out for garbage with one eye and for clubs and brickbats with the other. He is intent upon reform; upon cleansing the sewers; upon saving grain and other provisions from rats, which are the emissaries of Fermentation and the imps of Drunkenness. He bears a resemblance to Father Mathew in character and physiognomy, in all the qualities enumerated above, in the features, and particularly in the expression, as Father Mathew bears a resemblance to Fénelon. The likeness between these two noble catholic priests is indicated in the countenance, in the signs of benevolence, disinterestedness, courage, magnanimity, purity, virtue, refinement, gentleness, and internal peace, breathing "peace on earth and good-will to man."

It is perceived from these examples, and from every-day observation, that sobriety is an essential quality of the gentleman, and that the least degree of intemperance is ungentlemanly; yet conviviality is essential to sobriety, and inseparable from gentility, just as imagination is essential to reason, and is inseparable from refinement and intelligence. Conviviality keeps company with nobility and courage. No truly brave person ever lived who was not convivial. Father Mathew is eminently so, and it is not at all inconsistent with his gravity, his earnestness and zeal; and who can look at the face of Fénelon and not say that it is true of him? In the countenance of that terrier, too, there is conviviality: how bright and sparkling, and yet how gravely earnest! Earnestness is the silken tie that unites these two apparently opposite traits together. A man to be convivial must be in earnest, he must have life about him, and he must be in "sober earnest" in order to be sober. The sober man, therefore, who does not labor to destroy intemperance, and to promote sobriety, as the terrier does, is but a sober *thing*, the principal attribute of which is inertia; he is doomed to be a numbskull, in the degree that he is insensible in heart to the emotion of philanthropy, which is convivial.

Nature has provided for this conviviality most beautifully, and it is the perversion of her admirable provision that con stitutes drunkenness. She has formed the patterns from which wineglasses and goblets of every description are derived; and she has formed the nectar, in cups of her own, from which wines, cordials, and intoxicating liquors of every variety, are concocted and brought into existence. She is counterfeited with such skill, that people fancy they are sipping nectar, like the bee, when they are quaffing poison; that they are making themselves brave, when they are making themselves cowardly; that they are growing convivial, when they are growing riotous; that they are acting the part of gentlemen, when they are acting the part of vagabonds; that they are promoting cheerfulness, when they are promoting gloom; that they are improving their wit, when they are becoming foolish and insane; that they are ministering to health, when they are paying tribute to disease; that they are giving themselves freedom and the love of independence, when they are making themselves miserably servile; that they are, in fine, doing everything right, when they are doing everything wrong. To such perversions does the counterfeiting of Nature's beneficent provision, and the perversion of conviviality, lead! Conviviality, companion of all graces and human excellences, how beautiful thou art! Welcome art thou at the fireside, at the social board, if there is moral courage, truth, and honesty, enough to preclude and expel the base hypocrite who has counterfeited thy likeness! welcome art thou at "the feast of reason and the flow of soul," and at the home of peace, virtue, and domestic affection!

But what shall we say of sobriety that is the result of selfishness? There are those who desire to prolong life, and to escape suffering and disease, whether others fall victims to intemperance or not. The want of benevolence in such people shows itself in the want of conviviality. Life with them is such a life as cold-blooded animals enjoy. In their temperance they are not much better than vegetables, and make an approach to stocks and stones. The truth of this observation is better exhibited in these two heads, the one of an Irishman and the other of a terrier, than can be expressed in words. The first is somewhat exaggerated, but the latter is true to life. There

is no vivacity in either, no conviviality, but dullness and stupidity. The unmitigated sobriety of both countenances is easily perceived. There is more of interest, of warmth, of gentlemanliness, in the face of an Irishman who makes himself merry over his cups, than in this of one who takes the pledge because he has no disposition to break it. It is as if this dog should pledge himself to his master in a wink of the eye that he would never taste of a rat, having become too old and sober, if not too lazy, to catch one.

Virtuous sobriety manifests itself in the temperate use of the beverages which Nature herself has provided. What preparation, earnestness, delicacy, boldness, and precision, are manifested in the humming-bird, as he hovers about a flower, and passes his slender bill into the cup that contains the pure spirit which so enlivens and thrills him! The conviviality which belongs to true sobriety, or to temperance, corresponds to the revelry of a bee in the heart of a flower, and to the antics of a humming-bird as he approaches a blossom, and threads the honey-cup with his bill in search of the nectar that delights him.

But each stage of fermentation, as to the appetite that demands it, is a stage in the down-hill course of deception and mockery, of cowardice, cruelty, and degradation. The saccharine fermentation is a perversion of the secretion in flowers that produces honey; and, corresponding with this, cowardice is the perversion of caution, and cruelty is the perversion of courage. All animals that live on honey, or are very fond of it, are remarkable for courage, and also for carefulness, which is another name for caution, as, for example, the bee, the humming-bird, and the bear; but animals that are in the way of eating sugar instead of honey, and seem to prefer it, are deficient in those qualities, as, for example, the house-fly, the ant that lives in the sugar-bowl, and not unfrequently the wasp, besides which we may mention children that live on cakes and confectionery, and people who are very fond of sweetmeats and preserves. The red Americans made sugar from the maple, and the white ones manufacture it very extensively from the cane, and use it, too, as a substitute for honey, which their resemblance to the bear includes a particular love for; and this appetite for "sugar" (as if one species of saccharine matter were as good as another) indicates a difficulty of feeling the distinction between courage and cruelty, and between caution and cowardice.

The use of sugar is the stepping-stone to intemperance. The appetite grows upon a man by indulgence, and seizes him periodically like the propensity for strong drink, so that he is finally made aware that his condition is like that of the drunkard. He requires larger and still larger potations of sugar to satisfy him; he resolves against the intemperate use of it, and re-resolves, but he can not see and resist the temptation; and when the appetite comes upon him, like that of the drunkard for his cups, he wanders and almost rushes in search of it, and goes from one candy-shop to another as the toper goes from one coffeehouse to another to satisfy himself with drams. This is no fancy sketch, but is taken from life. The appetite for the result of the saccharine fermentation is like that for the result of the vinous; but with the appetite for honey or for any wholesome article of diet, unperverted by the use of sugar or intoxicating drinks, it is not so.

Yet the deterioration connected with the first degree of fermentation is very slight compared with that which is connected with the second, and would be hardly worth mentioning if it did not lead to the latter. When the craving for sugar refuses to be satisfied, and when the anxiety of the appetite demands relief, there is a feeling that strong drink would be good; but it is the sugar that renders brandy, gin, and toddy, palatable in the first place: nevertheless, when the mixture and the second degree in artificial courage are taken, those articles are loved raw. Of the cowardice connected with drunkenness, we have abundant examples in the Irish; and as the appetite for alcohol is a greater perversion in those who resemble bears than in others, the Americans, both the Indians and the whites, when they take to drink, are the greatest drunkards in the world. The bear is by nature courageous in the extreme, and is in no need of having his courage stimulated; he wrestles and fights hand to hand, and cuffs with his paws like a man with his fists, and will prey upon nothing that has not come to its death by his own hands; and for *him* to touch fermentation would be a much greater perversion than for the dog, that is inclined to it. Hence the Irishman is excused for being a drunkard, but the Yankee never.

If you are going to excuse anybody for indulging in intoxication, it will be one who feels under the influence of it as does the Irishman who is represented on the following page.

His combined gestures are an imitation of the humming-bird over the honey-cup. Yet it would be hard-hearted to indulge a feeling of gratification at seeing him so merry without cause, especially when we reflect that "wounds and bruises without cause" are sure to follow. The sober, second thought refuses to be gratified at the exhibition of a tragic farce. The contagion of this poor fellow's intoxication is worse than the original disease. The man who deals out intoxicating drinks, but abstains from them himself, reaps his enjoyments from the fictitious enjoyments of others, and intoxicates his own mind in the degree that he intoxicates the bodies of his victims. This is a species of intoxication as much worse than the other as the soul is superior to the body. The preceding gentleman would never be engaged in so mean an employment as keeping a drinking-house: he would not steal the pleasure and the profit, and leave the penalty to another. On the next page is a dog that looks as if he would like to join him in his gambols; and the resemblance between them shows that they would be fond of each other's society. He is a drover's dog, and may meet this gentleman at a country inn. The character of his business is such, that he must from necessity be unfeeling and cruel, though you can see by his good-natured countenance that it is superinduced, as it is in the man; it is not so much *his* fault as the fault of circumstances. He has a sense of duty, in spite of his perversions, and is governed by that; so that his conscience does not trouble him, the responsibility being laid off upon his master, whose mandates he obeys; his

master, by-the-by, will have a great deal to answer for! This same dog resembles the paddy given below, and the animal characteristics are the same in both. To a face like this what could be more becoming than a pipe? When the dog is made to "sit up," a short pipe is sometimes facetiously placed in the corner of his mouth to heighten his resemblance to an Irishman—of which resemblance there appears to be an intuitive perception in the mind of the operator.

After the vinous fermentation, comes the acetous, and with it a degree of cowardice and cruelty greater than the last. When a man's temper gets thoroughly spoiled by intemperance, he has passed the stage in which pure whiskey is grateful to him; he fairly loathes the taste of it, and drinks it only to allay trembling and the fear of death, and to give him courage to live on. The spirit that he has steeped himself in has turned to vinegar, and his taste is for that which gives him more cowardice than courage. Wretched man! he no longer drinks liquor, but *swills* it, and swill is sour: the vilest liquor of the still is nearer to his taste than that he once approved, and now vinegar is his taste, and his need of alcohol the same as before. If hard cider or vinegar would support his nerves, he might still fancy himself in Elysium; but his nervous sensibilities are sharpened, his teeth are set on edge, he is tortured with dreadful apprehensions, and makes a slimpsy show of a gentleman; he is all unstrung, he can scarcely hold himself together; his endeavor to pluck up courage turns into a plea for mercy; he is fain to fawn, to beg for quarter, and to have a dog for his master. He has nothing but his dependence and misery to rely upon. He has nothing of the gentleman left to him, except the court-dress (if he be an Irishman), and this serves to make him contemptible by the contrast of what he is with what he should be. Observe how truly Nature intended the Irish to be gentlemen, lords, and nobles, in the fact that the poorest of them who come fresh to this country make their appearance in court-costume!

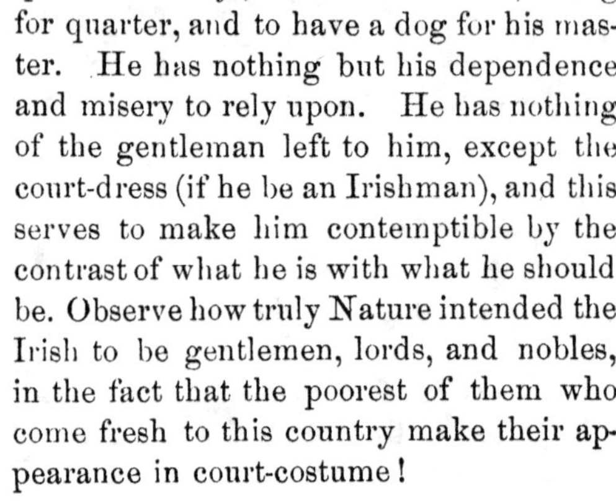

We have heard it said that drinking hard cider makes a man more cross and crabbed than drinking rum. We doubt not but that it is so. A crabbed disposition is a miserably cowardly one: the man who owns such a trait is cruel without courage; he can not delude himself for a moment into the idea that he is brave, or has the least particle of heroism. The same is the case with the person who is addicted to the use of vinegar, which, like the use of sugar, induces all the symptoms of intemperance, with the exception of intoxication. The individual can not deny that he is a coward, and he is not ashamed to own it, but makes it a plea for a thousand indulgences. He likes others to feel his alarm, and all the consequences of his cowardly apprehension, and to be governed by fear as he is; and therefore even in his benevolence he is cruel, and in his morality he is a hard master, as he conceives God to be. In his goodness to others, and in his religion, he is a "hired servant." His reverence and humility are such as his evil appetite in exciting cowardice and cruelty will allow them to be. He feels as if something is not right, as the drunkard often feels, and as if he would dare to be told of his faults by one who is blind and can not see them; but the truth is, he can not bear to be told of a single one. He has not the courage to look upon it; it would frighten him to death; and therefore to set it forth would be an unpardonable offence. He hates the person he is afraid of, but quails at the sight of him, and wishes to appear his friend.

The dogs that bear a resemblance to the class of persons of whom this is a description are of the sheepish variety, and are allied to wolves. Cruelty requires to be gratified, and they have a feeling that, inasmuch as they look for it to be practised upon themselves, they ought not be disappointed in the apprehension; but they have not the courage to face their masters, and to confess their crimes. The favor which they show to cruelty they exhibit in making an attack upon sheep, and this for the reason that sheep are their oldest and most innocent companions. They can fancy that in the sufferings of sheep their own crimes are expiated, and that they suffer punishment by proxy! They practise this species of deception upon themselves for the reason that they are cowards; and for their success in making capital out of nothing they rely upon the gullibility of others. They are "sly dogs," for the simple reason that cowardice leads to prevarication and falsehood, and that cruelty is not gratified in any way so completely as by stratagem. Who can not see the unfeeling cruelty and the cowardice in the eyes of the individual whom

we have represented above, to be compared with those of the wolf?—also the dishonesty that in the countenances of both is too intense for words? The "wolf's clothing" is more conspicuous in the man—in the crape on his hat, and in the entire face—than in the wolf; but what a villain is the latter, that stands there to give countenance to the proceedings! You might be hoodwinked so thoroughly by that man as not to know that he is a coward; but imagine a person taking him by the collar, and you can see that he will endeavor to slink away, will beg to be let go, and will promise solemnly to be seen in those parts no more!

The taste acquired for the vinous fermentation leads to the putrefactive. Following the stage of drunkenness last described is that in which the fluids of the body are on the eve of losing their vitality, in which the breath is already putrid, and in which the body itself has been known to undergo decomposition, called in this case "spontaneous combustion." The man whose vitality holds out to this stage of drunkenness has scarcely anything left of a soul but suspicion and cowardice. His voice is sepulchral, and warns us not to get within the sphere of the breath that accompanies it. The appetite accepts of food that is half rotten, and the degree of suspicion and cowardice is equal to that of the crow. Death stares him in the face, but does not stare him out of countenance, for the Death that he sees is a reflection of himself. He puts on the appearance of the grim monster perfectly.

"Hark, from the tombs a doleful sound!"

is a voice from his own breast, the breath from which is fetid, showing that he is "full of dead men's bones, and all uncleanness." He looks as though he were frightened out of his seven senses, and no wonder: he does

not see that it is himself that he is afraid of; it were well if he did; but that it is himself is evident from the fact that he *looks* all the dreadful things that he sees. He is himself the monster that is to be dreaded. He is cruel, hard, unmerciful, like the dog beside him—an animal that ought to be shot for his own good and for the safety of others. Is this cruel? We do not say it of the man, but of the dog, the very embodiment of a thirst for blood. It is only in France that the dog can be perverted to the degree that may be called infernal, and even there it is only in the employ of a butcher and in the atmosphere of a slaughter-house that a dog can be made as this one is. The man, too, who is evidently an Irishman, has undergone a metamorphosis that gives him a resemblance to the Frenchman, and also to the frog. It is natural to the French to be fond of tainted meat and of fermented drink, but it is less natural to the Irish; and for these to attain to the appetite for carrion is to become exceedingly perverted. You can see by this man's countenance that putrid meat can go into his mouth as well as not. But anything fresh would go in with reluctance; even whiskey is not easily swallowed. Imagine a man with the hydrophobia compelled to drink water, and you have an idea of the wretched condition of the man who has carried drunkenness to the last degree.

But "iniquity will have an end." The man who is not already dead can be redeemed from intemperance even in the last degree. He will be a different person from what he would have been if he had never become intemperate, but he will be reckoned among the sober, and an honorable position will be assigned him. The difference between him and the person who has never perverted himself will be as the difference between the humble-bee and the humming-bird. The one will have a rioting, rollicking, savage, ungentlemanly way with him, while the other will be a perfect gentleman in all his manners. The drunkard on his last legs may be compared to the blow-fly when it has come to the degree of perfection in the fondness for carrion, at which time it has so strong a resemblance to the humble-bee as almost to be mistaken for one. When the drunkard is in the corresponding condition, it is the time to save him. It was not known until a few years ago that the "confirmed drunkard" could be saved: the "Washingtonians" proved it to be practicable. We may suppose with good reason that the noble mastiff was derived from a dog like the preceding; and the drunkard when he is reformed has a mastiff-like countenance, the wild, furious,

ferocious aspect being tamed down into dignified courage and sobriety. The savage traits which he has acquired will be swayed by higher faculties; but in spite of these they will render him harsh, and inclined to rend and tear, and to use his wit sarcastically against the very vice that he has been addicted to. He can learn to be magnanimous, and even forgiving, but he will never be very amiable. He has that kind of character and physiognomy that are seen in the portrait of Ben Jonson, and particularly in Irishmen, most of whom were born of intemperate ancestors — the reformed drunkard and the child of a drunkard being alike.

CHAPTER XXXIII.

By knowing what animal a man resembles, we possess a clew to his character that may be of great use to us. We can judge of the secret springs of his conduct, of those motives of action that have their origin in nature, and that are almost as inevitable in man as they are in the lower orders of the animal creation. The knowledge of character by the signs in the face will be very materially assisted by a knowledge of the animal nature that is made up of a man's ruling traits. You must understand what his character is by nature if you would understand how various rational and moral influences would affect him; and this nature of his is something homogeneous, something that is presented individually in some department or other of the animal kingdom. The ability of getting at this resemblance will improve by use. At first you do not see that one man in a hundred has any resemblance to any particular animal, but the habit of study and observation will make it plain.

In this lady, for example, you would not at first sight discover that she resembled a dove, but you perceive something in her that produces the effect upon your feelings that you experience in relation to that bird. You may even call her "Dove," and be as familiar with her as lovers are with their lady-loves, and yet suppose that it is a mere fancy that leads you to call her by that endearing appellation. But you may be sure she is like the dove in disposition if she is like in face and in the sphere that she throws around her. She has the element, as the basis of her character, that is embodied in that bird; and it is her ruling trait, so far as her animal nature is concerned. And it is very likely that her moral character will correspond to it: it would be strange if it did

not. The moral and intellectual character has less to control in one who resembles a dove than in one who resembles a lion. The signs of the higher faculties exhibit, therefore, more refinement in the one and more strength in the other, and this places them on a par in respect to virtue and intelligence. In this character goodness finds a congenial soil, and it is therefore luxuriant but tender. In a character that resembles the lion, goodness finds a rock to grapple and a furious climate to contend with, and it is therefore strong and rigid like the oak.

There are, however, a great variety of doves and pigeons, as there are of frogs and toads, and they constitute as great a variety of character.

A certain likeness and apposition is to be observed between the person who resembles a dove and the one who resembles a hen. The relation is something like that of octaves in music. On the following page is the portrait of a Spaniard who resembles a cock. The Spaniards resemble cocks as the Irish resemble dogs. Love of contest, and love of triumph, and subserviency, are ruling traits in both characters. Cock-fighting is a passion with the Spaniards, as it is with the cock. In some of the provinces of Spain it is the favorite game; in others, bull-fighting is the favorite diversion; but contest in some form or other is a passion. The Spaniards and the Irish are as much like each other in their fondness for fighting as the cock is like the dog. But they differ in the mode. The dog gives no quarter: the cock beats his antagonist and then runs, and the conquered party runs after him, and in his turn becomes the conqueror. This is the way with the Spaniards, as exemplified in the contest between Don Carlos and the late regent Queen Christina.

In bull-fights it is the same. There is advantage allowed to both parties, though that which is shown to the bull is a mockery rather than otherwise. With the Irish it is not so. They fight like dogs, as if in a contest with "grim Death," to whom, as they expect no quarter, they will yield none. The Irish have to be parted. Not so the Spaniards: they fight upon the principle—

> "That he who fights and runs away
> May live to fight another day!"

The military ambition of the Spaniard is concentrated in a victorious contest with John Bull—always was, and always will be. The rules of honor in a bull-fight are a specimen of the magnanimity with which he regards that formidable power that it is his glory to contend with.

One of the most singular things about the cock is his crowing when he considers himself in the long run to have gained the victory. Both crow, and the contest has turned into one of lungs. Precisely so it is with the Spaniards. They blow the trumpet of fame in honor of a victory louder than anybody else, and that is saying a great deal. It is all the same whether they *anticipate* or *have gained* the victory, or whether they *might* have gained it had the circumstances been different.

Of the many instances of the confident boasting and triumphant exultation of the Spaniards which might be given, we quote the following "from an ode by Luis de Gongora:"—

——"Raise thy renownéd hand,
O Spain! from French Pyrenee to the land
Where the Moor Atlas lifts his mountain height,
And at the martial trumpet's lofty sound
Bid thou thy valiant offspring cluster round
Beneath thy old victorious banners, bright
In hardest adamant, a fearful sight!—
Such that the lands of languid power,
The nations leagued against thy faith, dismayed
At the strong radiance of thy beamy arms,
At the fierce splendor of the falchion-blade,
With looks averted, in alarms,
Shall turn at once their eyes and backs for flight,
Like clouds before the deity of day;
Or even, like yielding wax, dissolve away
Before the luminous and golden fire
That from their graven helmets forth shall fly;
As blind of faith, so blinded then in eye!"

An equally vivid representation of the cock, with his scarlet crown, his valiant look, his martial feathers, his savage beak, his shrill clarion, his solid spurs, lifted with pride, energy, and scorn, would be parallel to the above; but he has more of defiance and victory in his aspect than can be expressed in words! The young cock crows in a *strain* like the following. (It is a "poem written in the character of a child; a species of playful composition popular among the Spaniards" at the time of the great "Armada" for the invasion of England in 1585–'88.) A little girl is speaking to her playfellow, and tells him—

"My brother Don John
To England is gone,
To kill the Drake,
And the queen to take,
And the heretics all to destroy:
And he will give me,
When he comes back,
A Lutheran boy
With a chain round his neck;
And grandmamma
From his share shall have
A Lutheran maid,
To be her slave!"

Thus, in the Spaniard, is illustrated the proverb that "as the old cock crows so crows the young." Whether his giving a chance to the enemy is the result of what pugilists call "honor," or is the result of a desire to have an excuse in case of defeat, does not appear. It is doubtful, however, whether the cock would think so far as that. It is more probably the action of his wonderful subserviency, indicated by the wattles under the jaw. When a fellow-being is weak, this subserviency is prompted to help him; and when the antagonist is "wamble-cropped" and beaten, the victor regards him in the light of a hen, and instantly gives quarter; and then being turned upon when his anger is at zero he runs, and his ugly Xantippe after him. And thus the fortune of the game passes from one hand to another.

The Spaniards are famous cavaliers. They were the greatest knights-errant in the world. The cock is famous for his gallantry and his chivalrous bearing, and for his spirit in defending the females whose safety he is responsible for. But in spite of this, or perhaps on account of it, he is inclined to be jealous. He regards his lady-love as under excessive obligations to him, and he expects to be rewarded by the most devoted attachment. If he has delivered her from a castle, he considers that he has a right to lock her up in one; he does not expect, neither will he allow, the least wandering; but he is apprehensive that she may be stolen from him, and therefore he is excessively jealous. And it must be confessed that he has reason to be, for his neighbors have as much gallantry with respect to imprisoned females as he himself has! When he fancies that his treasure is in danger of escaping him, he plucks her by the head, and having done it once he is sure to need to do it twice; and thus his true gallantry particle by particle escapes from him, and he becomes a petty despot. His gallantry takes a wider range; it shows itself in a bad sense: his business is to deliver ladies from their cruel lords, and he finds that he has a plenty of it to do, and that the females whom he is inclined to take under his protection are very numerous. Of course, he is aware that the same disposition exists in his neighbors, and that they will look upon him, and justly too, as one of

the cruel lords who holds one or more of the fair sex in confinement. If under these circumstances he can catch one of them in the neighborhood of his domains, he is sure to chastise him, if he is able to, and for this he claims the merit of a chivalrous action. Such a chance to display his gallantry is a rare fortune, and he sounds aloud his exploits in the ears of his greatly-obliged and admiring hens, with his face toward home, and on his march thither. In other words, and placing it in the past—

> "Gayly the troubadour touched his guitar
> As he was hastening home from the war,
> Singing, 'From Palestine hither I come,
> Lady-love, lady-love, welcome me home!'"

Only for the knight-errantry of the Spaniards, some few of their number would have more wives than the sultan.

As Spaniards of the best quality are produced in Spain, the cocks that are produced there are of better quality than those of any other country. The Spanish cock is superior game, but its highest excellence consists in the quality of its flesh, which is said to be superior to that of any other of its kind. It is to be expected that the country that is best for the cock should favor a likeness to that animal in man, and should develop national characteristics founded in that resemblance. The same principle holds true with regard to the ox, the hog, the bear, the goose, the swan, the frog, the dog, and we believe with regard to all the other animals that have been mentioned. The people who resemble a particular animal naturally prefer the country that is suited to that animal, but do not always live there; and as it is the animal that becomes suited to the country, and not the country to the animal, we may suppose that it is the man that becomes suited to the animal, and not the animal to the man.

CHAPTER XXXIV.

Among the variety of human faces a resemblance to the goat is very frequently to be met with. This resemblance is plainly discoverable in the face of Sforza; and the prominent traits in the character of the goat are easily traced in his.

Large combative faculties, energy, perseverance, and precision, are discoverable at a single glance. In the man who resembles the goat, the most prominent traits are indicated in the most prominent part of the countenance. In these two profiles the ridge of the nose is distinguished for something more than prominence and convexity: it has a peculiarity of its own, indicating a manner of exercising the combative faculties that may be called *dogmatic*. Pugilism in a nose like this takes a particular direction: the bent of the reasoning faculties is indicated in a certain bend of the nose, which furnishes a sort of channel for dispute and polemical controversy. The "doctors and lawyers" of the olden time are represented always with features like these; and because the representations are thus true to life, they seem like portraits. In such noses and in such a form of the ridge of the eyebrow as the preceding, there are elastic energy and activity, and a strength that overcomes resistance. Such heads are formed not only for striking with great force, but for pushing; they present a hard front to whatever obstacles stand in the way, and are ever upon the lookout for a challenge, and ready to receive one. They join battle with canons and creeds rather than with windmills and inoffensive sheep; yet they reflect upon themselves, for all their labor and warfare is to show that what they are fighting with is a man of straw.

In proof of the correctness of these remarks, we would refer the reader to the portraits of distinguished controversialists, such as Calvin and John Knox. The age of chivalry abounded with such; and it should be observed here that they are similar in many respects to those who resemble cocks. The difference between them is that which exists between chivalry and the crusades. In nothing, but in what might be called the crusades of the Jews (for example, in driving out the Canaanites, Hivites, Hittites, Jebusites, Philistines, &c.), could the goatish propensity be more strongly exhibited than in a crusade to the Holy Land: this was the result, not only of the goatish action of the combative faculties, but of a likeness to the Jews, and of a liking for Judea, and for whatever the Jews were particularly fond of; for the Jews have a striking resemblance to the goat, as will be shown in the sequel. Under the influence of religious enthusiasm they made impetuous or goatlike descents upon the possessions of others, and the history of the crusades bears a striking analogy to theirs. As the cock and the goat are attached to the barnyard and the dunghill, and have a similar air and manner, and resemble each other in profile, so those who resemble these animals are intimately related to each other in character and physiognomy.

The word "striking" is particularly applicable to the goatlike face, as illustrated in the preceding engraving and in the following portrait of Beza. This old reformer, the associate of Calvin, and one of the most learned and zealous controversialists of his time, shows in his countenance the character of the goat as plainly as he exhibited it in his actions. Who can not see that of him, and of the class of which he is a worthy representative, it may be said —

"By apostolic blows and knocks
They prove their doctrines orthodox!"

By-the-by, the apostles were Jews, and some of them fine examples of the peculiarity in question.

A faculty which contributes more than any other to render the action of the combative faculties in the goat peculiar, is subterfuge. This is indicated by the falling or overhanging of the ridge of the eyebrow over the inner angle of the eye, as seen in the figures preceding. In that ridge of the brow there is always something striking in the person who resembles a goat; it looks as if it were formed to make a hole in the wall, so that the enemy might enter in martial triumph with all his hosts. How proudly he proceeds! It is because his subterfuge is subservient to his combativeness: if it were not so, it would make him sneaking and cowardly. It is this faculty which causes the goat to make his attack in the rear, whenever he has an opportunity; but his attack is so large, and is exercised so boldly, that he carries his head proudly, as if he had not been guilty of a meanness, and did not meditate the cowardly act which at any moment he is ready to perpetrate. The principle of action with the goat, and with the person who resembles that animal, is *vis atergo*—it may be set down as their governing motive. They *drive* things, or, in other words, they are *dogmatic*. They do not lead, or persuade; and yet they do not come up boldly as antagonists, but manage to get behind, and there to attack so boldly, that they mistake the back side for the front, and claim to "have done the thing fairly," and to have carried the redoubt courageously!

But subterfuge favors cowardice more than bravery. It runs to refuges and retreats, to prevarication and falsehood (which is always cowardly), and "crawls out at the little end of the horn." It has a thousand resorts, and most of these are confined places, or under-ground passages, where the air is polluted by excretion and putrescence, and is not relieved by ventilation. Thus cowardice, which is favored by subterfuge, is still more increased by the causes of stench, as before explained. The habitation of the animal that has large subterfuge "smells old," and the animal himself does so; he is "in bad odor" with all who have true courage and magnanimity, and not the mere pretension to it, like the goat. This animal has the odor alluded to in greater perfection than any other; it is the sphere of cowardice, and of traits worthy of being distrusted; and the sphere of the person who resembles the goat has a repelling influence upon those of a different character, and is of the kind to "knock a man down." Thus there is an agreement between subterfuge and combativeness; and every goat, as well as "every cock, fights best on his own dunghill."

It has been frequently observed that in certain characters there is a singular meeting of opposites. The love of climbing is diverse from subterfuge, but it acts harmoniously with that faculty, as combativeness does. The goat is fond of taking his station where he can get under a rock or mount to the top of it, and is familiarly seen at the side of a flight of steps, where he can get under or ascend, as one or the other of these dispositions happens to predominate. The sign of the love of climbing is the anterior projection of the ridge of the eyebrow over the centre of the eye — large in the goat and in those who resemble him. In human beings the ambition to rise includes this faculty, together with the love of eminence, indicated in the elevation of the wing of the nostril by the muscle called the *levator nasi.* The love of climbing may be so strongly excited as to produce an inflammation of the membrane that lines the frontal sinus in the place which indicates this faculty, and in this case there is pain and distress in that portion of the forehead. This remark is applicable to the person of whom this is a profile, and whose "synonym," if we mistake not, is a mountain-goat. The faculty of weight is intimately related to the love of climbing — and hence Nature has given to animals fond of clambering heavy horns, as in the case of the ibex. In the example before us, Nature has slung, not a bottle, but a horn —

——— "upon each side,
To keep his balance true."

There is a sympathetic spirit between these two, the person and the animal.

Now consider what must be the effect of this combination of combativeness, subterfuge, love of climbing, love of eminence, and balance and sure-footedness. It must be something very nearly allied to *diplomacy*. How nicely everything must be weighed, measured, and adjusted, by the man who resembles the animal that climbs precipitous rocks, and spends his life in perfect safety among cliffs and crags, caverns and pitfalls! The important office of the diplomatist may be assigned to him with the greatest propriety. It is a rare talent that distinguishes the man who resembles the mountain-goat, the ibex, or the chamois. He is often called upon to take a leap where the greatest danger is involved, and where not a moment is to be lost; and it is never into an oozy bed, like that of the frog, and is never therefore a leap in the dark. The man who resembles the goat always knows what he is about, and is always prudent so far as policy and expediency are concerned. A single reflection will satisfy the reader that the Jews possess the faculties here referred to in a super-eminent degree.

The connection of subterfuge and combativeness with the love of climbing is seen in the disposition to undermine natural and artificial walls and eminences, and to strike against those solid substances that compose an ascent and offer resistance to progression. Hence the goat and those who resemble him are suited in their tastes and habits to ruins and to everything which savors of the old. A mountain, with

——"ruined sides and summit hoar,"

is especially pleasing to them, and ivy-mantled towers and the fragments of ancient temples are their delight. There is an aristocratic bearing about them, and their thoughts are associated with grandeur, in which the eternal and the perishable are equally mingled; the contemplation of immortality being assisted by the emblems of frailty and of the insubstantiality of sublunary things. The love of his "holy hill of Zion," of his "beautiful temple," and of the rites and ceremonies of his religion (so remarkable for their accuracy and precision), is a characteristic of the Jew.

The faculty of acquisitiveness operates as a leading motive in the character of the goat and of those who resemble him, and it dovetails with the faculties before mentioned most admirably. Who has not observed the thievish propensities of this animal, and how boldly he exercises them in connection with combativeness, and how impudently in connection with combativeness and subterfuge? We could not bring a stronger example of the action of this faculty in the particular way which constitutes a resemblance to the goat, than in the Israelite. Boldness and impudence are cheap in those places where the "old-clo'" men congregate; and what we have already said of the love of antiquity, and of old smells, and of bodily excretions, explains the partiality manifested by these people for trading in cast-off garments, old furniture, and the like. The goat which this person resembles is similar to a sheep, but the similarity serves to heighten the distinction. The person who resembles the goat has a mouth

which indicates a taste for tobacco—a self-complacent appreciation of the quality which he calls "sweet," and which others are insensible of, in the nature of that weed. It is a Charles Goat rather than a Charles Lamb who says in earnest to tobacco:—

——"Plant of rarest virtue!
Blisters on the tongue that hurts you!"

A likeness to the sheep betokens spiritual perceptions, and the ability to distinguish between the peculiarities of one person and those of another; but a likeness to the goat betokens an external mind, and hence a deficient knowledge of human nature. Of course, such a character is a very superficial one; it is hardly worth the trouble of analyzing.

In the preceding figure it is easy to see that the eyes are mere windows to look out of. They observe the clothing of the spirit, and to them it is true that—

> "Nature has made man's breast no windows
> To publish what goes on within doors,
> Or what dark secrets there inhabit,
> Unless his own rash fury blab it!"

Hence they are interested in clothes and superficial ornaments, and the Jews trade and traffic in these the world over, particularly in jewels, which are well named, being the favorite merchandise of the Jews. They are no judges of character, and think that others will not know anything more of them than they blab. They make no distinctions, but address all with the same ridiculous familiarity, or formality, as the case may be. In Chatham street they do not distinguish you from a common loafer; you are not supposed to know the profession of the person who calls after you until he has pointed at his wares, nor to know whether you want anything or not, nor to have any mind of your own, for a mind is a thing which a Jew does not recognise. Look at those eyes: they catch every object that passes, that may be converted into gain; they are as full of business as a squirrel's cheeks are of nuts; they speculate on the solid attractions of woman, and may possibly see jewels in her eyes. His mouth is the figure of a tulip, and is fond of ruby lips and tobacco, the ruby of his own being the stain of the juice. Love with him is a gratification of the senses; it does not go deeply into his heart, and hence he makes no demands upon the hearts of others; he is a favorite of the ladies rather than otherwise, for, as he asks no heart, he puts them to no inconvenience to find out whether they have any. If he ever heard of "heart-strings," he thought of "purse-strings;" and when he hears of "a man of worth," he thinks of riches. The correspondent of all these traits is in the goat. This animal is all attention to the external; he has uncommon quickness of the senses. You never see a dreamy or abstracted look in his countenance, as you do in the sheep and the cow, and other domestic animals. He sees every motion you make, and so quickly that he seems almost to perceive your intention; but if your motive is pacific he does not know it; his nature compels him to act upon the principle of treating every man as a rogue; his countenance, be it ever so full of honesty, goes for nothing, unless he be himself in an honest mood, and then even the basest usage can not destroy his confidence; he may be seized repeatedly by a dog, and cry bitterly, but in the intervals will make no attempt to escape.

CHAPTER XXXV.

In traversing the thoroughfares and by-ways of a great city, we are impressed with the conviction that there are multitudes of people who resemble goats. There is a variety of

countenances that forcibly remind us of "some sort of animal," though we can not say that there is anything very gross or beastly in its appearance. An example is herewith presented, and on closer inspection it is the physiognomy of a goat. The individual before us is the representative of a class, who look so very innocent of any relationship to inferior creatures, that we do not at first sight form a very distinct idea of the animal they resemble. They give you to understand that they are descended from an ancient and honorable ancestry, and carry their heads with such an air of knowing what they are about, that you begin to accuse yourself of unpardonable irreverence in harboring the suspicion that they have a family likeness to the goat. The more you peer into their countenances, the more you are mystified and perplexed with a "lawless and uncertain" imagining; a vague impression steals over you that there is some sort of connection between beard and tobacco, and of these with goat, but you are determined not to credit the evidence of your senses.

It is a physiognomy like the preceding that excites this sort of metaphysical discussion in your mind. A proper use of the faculty of comparison would place this specimen of the *genus homo* where he belongs. He is cut out and formed specially for "dancing attendance" upon the ladies; and the ladies, dear souls, are quick to perceive the intentions of Nature. He is the very person to dance with when it is a *partner* that is wanted. That great prominence of the bone under the eye is an indication that he sees everything: hence he is the very person that is wanted in the cotillon, when it is needful that everything should be seen to, and that the dance should go off respectably. The motions in the ballroom are like those that are exercised in "dancing attendance," and the grace and elegance of the latter are greatly enhanced by the systematic exercise of which they are the original. The goat has a "light fantastic toe," and "trips it lightly." The performances called dancing, *par excellence*, are derived from a resemblance to the goat, which no person need be ashamed of, unless this element in his nature be in too great proportion, or too literal. The actions of this animal upon which we predicate our assertions are thus described: "She walks, stops short, runs, jumps, advances, retreats, shows, then hides herself, or flies; and this all from caprice, or without any other determinate cause than her whimsical vivacity." A very correct description of a dance certainly, and it may be true also that these "irregular" movements show "inconstancy," as natural history supposes; but when they are regulated by music, which brings order out of confusion, they show the opposite.

A word upon this subject. A resemblance to the goat argues a vast deal of amativeness, with very great impulsiveness of this faculty; and this sort of love is fickle and inconstant. The very motions described above are indications of this, and are lewd and vulgar; but in the degree that they are various and complicated they are subject to the influence of music, and become finally amenable to its laws. Music in this connection is first an element of bacchanalian revel, and is prostituted to debauchery and licentiousness by the superiority of that which it attempts to reform; but after a time it acquires the mastery, and governs the motions, and makes them, like itself, the language of constancy, purity, and love —expressive of the most delicate relations of the sexes, of refinement, friendship, and affection. As love and happiness are united, so are music and the poetry of motion, and it is natural to sing for love and to dance for joy.

Look again, if you please, at our hero. If you are not a woman, you can see by his countenance that he has in his mouth something delicious; you are sure that it is a quid, and that he "rolls it as a sweet morsel under his tongue." That in the muscles of his cheeks, and in his lips and tongue, there is the power of extracting the juice, and also of projecting it, is all plain to a masculine judgment; and his face is so largely concerned in his duties to the weed, that there is something delicious in his *countenance.* He says, when he stuffs a chew through the aperture appropriated to that purpose, that he "puts it into his *face.*" And yet not one woman in twenty would know that he chews. He looks with doating eyes on the lovely fair, and that is sufficient to withdraw their attention from everything but the eyes that are capable of such appreciation. But the eye indicates taste, and such taste as corresponds to that of the tongue. The ideas which a tobacco-monger forms of a sweet face and of a sweet disposition correspond to his ideas of sweetness.

Why it is that one who resembles the goat is fond of tobacco, we have not yet discovered. Certain it is that a person with features like the preceding, and with such a beard, can not be otherwise than fond of the drug. The appetite is natural to him, or rather we should say that it is easily acquired, and that he holds it with more tenacity than he does his saliva! He is one who does everything with an air of *nonchalance*, and is "well to do" in the world, and has something to chew upon, like the goat that retires and ruminates upon the stock of food that he has gathered. Here is a lot of people who resemble goats, and have all of them the air and manner that have been described. The resemblances are most admirable, as may be seen by comparing them one by one with the individual goats we have met with and have seen in print. Yet the artist had only the intention of representing a company of persons under the habitual influence of tobacco, and has evidently drawn from his observation—so

much so, that we are inclined to think that he has given us portraits, or, better still, that we have seen these portraits before. They speak for themselves, for countenances will speak even in church. It is easy to see rumination in the faces of the men, and perception in those of the women, which must be highly gratifying to the preacher, whose expression is that of delivery. The man nearest the desk is taking in an idea, and it is evidently a great one. The man with his back to us, and facing the speaker, is on the verge of apprehending, and is pausing and deliberating upon the event, as if there were no weightier consideration than that of listening. The man with a profile is cogitating upon the probable quantity of tobacco-juice he will be able to express from the cud that he has now in his mouth before he will be obliged to throw it away. The remaining, fat-faced, good-natured individual, is the only respectable person in the congregation: he extracts sweets from his tobacco and from the sermon as skilfully as a bee does from poison flowers, and is hospitable with pipes and tobacco to others more than to himself, thereby exceeding the requirement of the golden rule. The preacher is one who asks "a chaw" from every man he meets, as is plainly indicated by his countenance; and he patronizes the last-mentioned individual especially, and is blessed with an instinct in his fingers of seizing a pinch of snuff without knowing it, and of conveying it to his nose during one of his emphatic courtesies.

But the female part of the congregation — we leave them to an abler pen than our own. The speaker addresses all his eloquent words to the men, for they have reverence — and are of the opinion that such a sermon as that is "not to be sneezed at!" A woman, considering his "pinching wants," is offering to supply them, not dreaming that she is wanting in veneration; and just now the preacher is touching upon the sublime, and making an appeal to the organ of veneration rather than to that of benevolence, which makes the offering of a pinch of snuff highly improper, especially as he might say: "I am not speaking to you, ladies, but to these gentlemen; when I have something to say on *charity*, I will turn to you!" But it is a hard thing for women, who are so fond of attention, to see it bestowed on others, and not make an effort to gain it. *That* woman, especially, shows by her countenance that she is ever ready to thrust herself upon the attention of others, making herself officious, and in the face of reluctant admiration and cold indifference acting upon the principle, "Never give up the ship!"

We opine that the preacher is haranguing from a text from

Paul, and that the subject is "justification by faith." Paul was a converted Jew, and he would have been a strange Jew indeed if he had not preserved the national characteristics. The intricacy and subtlety of his reasoning, his discussions about the law, his manner of dispute, his cross-questionings and answers, show that he was "a Hebrew of the Hebrews," and that it was not for nothing that he was brought up at the feet of Gamaliel, and that the manner of his life was after the strictest sect of the Pharisees. He was the lawyer before Festus; the doctor in his epistles; and fully and thoroughly Jewish, in being "all things to all men, that he might win some." The Jews, scattered among the nations, are admirable diplomatists, for "when they are in Rome they do as the Romans do." All the Jews that are converted to Christianity are converted through the instrumentality of Paul; and it may be that that class of Gentiles who seem to say, "I am of Paul," are slightly Judaized.

The long beard of the goat indicates the impulsiveness of those faculties the signs of which are in the chin. The person who resembles this animal is remarkable for the same manifestation of the faculties of love. The disposition which more than anything else renders the goat a disgusting animal, is indicated in the breadth of his lower jaw, his peculiar odor, his prominent sacrum, the action of his head in the direction of the lower jaw, and the wanton manners, or "whimsical vivacity," before alluded to. This, together with the fondness for external objects and for the gratification of the senses, renders the person who resembles the goat exceedingly sensual, and a very perfect example of the "lusts of the flesh, the lust of the eye, and the pride of life."

Amativeness, with nothing to counteract it, and with subterfuge and suspicion to favor it, leads to "filthiness of the flesh," and to stimulant heats of fermentation and beds of filth, where whatever is engendered is the vilest of the animal creation, together with pestilence, contagion, and disease.

But this is applicable only to those who resemble the goat of the stable (see next page) more than the wi.d. and free, and

unperverted animal that inhabits the mountains. The goat has only to exercise his faculties of love of climbing and love of eminence to remove the popular prejudice against him; and the Jew, against whom there is a corresponding prejudice, is greatly admired when he aspires to a high position, and attains an eminence where he can exercise his noble gifts.

In such a case, even the natural grossness of the character becomes agreeable; there is abundant provision for the body, and the corporeal necessities of others are attended to: the ancient hospitality, so beautifully exemplified by the patriarchs, is still observed, and the Jew is deserving of the name which is freely given to him, and which he accepts without ostentation, of being "good-natured and hospitable." Yet his hospitality is seldom returned, except in the "Welcome, strangers, to dwell among us, if you will," which sounds so pleasantly to the "strangers in a strange land."

Yet it is natural that the hospitality that is extended to the

Jews should be stinted, and nobody is to blame for it. They are *scattered* among the Gentiles, and are nowhere tolerated in large numbers. In like manner, goats are scattered, one in this flock of sheep and another in that, a few here and a few there, though it was once their right and their custom to live together. There is a sphere about them that, concentrated, would be intolerable; and so they are spread abroad, notwithstanding they are naturally gregarious. The Jews have very great inhabitiveness, and wherever they are scattered they are a distinct people, and think of a return to their promised land, which is their home still. They are still animated by the spirit that prompted that beautiful psalm:—

"By the rivers of Babylon there we sat down,
Yea, we wept, when we remembered Zion!
We hanged our harps upon the willows
In the midst thereof.
For there they that carried us away captive required of us a song;
And they that wasted us required of us mirth,
Saying, 'Sing us one of the songs of Zion.'
How shall we sing the Lord's song
In a strange land?
If I forget thee, O Jerusalem,
Let my right hand forget her cunning;
If I do not remember thee,
Let my tongue cleave to the roof of my mouth;
If I prefer not Jerusalem above my chief joy."

In this charming expression of the love of home, is included whatever is domestic and social. Music and dancing are so —the first expressing love, and the latter the happiness attendant thereon; and they are mentioned in order, and with poetic allusions; the instrument of music, the song, and the dance. The *harp* is hung upon the willow, for its music should be like that of the wind-harp, plaintive and sad, and the willow is the emblem of mourning. The *song* is like that of the captive bird—

"Warbling its native wood-notes wild"

with a sad memory of its wild-wood home, and gratifying the unreasonable requirement of its captors. The *dance* is performed with wasted strength; and the "sacred mirth" of holy love and worship, joining the harp and the song, is required by those who enfeeble them, and is the saddest token of all. How shall the bird sing the song of the wild-woods in its wiry prison? and how shall the Jew sing the Lord's song in a strange land? He can not; and yet his practice upon the harp shall prove that he does not forget Jerusalem; the use of his tongue in singing shall prove that he remembers her: if he *can* forget her, let his hand forget its skill upon instruments; if he ceases to remember, let his tongue refuse to sing; if he prefer not Jerusalem above his chief joy, let him never again "joy in the dance."

It may be supposed that we have wandered quite beyond our province, which is the resemblance between the Jew and the goat. The goat has very great inhabitiveness, as all animals have that inhabit mountains and are sheltered by rocks; but the strongest love of home is that of mountain and valley combined, and this is particularly manifested in the goat. Jerusalem was built upon a steep rock in the midst of a valley. This is such a place as the goat would choose, as best suited to the gratification of his nature, which combines subterfuge with the love of climbing. Moreover, the goat seems to have a strong sense of his individuality, everywhere standing alone, and shunning contact. Now, place and individuality are essential to each other, and both are essential to music and dancing. Individuals can be placed in harmonious relations to each other, and harmonious relations can confer individuality even upon sounds, as is the case with the notes in music. Place and individuality in the goat cause him to be possessed of the faculties of "time" and "tune." It is evident that he has a good knowledge of metre, for in leaping from rock to rock he combines an accurate perception of time and distance, and we can testify that he has a perception of tune, for we have heard him at night utter sounds that were musical in their combination, so much so as to convince us that there is "music in him." The sounds were singularly human and pathetic, and touched our souls with a sympathy that the notes of no other animal ever awakened. We presume that those who are accustomed to sleep in the neighborhood of goats have often heard them.

The reader may be disposed to laugh at the idea that a goat can sing; but there is the same approach to singing in the cries of this animal, that there is to eloquence in the barking and howling of the dog. That the goat is possessed of the elements of the art and science of dancing we have before observed. The ancient Jews excelled in this accomplishment, as they did in music, and their descendants are equal in these respects, if not superior, to the people with whom they dwell.

Music is the language of love, and "perfect love casteth out fear;" hence the cultivation of music gives increase to courage, and whatever diminishes bravery diminishes the love for music. Of animals that are fond of fermented food the notes are discordant and harsh, and these animals are cowardly; but of animals that will not eat and drink unless their food and water be fresh and pure, the notes are soft and musical, and these animals are not cowardly and cruel, but cautious and brave. Fermentation is disorder and confusion, and it corresponds to and is promotive of discord in the person who allows it in the food and drink that he uses. Music inspires courage, and cultivates it. The schoolboy whistles to put down the fear that haunts him when he passes a graveyard at night. Tam O'Shanter in the neighborhood of Kirk Alloway is described —

> "Whiles holding fast his gude blue bonnet,
> Whiles *croning o'er some auld Scotch sonnet*,
> Whiles glow'ring round wi' prudent cares.
> Lest bogles catch him unawares."

The soldier, with all his boasted bravery, requires

> "the thrilling fife and pealing drum"

to nerve him to the dread encounter; and the music is first and foremost, the warriors following behind, with the expression "Who's afraid?" legible in their faces.

There is no disputing the courage of the goat: his indisposition to run when there is a provocation to fight is well known, though, as before stated, he has a peculiar way of making his assault. The Jews are courageous; they always were, and always will be. They have no need to "pluck up courage," and hence no need of a "brandy smasher." A drunken Jew is a rare commodity. In dealing with you, they make up their minds at once what they will do; and though they invariably conclude to make a large profit, they are, on account of their courage, fair people to deal with. They keep their eye upon the "main chance," which they could not do if they shrunk timidly away; and they are always ready for that

> ——— "tide in the affairs of men,
> Which, taken at the flood, leads on to fortune."

Here is the "Jew boy, by Mark Lemon." You may trust him to earn a living, and to live easily without seeming to be

busy, for he takes after his seniors by a kind of instinct. The philosophy of living is known only to the Jew: it is to live free from care, to be never troubled with business, to live easily as if the means of living were abundant, and by seeming to do nothing to show that business is prosperous. This is the air and manner of the Jew boy; he has nothing of the loafer about him except the appearance.

It is curious to trace the likeness between the Jew and the goat in the general appearance and in the features and expressions of the countenance. The signs of attack and relative-defence in the convexity of the nose, the large signs of acquisitiveness and love of clothing in the breadth of that organ, the love of eminence in the elevation of the wing of the nostril, the want of concentration in the shortness of the upper lip, the strength of the love of home and of family pride in the length and stiffness of the under lip, the energy and impulsiveness of love and will in the beard and chin, the signs of substitution, subterfuge, and the love of climbing, in the ridge of the eyebrow, the look of attention to external objects, and many other things, betray the relationship between the Israelite and the goat.

The fondness of the Jew for things "as old as the hills," has been already spoken of. He has the strongest possible attachment to the religion of his forefathers, as well as to the country they inhabited. He has no ability to change his creed. The goat is equally attached to the remains of the

generations that are past, as for example old castles, mouldering walls, the ruins of temples, and

> "Rocks, knolls, and mounds, confusedly hurled,
> The fragments of an earlier world."

He has "antiquity" written in his visage, and expressed in his sage demeanor, and in that long beard that has always been the badge of wisdom and patriarchal dignity. Who more than the Jew has defended this mark of manhood amid all the obloquy that has been heaped upon it? He inclines to preserve it as a token of age, of wisdom, of experience, and of matured and masculine intellect. It carries with it the impression of authority, as of something that grows hoary with age, and resists the liability to decay. "Wo betide the hand that plucks the wizard beard of hoary error!" That hand —

"Might wish that it had rather dared
To pull the devil by the beard!"

The Jew had ancestors that lived from two to nine hundred years; and nothing could be more sure to offend him than the representation that one of these was wanting a beard. The profession of a barber finds no followers among the Jews. And yet the Jew is a notorious *shave*, or there is no truth in the common opinion. He takes the whole or none; figuratively speaking, he "grinds the faces of the poor." This kind of business is very thoroughly done in a pawnbroker's establishment, and the Jews are the people to do it. In this degraded condition they resemble the goat that is smelled as far as he is seen, and is classed with skunks. "The smell in a pawnbroker's store is sickening; it nearly resembles what the Spaniards call *aroma de bacallo.*"

CHAPTER XXXVI.

Let the individual here presented be described according to the signs of character in the "Outlines of Physiognomy," and we shall see that his traits agree with those of the sheep, to which animal he is seen to bear a marked resemblance. Such a face speaks very great mildness and amiability, refined and ar-

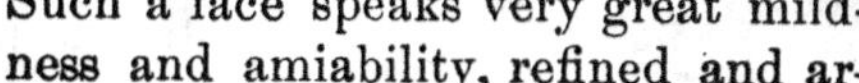

dent affections, unaffected modesty, and the total absence of ill-will. It expresses the love of children, of parents, brothers and sisters, and the social affections grounded in the domestic. Children are regarded by him as "little lambs," and he teaches them by his own meekness and dependence the force of the petition, "Lead me to the Rock that is higher than I." To trust in the "Good Shepherd," and to commit his charge to the Power that protects himself, is his first concern.

In the man who resembles the sheep, the signs of attack, relative-defence, and self-defence, in the ridge of the nose, are generally large, though less than in the man who resembles the goat; and, to confess the truth, he is never backward to engage in a fair and honest discussion, but it is always with mildness and courtesy, and without the least disposition to take the advantage of his opponent. In this he is very different from the person who favors the goat; for the latter, though "all things to all men," makes it a point to take the advantage in an argument, and is often captious. The one has large subterfuge, retaliation, and love of contest, and the other is exceedingly deficient in these, and has great love of preserving.

Men of true courage and heroism more frequently resemble sheep, goats, hares, and other timid, inoffensive animals, than lions, tigers, and animals of the savage variety. This can be easily seen by looking at our own revolutionary heroes, and at the truly brave and patriotic men of other countries, and by contrasting these with the tyrants and rulers who hold the same relation to the former that the savage animals do to the inoffensive. The destructive instrument is like the passion that employs it. "Battering-rams" are bolder instruments of war than pikes and guns: they seek to conquer at once, without the shedding of blood; they are levelled against inanimate objects—and are the very instruments to "conquer a peace." We use this as figurative of the warrior who resembles a ram. He is essentially peaceful, and the exercise of his superior tactics and bravery in war is for the sake of peace and repose, as is truly the case with the

sheep. In the warrior represented on the preceding page, the similarity in the air and expression of the countenance to the peaceful and gentle animal with which he is compared is easily perceived. There is a striking resemblance to the ram in the profile of General Scott.

The sheep makes good use of the fine developments along the ridge of his nose — sometimes in a friendly argument with his fellow, in which he gives and takes without any tokens of savage anger; and sometimes in a tug of war with some inoffensive post, which his imagination seems to convert into a hostile champion. The part of his head which is brought to bear upon the object of attack is the sign of *substitution*, or the lower part of the forehead in the place called the *frontal sinus*. It is, in reality, the faculty of substitution that is particularly exercised in this case, the post being substituted for an individual, and the wall for an army of soldiers. By the exhibition of martial prowess against inanimate objects, the enemy, if he have ordinary prudence, is convinced that resistance would be vain, and that it is owing to the magnanimity of the injured party that he is not severely punished. As it is not the love of triumph that prompts the sheep to an onset, he is satisfied to try his strength on some insensible object, and this he regards with a friendly feeling, as the means of his making a demonstration. It is a singular trait of character that we are speaking of, for those who resemble the sheep are not much observed. In such it might appear as if it were the effect of education and discipline; but observe, and you will see that it is a natural disposition. The love of *preserving* is uppermost in the animal we are speaking of, and in those who resemble him, even when the warlike faculties are called into exercise.

The bearing of the head in those who resemble sheep is independent, but not proud. He who, with the appearance of belonging to the *genus ovis*, hangs his head meanly, has in his composition something of the character of the wolf; he is in the habit of "casting sheeps' eyes" upon the lamb, the emblem of innocence and virtue, and this has given him the "hang-dog" look that is observed in the dog that is to be hanged for stealing sheep. The sneakish look that we are speaking of is conspicuous in the canine animal that hangs about the sheepfold, and says —

> "'Tis conscience does make cowards of us all;"

and pronounces the sentence of hanging "by the neck till he be dead, dead!" But even this, mean as it is, is better than deception, or the wearing of "sheeps' clothing," by which wolves endeavor to palm themselves off for sheep. It must not be forgotten that we are to distinguish between the look of "sheepishness," as it is called, and the looks that are peculiar to the sheep; but there is hope of reformation in the man who is not insensible to shame.

In the person who properly resembles the sheep there is a forward position of the head, indicating a certain degree of diffidence, or a susceptibility to shame, should there be an occasion for the exercise of this feeling. Large and prominent eyes, in which there is the expression of heroic daring enshrined in peace; great activity; a high and gently-retreating forehead — grace in feeling and action; a light form and elastic step; admirable precision in hitting thoughts upon the wing, and in clothing them with language; great consciousness and capacity of suffering; tenderness of the feelings of others, and a disposition to lay the burdens of human beings upon inanimate objects; comfort and simplicity in dress; great refinement of feeling and manners; freedom, simplicity, and copiousness of ideas; poetry, and sublimity, and elegance of expression; great love of liberty, and indignation at the wrong done to others by the right of the strongest

—are among the traits of character in the man who bears a worthy resemblance to the sheep. In his dress he is studious of comfort, and all his efforts are directed to contentment. He trusts in Providence: he scarcely knows the meaning of the term want or stern necessity; he does not complain of his lot, nor fear that the world should know that he is set aside to make room for others. In many of these things (but not all) he is the very opposite of the man who resembles the goat.

As all sheep are not equally improved, or preserved from deterioration, so all men are not equally noble. On the following page is a profile of Alexander the Great, who for some reason or other, in the coin from which this cut was taken, was represented with ram's horns. In his youth he answered to the description above, but perversion changed him into the very opposite. The horns, which should betoken moral and intellectual power, like those which threw down the walls of an ancient city, are converted into serpents, coiling around the seat of infernal passions, and whispering in his ear. Spiritual-mindedness is displaced by sensuality, mildness by revenge, and contentment and humility by ambition and pride. His face is Grecian, and the Greeks as a nation resemble sheep; but far superior to this is the face of old Homer.

whose resemblance to the sheep is likewise observable. His is a face knotted and gnarled like that of the patriarch of the flock, or like the oak in whose shade the flock reposes, listening to the shepherd's pipe, or like the craggy cliffs where the oak braves the lightning and the tempest, and where the sheep is safe from danger; but it is a face full of feeling and sentiment—a face from which the noble character has not been worn off by the chafing of ambition and insatiable desire. It is something altogether different from the mere "battering-ram" which that man is made to be who substitutes physical power for moral and intellectual. And we may observe here, that where Nature is most capable of giving birth to a Homer, a Sophocles, or a Plato, she is most capable of bringing the sheep to perfection. It is a meditative, philosophical sheep (see next page) that resembles Plato.

The scenery that is best adapted to refinement and the delights of imagination is best adapted to the sheep, and *that* is the mountain scenery of Greece. This may appear from history, and, as there is truth in poetry, from pastorals also. A certain writer says that Attica "might rival Spain in the fineness of its wool; the goat thrives on its hills; the uncultivated lands are overrun with thyme, serpillum, and marjoram; the Albanian shepherds lead their flocks in summer to these pastures."

Now, the excellence of the honey that is brought from that country is not the only excellence that is derived from the aromatic plants which cover the soil: the flavor of mutton, which is savory beyond that of any other meat, makes a demand for aromatic substances, and is increased by them, and therefore we aver that the country which produces the Greek is particu-

larly suited to the sheep. The animal that is superior to all others as a sacrifice of a "sweet-smelling savor" is the sheep, and the Greeks were particularly fond of such sacrifices, and therefore required them. The aromas of flowers are like the breathings of the soul in praise and prayer, in gratitude and love, and in pure and pious aspira-

tions; and hence is the offering of incense in religious worship. The sheep is a correspondent of good affections, not only on account of the qualities before mentioned, but because his flesh is refined and flavored by substances that correspond to what is spiritual and heavenly, as the animal faculties in man are purified and governed by the moral and religious.

For these reasons, and on account of innocence, the lamb is typical of the Christian sacrifice, as it was also the sacrificial offering of the Greeks. The character that is most perfectly represented by the sheep is that of Christ; and as Christians are like him, there is the same difference between the Jews and Gentiles that there is between goats and sheep. Also the term "Greek" is used synonymously with "Gentile," for the simple reason that the Gentiles in acquiring a character corresponding to the innocence, purity, and excellence of the sheep, resemble Greeks. They are called Greeks for the same reason that they are called sheep. "The sheep on the right hand and the goats on the left" is the contrasted position of the Jews and Gentiles in respect to

Christ. The propriety of this figure has been sufficiently shown in the resemblance of certain persons to the sheep, and of others to the goat, in both character and physiognomy. The portrait above is that of Oberlin. The man who resembles the sheep in natural disposition, if he be a Christian, can say with the utmost degree of truth and feeling:—

"The Lord is my shepherd; I shall not want;
He maketh me to lie down in green pastures:
He leadeth me beside the still waters.
He restoreth my soul:
He leadeth me in the paths of righteousness for his name's sake.
Yea, though I walk through the valley of the shadow of death,
I will fear no evil: for thou art with me;
Thy rod and thy staff they comfort me."

As to the Greeks themselves, or the better class of them, we can not do better than to take the following description: "The Athenians have not lost their ancient urbanity; their accent is more harmonious than any o her in Greece; their language is less diffuse, and for that reason more energetic. Their appearance is nearly the same as that of their ancestors; the women of Athens are still distinguished for their light figures, the oval form of the face, the regular contour, the straight line that marks the profile, full black eyes, high forehead, red lips, small hands and feet; they are equally graceful in the mournful dance of Ariadne and in the rapid mazes of the Romaika. The simplicity of the ancient dress is in some degree retained: a white tunic descends from the neck, and a white mantle covers the arms and falls over the shoulders; a handkerchief tied loosely around the head does not conceal their jet-black hair, but the barbarous *empire* is typified in a clumsy and ill-placed girdle, red trowsers, and a heavy Turkish cloak." The resemblance to the sheep is here sufficiently described, and it might be very well contrasted with the resemblance between Turks and turkeys.

The reason assigned for the language of the Athenians being more energetic than that of other Greeks is that it is less diffuse. We see the correspondence of this in the motions of the sheep, which are short and quick. What is lost in strength, or "the long pull, the strong pull, and the pull all together," as they say at sea, is made up in quickness, elasticity, and energy; and this is especially suited to expression, or to being the medium of moral and intellectual power: for as grossness is necessary to the former, so refinement is essential to the latter. Sailors are consequently clumsy and gross, and so are all those whom society condemns to the galleys, or, in other words, to hard labor; but those who study grace in action, and engage in such employments as require bodily and mental activity, will acquire moral and intellectual refinement with much more facility than those with whom these conditions are not attended to. The relation of analysis, and consequently of refinement, to language, is very evident; and the man who resembles the sheep in a marked degree is interested in language as the means of expressing the most refined and delicate shades of thought and feeling, and will probably do much toward perfecting it. He will wish to free it of all that is unmeaning and cumbersome, for these things are clogs to the wheels of progress, and he regards them as sand in sugar or a sinecure in a government.

The sign of architecture and the memory of names in the Greek contributes very much to his resemblance to the sheep. It is architecture, probably, together with large attack, which inclines the sheep to brace the top of his nose against a pillar or post; and when he wishes to make a forcible *entrée*, he calls into exercise his large endurance, and, like certain woolly-headed gentlemen, tries the strength of his skull. In many more amiable traits than this does the negro resemble the sheep, but we need only say that with proper advantages he becomes a good Christian.

The rocks with which the sheep is surrounded in his mountain-home are natural fortifications, or embrasures, where liberty is often better protected than in castles and fortresses. They are the foundations of the beautiful temples and palaces in the higher world which the Greeks took and handed down to earth after they had peopled them with gods and goddesses, and with the sublimest of their heroes. The Grecian deities were the embodiments of their own exquisite and refined natures; and what the horse is to Italian art, the sheep is to the Grecian. Painting and dramatic representation are more perfect in the former, and architecture and sculpture in the latter. The man who stops short of the perfection which the Greeks attempted to embody in their deities (and in which they failed), stops short of the spiritual beauty of which the sheep is a correspondent. That perfection is reached in the conception of the Divine Man, and is aimed at by those who follow his example. It is with them as with a flock of sheep —where the Leader goes, the flock is sure to follow. "He leadeth them out, he calleth them all by name, and they follow him, but a stranger will they not follow, for they know not the voice of strangers." Where the people are unanimous, and will not be diverted from following their leader, what victories can they not accomplish?

One other trait of character in the sheep we must mention, at the risk of being tedious. It is irritability and indignation. The sheep when offended stamps indignantly with her

foot. This comes from relative-defence and love of liberty. It is a noble trait of character, one for which the Greeks distinguished themselves in ancient times, and which their throwing off the Turkish yoke shows that they are still possessed of. Spirit and gentleness are united in this face of Kalergi, the Greek patriot. The gentleness of the sheep does not entitle him to the name of "good-natured," which is often a doubtful compliment. "Hogs," says a newspaper paragraph, "are patterns of good-humor. Hit 'em a kick, and they forget it as soon as they are out of reach. Dog 'em, and they root as happy as ever the minute they are left alone." This comes from the insensibility of the animal, and from his incapability of feeling a "righteous indignation," and not from a lack of retaliation and self-defence. Let an injury once penetrate the crust of his insensibility, and he will revenge it on the spot, or show that he is not so forgetful of injuries as you supposed. But the indignant person is not implacable; he is merciful and forgiving. That which rouses indignation is an offence against truth and goodness, purity and innocence. or some other person than one's self; and it was exhibited perfectly in Him who was called the "Lamb of God," and prominently in the characters of the gods, who were a foreshadowing of the Divinity that was to be restored.

The goat is very like the sheep, notwithstanding the paradox, and in like manner the Jew has points of contact with the Christian; Moses is the representative of Christ, and the Old Testament is typical of the New. The corporeal senses are the inlets to the mind, and through the "letter" of a communication we arrive at the "spirit" of it. The Jew is literal. Shylock says simply, "It is in the bond;" but the converted Jew says, "The letter is of no profit—it is the spirit that quickens." The Christian "puts off the old man," and the Jew puts it on; the literal of which is, that the Christian throws off his old garments, and the Jew takes them!

CHAPTER XXXVII.

We often hear of children learning to repeat like parrots. The gift of language ought, indeed, to entitle the parrot to comparison with somebody. But it is not the ape that we are speaking of. As for saying a man's words after him, the parrot is entirely above it, except it be with the expectation of a reward. There is nothing in which originality is so much exercised as in the use of the tongue. Language is artificial, and the constant effort to invent new languages shows itself in 'provincialisms,' not only in provinces but in districts, the world over. You may try to get the parrot to say, "Pretty Poll," or "Polly want coffee," by setting her the example, but you will fail in the object.

It is only to the words "Polly want *cracker?*" that she deigns a response. She despises servile imitation, and aspires to originality. Think you she is going to make a ninny of herself by showing her weakness and dependence? Rather than not talk at all, she will say what she has heard others say, but it will be when she supposes you have forgotten it. She would much rather do what you do not want her to do—to imitate your infirmities, for example—as therein she shows she is not indebted to a master. She aspires to originality in everything. You see in her all sorts of one-sided, strange, outlandish motions, the results of her unwillingness to follow in the footsteps of others.

In inferior minds the love of originality shows itself in oddity, and, when this is connected with a taste for wit, in a constant exhibition of drollery. There is a perfect agreement between the parrot and the clown, and the value that is attached to them is the same in both. They are *tolerated* for the same reason, viz., the amusement they afford by the constant exhibition of something new and startling, and by their buffoonery. It is a vulgar taste, identical with that which gleans the "horrible and awful" in newspapers, and prefers a *lusus naturæ* to what is orderly and beautiful. Those who patronize clowns are people who have the same traits, but are in too high a station, or consider it a little below their dignity, to act the part of buffoons. Still the clown, though he makes a fool of himself, in compliance with the notion that a fool is a rare commodity in a court, has often more influence over those he amuses than any other man, and treats his master familiarly and even contemptuously. It is well for him that he can cry out, "I say, master," every now and then —for if his "master" were not his master in the art he

professes, he would be considered as deserving of banishment for every tenth witticism that he utters. Like the parrot, he never says anything you would put into his mouth to say—it is something else, or nothing.

It is laughable to hear the parrot laugh like the clown, or, what is the same thing, like some ridiculous old fellow who bursts out in spite of the unmusical quality of his voice, and whose laugh, therefore, is more laughable than what he laughs at! He coughs like somebody with the consumption, till he is apparently exhausted, and almost goes into a swoon; "tells on you," when you expected that your doings were a profound secret; shows a decided taste for whatever is unpopular; is grotesque, and in all respects a perfect clown. People who are like him are glib with their tongues, make a burlesque of singing and eloquence, introduce variations and high-flown language into their performances, all for the sake of originality; which shows that, after all, there is more harmony in the world than discord, or that order is the rule and absurdity the exception.

But all persons who resemble the parrot do not resemble him thus literally. The love of originality and the gift of tongues are not always connected with a sense of the ludicrous, nor with such mischief as lurks in the parrot. There is many a sober innovator, whose delight it is to ponder

"o'er many a volume of forgotten lore,"

that he may not be supposed to make use of the humdrum literature of the day; who introduces obsolete words and coins new ones, and makes a patchwork of all languages; makes use of execrable phrases, and invents a style that may be called his own. He has the appearance of great learning, of being able to run through the contents of musty libraries at a single glance; passes over modern discoveries, in search of things quaint and queer, which, being monstrosities, and buried out of the sight of man, he considers proper subjects for discovery. Whatever was forced upon the world as a *misfortune and a necessity*, he is particularly solicitous to bring to light. The impression that his *matter* is new, and out of the ordinary course of things, he enforces by the singularity of his style, and his verbosity and grandiloquence. *Invention* he makes synonymous with discovery, and discovery with invention; but his love of originality is gratified in his being

considered the author of his discoveries, and on examination they are found to be—

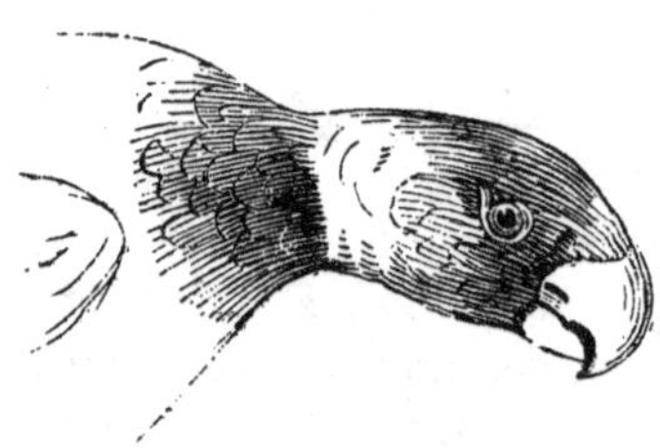

"The children of an idle brain,
Begot of nothing but vain phantasy."

His grand idea is *originality*, and as this is attained by raking up whatever is exploded, and by paying homage to Misfortune; and as language, in which he is so thoroughly engrossed, is the mere *clothing* of ideas—his philosophy is necessarily materialistic. His marvellous acquaintance with languages, and the multiplicity of his words, are as much a subject of wonder as is the gift of speech in the parrot. He bends all his efforts to excite the wonder of people more and more—

"Till they cry out, 'You prove yourself so able,
Pity you were not dragoman at Babel;
For had they found a linguist half so good,
I make no question but the tower had stood!'"

There is a character quite different from this, and yet closely related to it: it is that which resembles the mocking-bird. This bird is as wonderfully gifted as the parrot, but his gift is eloquence. Intonation, inflection, harmonious modulation, chords that waken echoes in the breasts of a thousand warblers, are as easy in his throat as motion in his wings.

Those who are gifted with eloquence possess a strong resemblance to the mocking-bird; they strike the chords in human bosoms when they waken their own, without producing a jarring discord other than is necessary to increase the harmony; they know the secret spring of feeling in the human heart. They possess extraordinary knowledge of human nature, and the reason is, they feel what others feel, intuitively, in a way they can not account for. They are better physiognomists than others, but how it is that they are seldom or never deceived in their estimate of character they can not tell.

The eloquence that the mocking-bird possesses in so extraordinary a degree is accompanied by a wonderful knowledge of character. He never fails to distinguish his friends from his enemies in the animal creation, and is almost equally sagacious in respect to human beings. He is as wary of enemies as the crow, but his confidence in building his nest close by a house, and a few feet from the ground, shows that he is not governed by suspicion in his relations with others. Of the cat-bird, which is a mocking-bird of very charming accomplishments, Audubon says: "In some instances I have known this bird to recognise at once its friend from its foe, and to suffer the former even to handle the treasure deposited in its nest, with all the marked assurance of the knowledge it possessed of its safety; when, on the contrary, the latter had to bear all its anger. The sight of a dog seldom irritates it, while a single glance at the wily cat excites the most painful paroxysms of alarm." This knowledge of the dispositions of others is very intimately connected with his gift of eloquence; for the notes of different birds are the sounds of their affections, and the bird that can express them all must have inspired the feelings which each one expresses the moment he heard them.

Another trait of the mocking-bird is his deadly hostility to oppressors, particularly the snake, and his readiness to take the part of the injured. This is naturally associated with eloquence. In all ages of the world, and in all countries, the theme that has awakened eloquence more than any other is Liberty, and the right of the weak to the protection and sympathy of the strong. A bad cause inspires something the very opposite of this. The eloquence uttered in the cause of humanity is divine, and only this is immortal. And those orators whose services were rendered to humanity, and whose fame is the inheritance of mankind, had wonderful knowledge of the human heart. The action of an orator is the earnest of his sensibility, every nerve and fibre of his frame being thrilled with the enthusiasm of his inspira

tion, like the bird, alive in every feather, "fast fluttering all at once," and unable to contain himself. The eloquence itself, as corresponding to the outpourings of the mocking-bird —it would be a letting-down to attempt to describe it.

It is man's freedom and his moral accountability that are indicated in the countenance. Technically speaking, the signs of the voluntary action of the faculties are in the face. For this reason, and because pathos and the ability to move the feelings of others implies a knowledge of nature, and of human nature in particular, eloquence is inseparable from physiognomy. The beautiful things appertaining to the latter that are always being introduced into the discourses of our finest orators, are proof of the connection. The knowledge of Nature in its widest sense is embraced in the term Physiognomy, and Nature is the theme of the most glowing descriptions. The crowning work of creation is the subject of inspiration.

CHAPTER XXXVIII.

THE reader who has felt a sufficient interest in our subject to accompany us to the last chapter, will have made a number of observations in confirmation of our own, and some, no doubt, that are really or apparently contradictory. We do not claim to be infallible, and the reader is not bound to believe anything that he does not see to be true. Of the statements we have made, and respecting your interest in them, we would say to you, gentle reader, as we heard an Irish apple-woman say to a boy who asked her for an apple: "If you see one at all that pleases yourself, take it." This conveniently illustrates the gentlemanly relation, as well in respect to ideas as in respect to bodily hospitalities, at the same time that it illustrates the natural gentility of the Irish, and, *à priori*, the gentility of the dog. The language used by that poor Irishwoman, and the common speech of Irishmen, is such as is heard when one gentleman addresses another, and of the kind that is used in genteel society.

Dear reader, we fancy you asking us mentally to let go your button, at the same time that you are attentive and polite. You must not suppose that we have inflicted upon you all that we might have done, had we been disposed to trace the resemblances between men and all the inferior animals of creation. We must receive credit for not having even mentioned all the resemblances between the men and animals that we have treated of. For example, we might have asked you to observe that, of the two classes of negroes, the one open their mouths like fishes, and the other their jaws like elephants. Then we might have directed your attention to the fact that the English are inclined to drawl, and to utter half their words in the inspiration of the voice; to use aspirates where they ought not, and to leave them off where they belong: like the cow in her long-drawn loo, in her moo-hoo; in her *h* as in *hoo*, when she takes back her breath; and in her neglect of the *h* as in *hoist*, when she has a potato in her throat, which gives her occasion to expel what she can not swallow. It is evident that other animals, the dog and the cat for example, when they endeavor to expel anything from the throat, give the sound of *h;* and that in inspiration they give only the vowel sound, if any. It is in consequence, therefore, of a resemblance to the cow, that the Englishman says, "'Ear me," and "Lend me your *h*ears." It is worth mentioning, also, that one of the most celebrated places in England is called "Ox-ford." Then, if we had said all that we might have said about the resemblance between the Chinaman and the hog, we should have remarked upon the similarity of sounds—as, for example, that the words Tchong-Koue, Ning-po, Hong-kong, Kwang-tung, and the Choos and the Foos of the Chinese language, partake of the nasal grunt and the *foo*-ing of an old hog; while Fu-keen, Pekin, Pe-chele, and the like, are akin to the squeaking of a little pig. As the life employment of the hog is chewing at first-hand (for he has no time to spend in chewing the cud), it is not strange that nearly every other word of the Chinese language has a "choo" in it, so that the Chinese in conversing do little besides *choo*. Then we might have spoken of the similarity of the French language to that of the frog, till with the twirling of linguals about our ears we might have fancied ourselves in Bedlam. We might have drawn comparisons between the languages of men and animals, as between the faces of these and those; but we did not, and there are many other things we did not touch upon.

It may be thought that in the preceding chapters there is no orderly arrangement; but there is an order, and it is according to harmony, and for that reason it is not easily perceived. Harmony is so delightful, that we perceive only that it governs us, and not that it governs us by laws. When we have unfolded the Science of Nature more fully, we shall analyze and understand that which we are now sufficiently happy in feeling. From feeling we shall glide into perceiving, from perceiving into understanding, and from understanding into something higher.

We are hard-hearted indeed if, having studied our relationship to the inferior animals, we are not disposed to treat them more kindly. We sympathize with them, for we perceive that the same faculties which warm our breasts animate theirs. We share with them our "creature comforts," for they are creatures more than we, and our superior reason enables us to provide for those comforts better than they. Our moral and religious inspiration, by which we are distinguished, prompts us to confer happiness on others. If we are not true to this, we are inhuman — that is, we are neither men nor brutes — and this never can be said of the inferior animals. *Creatures* are not bad. A person with a good natural disposition is called a "good creature," and it is in reference to our natural dispositions that we are called the "creatures of God." — "An unfortunate creature" we often hear of, but who ever heard of a wicked creature, except it were of some one whose wickedness is synonymous with ugliness, such as is observed in the cow or the goat? If we say to a person, "You wicked creature!" the word "creature" shows that we do not mean it. The word "wicked" is an absurdity in such a connection, and therefore it is applied wittily. Simply, "You creature!" is equivalent to saying of the person thus addressed, that —

"E'en his failings lean to virtue's side!"

A *perverted* character has never the term "creature" applied to it. It is evident, therefore, that our relationship to the lower animals is no disgrace to us if it is none to them. In this case, we are "children of Nature," as they are, but more perfectly, for we are also the "children of God." It is an honor to be the children of "the common Mother" when wisdom is given us to know our Father — which wisdom is not given to the lower animals. A true nobleman will not despise his poor relations: he knows that his origin is humble, and that all his riches and honors are conferred by his Sovereign. "Man is an animal." With this humiliating truth we commenced our subject, and with this we conclude. But for the use which we should make of this knowledge, we adopt the sentiments of an old author:—

"Man, considered in himself, and in his own *proprium*, is nothing but a beast, having like senses, like appetites, like lusts, and also like affections in every respect; his good and best loves are likewise very similar, as the love of associates of his own species, the love of children, and the love of his mate; so that there is no difference between them in any respect. But that he is man, and more excellent than the beasts, is, because he has an interior life, which beasts have not, nor are capable of having; this life is the life of faith and of love from the Lord; and unless this life were to influence and prevail in each of those properties which he has in common with the beasts, he would never be anything else but a beast: as, for instance, in respect to love toward his associates, if he loved them only for the sake of himself, and there were not in the love something more celestial and divine, he could not be called a man in consequence of that love, because it is similar with the beasts: and so in other instances: wherefore unless the life of love from the Lord were in his will, and the life of faith from the Lord in his understanding, he would in no respect be a man. By the life which he has from the Lord, he lives after death, because thereby the Lord joins him to himself; and thus he has a capacity of being in heaven with the angels, and of living to eternity: and although man lives a wild beast, and loves nothing else but himself, and the things which respect himself, yet the mercy of the Lord is so great, being divine and infinite, that he never leaves man, but continually breathes into him his life by the angels, which, notwithstanding his perverse reception thereof, still gives him a capacity of thinking, of reflecting, of understanding what is good or evil, whether it relate to moral, civil, worldly, or corporeal life, and thereby of discerning what is true or false."

Mankind in general find their resemblance in the ape, as was shown in a preceding chapter; while races of men, and individuals in particular, resemble animals of every species and variety. As to *animals* in general, we also find their resemblance in the ape: it is easy to see that the quadrumana resemble both beasts and birds, living as they do in trees, and grasping with the posterior members, as birds do, and belonging at the same time to the mammalia. It is evident, therefore, that every man, in resembling the ape, resembles the entire animal kingdom, and that by resembling each individual beast and bird he resembles each individual man to whom such beast or bird bears a resemblance. As all men have a resemblance in common, it is certain that each individual man has in himself the peculiarities of all other people — so blended, that only his own individual peculiarity is conspicuous. Also, as the predominant animal nature is *bovine* in one, *equine* in another, *canine* in another, *feline* in another, and so on — it is evident that there is in every individual a congregation of all sorts of animal natures, and that the difference between people is the predominance of one or other of these elements. Of course, it is the element that is most conspicuous in an individual that constitutes his resemblance to a particular beast or bird.

Being fortified by reasoning, we have no hesitation in saying, figuratively, that man's breast is a menagerie of animals, of beasts and birds, clean and unclean, wild and tame. To name them and to govern them by morality and religion, is his highest duty and his highest delight. He transforms them into the likeness of the higher faculties by which they are governed; and with these they are so admirably blended, that they are no longer animal, but human. The animals of the external world still resemble him, for he subjects them to the same discipline as those within. He masters them by love and kindness; he makes them beautiful and useful, peaceful, harmonious, and happy. He exhibits in himself (and it is shadowed forth in the animals around him) a fulfil ment of the prophecy: —

"The wolf also shall dwell with the lamb,
And the leopard shall lie down with the kid,
And the calf, and the young lion, and the fatling, together;
And a little child shall lead them.

And the cow and the bear shall feed;
Their young ones shall lie down together:
And the lion shall eat straw like the ox.
And the sucking-child shall play on the hole of the asp,
And the weaned child shall put his hand on the cockatrice's den:
They shall not hurt nor destroy in all my holy mountain."

The helpless condition in which man is born makes it necessary that he should be endowed with a superlative degree of that faculty which prompts him to look out for his own interests. It is difficult to see how a person could be possessed of individuality without self-love for its basis, or recognise the individuality of others without first recognising his own, or ever love his neighbor until he had first loved himself. "Charity begins at home." Man is required to "love his neighbor as himself," which proves that the standard by which he is to measure his love for his neighbor exists beforehand, and that it is right and proper that he should have loved himself first. Self-love, therefore, is good; it is necessary to a weak and dependent being; and *all* beings are weak and dependent, and the Creator has given them self-love that they may supply their other deficiencies. And what *are* their deficiencies, and what their wants? Their first wants are physical, their second sensual, their third rational, and their fourth supernal. As long as these wants continue, so long self-love must be active; but, in the degree that these wants are supplied, it becomes man to be charitable, and to minister to the wants of others. It is only after these wants are supplied that man can become wickedly selfish. The object of self-love is to prompt him to take care of himself; and if he desire that others may take care of him, he is selfish beyond what Nature intended. An animal requires all the self-love that Nature has given it to supply itself with necessaries; and it is contented to "shirk for itself" if its exertions are capable of supplying its wants. At the season of the year when it is capable of doing more than this, Nature bestows offspring, and the care of the parents is expended upon other objects than themselves. Thus self-love in animals is kept within bounds; and it is proved by this that the inferior creatures are good. But with human beings it is otherwise. They wish to be taken care of by others, and to be supplied with multitudes of things that are not necessary; and for this end they acquire artificial appetites, such as the appetites for tobacco, tea, coffee, opium, and alcoholic stimulants. This perversion of self-love in man is from the perversion of the privilege of dependence, which is extreme at the moment he is born, and which is again extreme at the moment of his departure from this world: it is from the perversion of his perfect dependence upon his parents for the supply of his bodily wants at the commencement of his life, and of his perfect dependence upon his Creator for those things which alone can satisfy the cravings of an immortal soul at the period of his transition into another state of existence. Between these two extremes of dependence there is abundant room for self-exertion, self-improvement, and self-dependence, and there is occasion for the exercise of benevolence toward others when benevolence toward self has accomplished its object. What, then, must be the depravity of man, when, instead of loving himself and taking care of himself for the sake of his neighbor, he loves his neighbor and has his neighbor in keeping for the sake of himself? Look at those who in all countries oppress and enslave the bodies and souls of men, and at those who in their weakness and poverty exercise their tyrannical selfishness in oppression of the inferior animals, and you will see. The animal which the natural man resembles, viz., the ape, is selfish and disgusting in the extreme.

THE END

www.ingramcontent.com/pod-product-compliance
Lightning Source LLC
LaVergne TN
LVHW020214110826
845151LV00003B/712